PAUL THE PREACHER

PAUL THE PREACHER;

OR,

A Popular and Practical Exposition

OF HIS

DISCOURSES AND SPEECHES,

AS RECORDED IN

THE ACTS OF THE APOSTLES.

By JOHN EADIE, D.D., LL.D.,

PROFESSOR OF BIBLICAL LITERATURE TO THE UNITED PRESBYTERIAN CHURCH.

"The words of St Paul are not dead words; they are living creatures, and have hands and feet."
LUTHER.

SOLID GROUND CHRISTIAN BOOKS
BIRMINGHAM, ALABAMA USA

Solid Ground Christian Books
2090 Columbiana Rd, Suite 2000
Birmingham, AL 35216
205-443-0311
sgcb@charter.net
http://solid-ground-books.com

Paul the Preacher
A Popular and Practical Exposition of His Discourses and Speeches
As Recorded in the Acts of the Apostles

John Eadie (1810-1876)

From 1859 edition from Richard Griffin and Co., London and Glasgow

Solid Ground Classic Reprints

First printing of new edition July 2005

Cover work by Borgo Design, Tuscaloosa, AL
Contact them at nelbrown@comcast.net

Cover image is taken from Gustave Dore's "Paul Menaced by the Jews," from 'The Dore Bible Gallery.'

ISBN: 1-59925-002-0

PREFACE.

The following pages are simply what they profess to be in the title—neither a life of Paul, nor a commentary on the "Acts," but an honest and hearty attempt to explain and apply in a popular and practical shape to the common reader, the spoken words of the apostle. So that there is no array of minute criticism or technical exegesis, no formal quotation of authorities, or classified enumeration of conflicting views. My uniform effort has been to bring out briefly and clearly the apostle's meaning, without much regard to the form which the exposition may assume; to give the result without detailing the process; to be in short as the dial of the watch, which shows the hour while it conceals the mechanism. The various chapters are not sermons bearing on the subject, nor disquisitions on allied or collateral topics, though my aim has been throughout to press the truth on the attention and conscience; for what brought salvation then is fraught with the same blessing still—the gospel of the first century being in no sense different from that of the nineteenth. Though I have endeavoured to realize the more striking scenes in the apostle's travels, and reproduce my impressions of them, still the labour has been almost wholly expended on the addresses themselves, and this volume, therefore, differs in contents and purpose as well from the excellent volumes of Lewin, Coneybeare and Howson, as from those of others of secondary note who have made a prey of these distinguished authors. Nor need I give a list of commentators which may have been consulted. The longer discourses will be found in new translations, not indeed claiming classical precision, but giving what is thought to be a broad, correct, and easy version of the original. When any words of the authorized version are printed in Italics, followed by a dash, some direct explanation of the term or phrase is subjoined.

It is humbly hoped, in fine, that the volume may be useful in giving ordinary readers a juster and fuller conception of the creed and preaching, the life and work, of the great apostle of the Gentiles, who, amidst all diversities of place, time, audience, and immediate theme, made it his constant business to preach Christ crucified. May we know Him to be "the power of God" and the "wisdom of God," and experience that change of heart which is only effected by such a manifestation of His truth and glory as He vouchsafed to Saul of Tarsus.

JOHN EADIE.

13 LANSDOWNE CRESCENT,
May, 1859.

CONTENTS.

		Page
I.	SAUL AT DAMASCUS,	1
II.	SAUL AT JERUSALEM,	23
III.	SAUL AT ANTIOCH IN SYRIA,	35
IV.	SAUL IN CYPRUS,	50
V.	PAUL AT ANTIOCH IN PISIDIA,	65
VI.	PAUL AT ICONIUM,	113
VII.	PAUL AT LYSTRA,	120
VIII.	PAUL AT PHILIPPI,	139
IX.	PAUL AT THESSALONICA,	159
X.	PAUL AT ATHENS,	177
	PART I.,	187
	PART II.,	203
	PART III.,	222
XI.	PAUL AT CORINTH,	243
XII.	PAUL AT EPHESUS,	270
XIII.	PAUL AT TROAS,	295
XIV.	PAUL AT MILETUS,	309
	PART I. INTRODUCTORY APPEAL TO THE PAST—HIS FIDELITY,	312
	PART II. ANTICIPATIONS OF THE FUTURE—HIS COURAGE,	316
	PART III. HIS CHARGE,	325
	PART IV. THE FAREWELL,	340
	PART V. CONCLUDING APPEAL TO THE PAST—HIS DISINTERESTEDNESS,	344

CONTENTS.

	Page
XV. PAUL AT JERUSALEM—	
I. SPEECH FROM THE STAIRS OF THE GARRISON,	352
II. BEFORE THE SANHEDRIM,	365
XVI. PAUL AT CESAREA—	
I. BEFORE FELIX,	379
II. BEFORE FELIX AND DRUSILLA,	393
III. BEFORE FESTUS,	404
IV. BEFORE FESTUS AND AGRIPPA,	408
XVII. PAUL ON THE VOYAGE TO ROME,	423
XVIII. PAUL IN ROME,	436

PAUL THE PREACHER.

I.—SAUL AT DAMASCUS.

HIS FIRST APPEARANCE AS A PREACHER.

Acts ix. 19–25; Gal. i. 17; 2 Cor. xi. 32, 33.

A PROFOUND and permanent change had suddenly passed over Saul in the immediate vicinity of Damascus. The Saviour had shown Himself in glory, and spoken a few words of gracious power to him. The brightness of the vision had dazzled him into blindness, and with a smitten heart and faltering step he was led by his companions through the gate into the city. He had hoped to make the old Syrian capital the field of new triumphs, as he beat down the rising faith, and punished with merciless rigour the adherents of Jesus of Nazareth. But "it is not in man that walketh to direct his steps." The sunny landscapes through which he was passing suddenly lost their charm for the sightless traveller, and his mind's eye was turned inward on his own heart and history; the noise of so many rills—"streams from Lebanon"—dancing and singing through the gardens that surround Damascus, must have fallen faintly upon his ear, for there still rung in it a louder voice—" Saul, Saul, why persecutest thou Me;"

and that was the knell of his previous life. As he moved along with all that awkwardness which one so suddenly bereft of vision must have exhibited, even though "the men which journeyed with him" guided his steps, his rapt spirit could be but little disturbed by the hum of the streets and the clamour of the bazaars. The scene of his fancied victories had in a moment become the scene of deepest anguish and self-prostration. Christ had waylaid him, and a brief challenge from His lips had at once arrested the present enterprise. For, it is only when Christ speaks that conversion really takes place; it is only when the soul apprehends His glory that it bows to His will, and feels the checks and impulses of His grace. Ananias was induced to overcome his natural scruples and visit Saul at his lodgings, in the street called "Straight;" and the first Christian face which Saul looked upon with complacency, was that of the "disciple" at whose bidding his blindness departed, and by baptism at whose hands he was formally admitted into the church. He had seen the serenity of Stephen's countenance when it beamed like that of an angel, but his rage had been whetted by his victim's composure. Now his eyes suddenly opened on a visitor, who had styled him "Brother Saul," and it must have been a troubled and mysterious gaze which he cast upon him as he heard him repeat the words—"Jesus who appeared unto thee by the way."

Saul had not been "forsaken," though he had been "cast down;" the three days of his soul's agony were to issue in peace. His spiritual life, like that of plant and flower, had germinated in darkness, and had been watered by tears and prayers; but it was soon to welcome the light, and be trained to a healthful activity and expansion. "Light is sweet," and ere the scales had fallen from his eyes, his inner vision had been blessed with a glimpse of the truth—"the light of the glorious gospel of Christ" had shined in his heart. He had undergone in an instant the mightiest of all changes the soul of man can pass through, and which, in general experience, is often as sudden as with him whom Christ had thus surprised. There may be meditations and resolves and deep searchings of spirit—a succession of those terrible pangs which make the heart stand still, or of those perilous balancings of probable destiny, when the soul sends itself forward to the judgment, and strives to realize it; there may be these anxious flutterings about the boundary, but still on this side of it—till in a moment the line is crossed, and "old things are passed away; behold, all things are become new." As there is a first throb of the heart in the implantation of physical life, so is there a first pulsation of the soul through the energy of spiritual existence. This phenomenon is no mental novelty. There is an instant in which one is frequently conscious of renouncing one opinion and entertaining another, preceded, it may be, by scepticism, struggle, and oscillation, the results of conflicting proofs. Conviction may work its way slowly, and up to a certain point, though in the end the conclusion is suddenly gained; the words may linger long on the tongue, till, by an impulse quick as thought, they are at length pronounced. Amidst the mysteries of the will, this palpable fact is often disclosed—that while one may take long to make up his mind, his mind is finally made up by one effort and in that second of time when preference loses its passive character, and inducement ceasing to be a potential becomes an efficient motive. The instant in which Saul heard Jesus name him was that of a total and immediate revolution, for the truth rushed at once upon him that Jesus was true and divine, dwelling in glory, and possessed of sovereign power. The miracle lay not in the change itself, but in the way in which it was effected; the ordinary agencies of argument and remonstrance being superseded by the vision, which, from its very nature, created instantaneous impression and belief.

Still unrelieved of all his astonishment, and, perhaps, scarcely able at times to believe or realize the change which had come over him, Saul "was certain days with the disciples which were at Damascus." What mingled sensations must have been felt on both sides—a wolf among the flock; he, scarcely able to identify himself in the midst of the new associates whom he had travelled all the way from Jerusalem to devour; and they with difficulty regarding him as a brother, at whose threatened approach they had been so terrified. What Charles IX. would have been to a trembling company of Huguenots after the blood and panic of St. Bartholomew, had he avowed himself a protestant, and, lowering his sceptre, besought their forgiveness and fellowship; what Laud would have been to a secret assembly of Puritans, had he owned himself a convert, and flinging his mitre to the ground, asked with tears to be admitted to their communion; what Claverhouse would have been to a nocturnal meeting of Covenanters, had he suddenly burst in among them, protesting that now he was one of them, and claiming, as he tossed his sword from him, their commiseration and prayers—that must Paul have been to the disciples at Antioch. The whole scene was so strange, that they must have been somewhat bewildered, while "they rejoiced for the deliverance." Where were now the letters and the commission from the inquisitors in Jerusalem? Where now the terror produced by the well-known project "to bind all that call on Thy name?" The thunder-cloud had dissolved as it approached.

On the other hand, there must have been in Jerusalem no little anxiety for intelligence of Saul's doings at Damascus, with high anticipations of his success. It must have been felt by his employers, that whatever ardour and an unflinching sense of duty could do, would be done by him. The business was felt to be safe in the experienced hands of him of Tarsus. But no tidings came—no roll of persons arraigned, imprisoned, or tortured. What then? Probably flying rumours preceded—strange whispers, the origin of which could not be traced; and yet each member of the Sanhedrim might, in his perplexity, be asking his neighbour if he had heard them. Something unusual must have occurred—something that could not well be explained. At last there burst upon them the news that Saul had turned renegade; that their trusted and favourite agent had betrayed them; nay, that he had actually gone over to the enemy, and was openly preaching the hated faith. The council would scarcely credit such a rumour, but it was soon and amply confirmed. No doubt they were stunned; and some might mutter in their rage and wonder—"The earth and all the inhabitants thereof are dissolved, we bear up the pillars of it." Who could have dreamed that one so deeply committed as Saul; one so high in confidence, and who had lived but to suppress the infant religion; one who had volunteered to go on such an errand, so fully equipped with credentials, ay, and so sharply goaded on by his own zeal and fury—who could ever have dreamed that he, of all men, should waver, far less apostatize? The riddle could not be solved, though many explanatory hypotheses would soon be in circulation, and every solution but the true one received. The frantic commotion at Jerusalem is the counterpart of the joyous amazement at Damascus. Judaism had lost, Christianity had won; the loss was deplored or cursed, but the gain to that age and all ages after it could not be calculated. For it was not simply the sudden stoppage of a bloody and malignant career, nor the mere peace of the saints in Damascus. There lay in that change not only the germ of a mighty power and many a successful sermon, but there also sprang from it toil and travel beyond the narrow limits of Judea, the conception of a gospel offered to men without distinction of blood or nation, and the composition of those letters of solace and warning, instruction and precept, which form so large a portion of the New Testament. Saul became the living repository of Christ's chosen purpose, as a "light to lighten the Gentiles," and he wrought out that ideal of a church which the Lord had sketched to him, and which, rising above what was local and temporary, gladdened Antioch and penetrated Rome, despaired not of Athens and shrank not from Corinth; which, in short, has hallowed Europe, and shall stretch itself over the world.

> "Lord! thou wilt surely greet
> Souls for Thy service meet;
> No bars of brass can keep Thine own from Thee.
> O! vainly Earth and Hell
> Guard their grand captives well
> Against the glimpses of Thy radiancy.
> Thou streamest on their startled eyes,
> And makest them Thine own by some Divine surprise.
>
> "Forth from the leaguer fell
> Wherein Thy foemen dwell,
> The glorious captains of Thy host Thou takest;
> The mighty souls that came
> To quench the sacred flame,
> The bearers of the Heavenly Fire Thou makest;
> And hands that vexed Thy people most
> Do wave the greenest palms of all the Martyr Host.
>
> "The light not vainly glowed
> On that Damascus road:
> O not for nought that Voice Divine was heard,
> The foeman was o'erthrown,
> The champion made Thine own
> When right against Thee in hot haste he spurred:
> Then streamed forth the world to win
> The mighty burning flame of Love which hate had been."

But Saul's mental temperament was neither blighted nor changed. A brief and single declaration of the historian reveals his nature, and portrays the first appearance of PAUL THE PREACHER—"Straightway he preached Christ in the synagogues—that he is the Son of God." So soon as his own opinions were formed, he began to urge them. He could as yet have no full or adjusted knowledge of the gospel; for he neither received it nor was taught it "of man, but by the revelation of Jesus Christ" in a series of disclosures, made to him in all probability during his subsequent long stay in the deserts of Arabia, where alone and without disturbance he was brought face to face with the Lord, and had laid bare to his inspection the truth and relations, the connections and evidences of that great scheme, in the "defence and confirmation" of which he spent his life and met his death. But in the meantime he acted up to his light— what views he had he dared to express. He longed to disentangle others from the errors which had so long enslaved himself, for his was one of those practical natures in which conviction is identical with action. "*Straightway* he preached:" no wasting of strength by oscillation of purpose—no pang of shame that he must teach the religion which he had laboured, with stripes, and chains, and blood, to exterminate—no compromise with his feelings, as if he should only hint his doubts, and try to bring the question to a quiet discussion. He would not wear any disguise —" Straightway he *preached*." He had come to the truth, and he instantly was in an agony to inform others; for he knew their wants and also their prejudices. The Master's commission pressed upon him, and he must at once make amends for the havoc which he had wrought in the churches. Therefore he entered on the work, heedless of what might be thought of him, of what opprobrious epithets might be heaped upon him, or what ferocious enmity might be excited against him. Name and fame, with all objects of youthful aspiration, he threw aside, nor once cast a longing glance at them. "What things were gain to me, those I counted loss for Christ." And he preached with constitutional intrepidity. He did not quietly ask a few of the more pious and peaceful Jews to his apartments "in the house of Judas" to talk over, without danger, the topics of dispute. He did not suggest such a timorous course, as if alarmed at his change, or doubtful of his tenacity. No. "Straightway he preached *in the synagogues.*" Fearlessly he entered into their religious assemblies, and preached in the places where he had expected to scourge and torture the Christians, making them, as he had uniformly done in Judea, scenes of violence and outrage, of tears and blasphemy. It was a novel spectacle, and his audience could scarcely believe in its reality. It was passing strange, even to disciples. He whose rumoured coming had so terrified them, was now their ablest and boldest advocate. Such a moral miracle can the grace of Christ achieve. The assemblies of the Jews must have been convulsed with agitation—wonder on one countenance, incredulity on another—the eye of one suffused with tears, and the teeth of another gnashing in frenzy; while some tortuous spirits might cherish a forlorn hope that possibly the whole was a deep intrigue—a piece of daring hypocrisy to detect the Christians, and sweep them off in one resistless shock. And yet that earnestness could scarcely be assumed—those calm and commanding tones came from the heart: life and spirit were in those weighty and well-chosen words.

And the speaker did not fence about the subject, suggest some compromise, or deal in vapid generalities; but he openly and distinctly preached "Jesus, that He is the Son of God." This was the pith and marrow of the controversy; not simply that Messiah was divine, or that the great Deliverer should be superhuman, but that Jesus the babe of Bethlehem—" despised and rejected " of the nation, seized and " hanged upon a tree "—was the Son of God. *Son of God* was, in fact, a name of the Messiah. Nathaniel uses it —" Rabbi, thou art the Son of God." Peter employed it —" Thou art the Christ, the Son of the living God." " Art thou the Son of the Blessed?" asked Caiphas, " and Jesus said, I am." " Whosoever," adds the beloved disciple, " shall confess that Jesus is the Son of God, God dwelleth in him, and he in God." The Angel of the Covenant, so often referred to in Hebrew narrative and oracle, and who is identifiable with the promised Saviour, was divine—no created Angel, but the Son of God often appearing in man's form, as if delighting to anticipate his future assumption of humanity. " I am Jesus," said the voice which arrested Saul, " the voice from the excellent glory ;" and, therefore, he argued that this Jesus who had spoken to his inmost soul, and filled it with a new life and power, was the Son of God. His first sermon only told in other words that " God so loved the world, that He gave His only begotten Son, that whosoever believeth in Him should not perish, but have everlasting life." The Son of Mary was the Son of God, the divine and divinely-promised Saviour.

Now the proofs that Messiah should be the Son of God must have been taken principally from the Old Testament. The references in " the Law and the Prophets" must have been the leading steps of the demonstration. Nor are they few nor unimpressive. The names of Messiah are significant and full of mystery, and He who wears them must be divine. Thus, in Genesis, He is the woman's 'Seed,' and He alone of all men was born of a virgin—the 'Seed' of Abraham, too, in whom all the nations of the earth were to be blessed—and 'the Shiloh' springing out of Judah, to whom 'the gathering of the people shall be:' in Exodus, the occupant of the burning bush—Jehovah's 'Angel' and yet Jehovah himself—'I AM THAT I AM,' the name of uncaused and unchanging Essence: in Leviticus, the God of that tabernacle, the splendour of whose golden furniture was dimmed by the resident glory of its divine Architect: in Numbers, the King and Lawgiver, with the cloud by day and the pillar of fire by night, the symbols of His awful and protecting presence: in Deuteronomy, the 'Prophet like unto Moses,' raised up from among his brethren, Jehovah speaking to him face to face—for so it was with the son of Amram: in Joshua, the 'Captain of the Lord's Host' with the drawn sword, before whom Jericho fell without the stroke of a battering ram, or the digging of a trench: in Judges, the 'Angel who did wondrously,' and went up in the smoke and flame of Manoah's accepted sacrifice: in the Books of Samuel, Kings, and Chronicles, the Head and Guardian of the Theocracy, for under it to fear God and to honour the king were one and the same thing: in Job, the 'Daysman who can lay His hand upon both,' and the 'Redeemer who shall stand at the latter day upon the earth:' in Psalms, 'David's Son and David's Lord;' the Priest-king 'for ever, after the order of Melchisedec,' whose body was prepared for him by God, and which, though it went down to the grave, did not "see corruption:" in

Proverbs, the incarnate 'Wisdom, by Him, brought up with Him, rejoicing always before Him:' in the Song of Songs, the august Bridegroom, whose royal splendour is equalled by his conjugal affection: in Isaiah, the 'Servant of Jehovah,' despised and scorned, 'wounded for our transgressions, and bruised for our iniquities;' slain, but yet crowned and compensated for His sufferings, having divided to Him 'a portion with the great,' Himself 'dividing the spoil with the strong:' in Jeremiah, the 'Lord our Righteousness:' in Ezekiel, 'the likeness of a Man' on the sapphire-throne, served by the cherubim, and guiding the mystic mechanism of 'the wheel within the wheel:' in Daniel, 'Messiah cut off, but not for Himself'—the 'Son of man coming in the clouds of heaven:' in Hosea, the plague of death and destroyer of the grave: in Joel, the Lord and dispenser of the Spirit: in Amos, the 'Repairer of the breaches' in David's tabernacle: in Micah, the 'Ruler' whose birth is to be at Bethlehem, and whose 'goings forth have been of old, from everlasting:' in Zephaniah, 'He who rests in his love, and joys over his people with singing:' in Haggai, the 'Desire of all nations:' in Zechariah, the 'Man whose name is the Branch;' and, the 'Sun of Righteousness,' in the book of Malachi. And then came the argument that these descriptive epithets met in Jesus, and that His whole life embodied them. The preacher must have heard often of Jesus, and may have, at a prior period, learned the leading facts of His career in a distorted shape. But a few days in Damascus must have given him detailed and accurate information, and his trained mind was soon able to arrange it, and use it to advantage.

A Christian teacher must not be a "novice" or recent convert, lest he be lifted up with pride by his speedy elevation. So the apostle ruled, and so he exemplified it. He had shown the Jews of Damascus the change which had come over him, and he had laboured to make them partakers of his own vivid and imperious convictions. What success attended his labours we know not; perhaps the suddenness of his conversion may have made him an object of suspicion and distrust; some might be disposed to wait for further explanations of it, as if some chain of subordinate and personal motives might have led to it; others might compassionate him as partially bereft of his intellect by the startling radiance that had enveloped him near the bridge where he and his companions had fallen; as in short labouring under some hallucination which might gradually pass off, so that, as soon as he should come to himself, he should return more fondly and fixedly to his original creed. From whatever reason, the apostle left Damascus, and retired into the neighbouring deserts, where, perhaps, he might maintain himself by his handicraft as a tent-maker; tent-cloth, or a coarse cashmere, being woven of the hair of the shaggy goats in that region, as in his native province of Cilicia. In those solitudes the apostle spent a lengthened period. There his soul must have communed much with itself and God, and there he enjoyed successive revelations of the scheme of mercy. Great disclosures have resulted from solitary study, and from musing in scenes—

> "Where woven shades shut out the light of day,
> While, towering near, the rugged mountains make
> Dark back-ground 'gainst the sky,"

discoveries in science, inventions in art, and forms of ideal beauty have flashed upon the self-rapt spirit as it held secret fellowship with nature. Dreams have fallen on it which indicate the dawn of a better philosophy, and it has given incidental utterance to hints which have proved themselves the seeds of a bounteous harvest. "An horror of great darkness" may have occasionally enveloped him, for the mighty change did not mechanically fortify him against all memories, or shut out from him all anticipations. His susceptible nature must have undergone a process involving every variety of emotion and soliloquy; casting up the motives of the past, and forecasting the possibilities of the future; taking the measure of itself in searching and repeated self-questionings; sounding the depths of its convictions and resolves; a lifetime in awfulness and intensity of feeling, and in depth, vastness, and pressure of thought, crowded into the space of a few short months. Such agonies of preparation are the prelude to valiant deeds: the Slough of Despond precedes the firm path, and the Valley of Humiliation lies in front of the Delectable Mountains.

Saul studied theology in no earthly school, and under no human teacher. He called no man master, and after he left the feet of Gamaliel he never occupied a similar relation towards any other human being. Nor yet did he think out the various truths of the gospel for himself, or with the assistance of kindred minds. The doctrines which he subsequently proclaimed were not evolved by such a secret and prolonged mental process as a daring and speculative spirit loves to indulge in; for they were in no sense "after man"—neither in man's style of creation nor expression. The revelations which the recluse enjoyed, suspended his natural powers only so far as inventive genius was concerned. He had not to excogitate a system, but he had still to connect and comprehend the disclosures made to him. What the Divine Teacher time after time communicated to him, that he would revolve and meditate on, viewing it in all lights and upon all sides; till being mastered in sum and in detail, it was inwoven with his spiritual constitution, and became a portion of himself. The great reformer of philosophy could truly say—Thus Bacon thought; but the apostle of the Gentiles could only affirm—Thus was I taught. On such revelations he casts himself when his authority is open to question, as when, in writing on the Lord's Supper to the Corinthians, and referring to his account of the first scene, himself not having been present, he affirms—"I have received of the Lord that which also I delivered unto you." So, when about to describe the free and full admission of Gentiles into the church—an idea that excited no little prejudice, and met with no common antagonism—he solemnly avers "how that by revelation He made known unto me the mystery;" or as when he portrays the solemn mysteries of the last day—the rising of "the dead in Christ" before the change of the living—he announces, "This we say unto you by the word of the Lord." After the musings and revelations in Arabia, the "chosen vessel" was so filled with divine communication, that his chiefest pleasure afterwards lay in giving it out. By a resistless law of his spiritual nature, he could not but speak what his soul was surcharged with;

and whether he thought of its truth or of its grace, its origin from God or its adaptation to man, it became a "necessity" for him to proclaim it. Saturated with evangelical truth, and urged on by the constraining power of the love of Christ, Saul returned to Damascus. And now, as he was more powerful in argument, his appeals must have been armed with a keener barb than on his first visit.

So that, after narrating the natural wonder and talk of spectators, the historian adds—"But Saul increased the more in strength, and confounded the Jews which dwelt at Damascus, proving that this is very Christ"—*proving*—forging link after link in a chain of argument. Opposition did not daunt him. No appeal to the tenor of his past life could shame him—no satirical remarks about consistency could put him out. He rose in intellectual and spiritual power. He was well aware, from his own experience, what were the strongholds of Pharisaic pride and fanaticism. He could anticipate every objection, remove every scruple, and so enter into the spirit of his opponents as to meet and refute every doubt. He had but to remember how himself had felt and reasoned, and he was armed for his task, and then, with his new and additional information, he confounded the Jews which dwelt at Damascus. As he heaped proof upon proof in intense accumulation, as he laid bare their sophisms and gave them a vivid anatomy of their inner nature, transferred his own experience to them, exposed every prejudice, and overturned every refuge of lies—no wonder he "*confounded*" them; that is, he so perplexed them with his reasonings, that ingenuity failed them—they were struck dumb, and could not reply. They "could not resist the wisdom and power" by which he spake, as he was "proving that this is very Christ;" that this man who passed among men by the name of Jesus, is verily the long-promised and long-expected *Christ* or Messiah—that is, the anointed One—having in the unction of the Holy Ghost the seal and signal of His commission, and the great element of His qualification; for God gave "Him not the Spirit by measure"—" the Spirit of counsel and might"—the Spirit which descended "like a dove, and it abode upon Him"—since He was "justified in the Spirit;" "by the Spirit of God" He wrought miracles; "through the eternal Spirit" He offered Himself; put to death in the flesh, He was "quickened by the Spirit;" nay, He was "declared to be the Son of God, according to the Spirit of holiness, by the resurrection from the dead."

The evidence must have rested on a comparison of Christ's life with the "prophecies that went before concerning" Him. That evidence is varied and convincing. He was born at Bethlehem, as Micah had predicted, and before the four hundred and ninety years had expired, as Daniel had foretold; born of a virgin, and of the family of David, as the seers had announced; walking and worshipping in the second temple, as the last of the prophets had pre-intimated; baptized with the Holy Ghost, and assuming a public ministry, for thus had He been heralded; speaking, and that by parable, as the Psalmist had avouched; working, and that by miracle, as Isaiah had chanted; living a holy and gentle life, as long ago pencilled by the Spirit; betrayed by His "own familiar friend which did eat of His bread;" apprehended and put to death, according to "the determinate counsel and foreknowledge of God;" His hands and feet pierced, and yet "not a bone of Him broken," for so had it been fore-pictured; offered vinegar in His thirst, as His suffering prototype had drunk before Him; "numbered among transgressors," for such had been the strange and awful utterance; a grave prepared Him with the two thieves, and yet laid in the tomb of "a rich man," who begged His body; the execrated of the world, and yet the Saviour of the world.

Such a demonstration was Saul's special work in the meantime. He upheld the claims of Jesus, as he was for the second time confronted with his countrymen, and there were fifty thousand of them in Damascus. He did not beat about the question, but brought it at once into earnest conflict. It was a question of life and death—it was the question of the age—the question for all ages—the identification of Jesus with that divine Emancipator whom the Hebrew bards had sung of in rapturous anticipation—with Him who, in taking humanity, was to redeem it, and in descending to the world was to lift it out of degradation and ruin, and elevate it to renewed fellowship with its Creator. It needed faith, indeed, to comprehend the mystery, for there had been no external manifestation. He was not born in a palace, nor swaddled "in soft raiment." The Babe did not sleep on a lordly couch, nor was there a glory round the head of the Youth. The Man was not surrounded with oriental luxuries, but He handled hammer and hatchet, when He earned His bread by the sweat of His brow and felt the primal curse. He wore no divine livery, as He wrought His miracles; and when He died, no choir of angels were heard singing hymns of comfort in His ear. What about Him, then, signalized Him? It needed a keen eye to watch Him, so as to detect His higher nature. But then, as you compare Him with the olden oracles, who can doubt their fulfilment in Him? Moses throws a halo over his successor "like unto" him. Aaron, clothed with the ephod and breast-plate, and carrying "the blood of goats and calves," represents Him dying and pleading. David, with his diadem on his brow, claims Him as his Son, and last and great successor. Yes, this is He, seen in the light of type and prophecy. O surely it is a sin of sins to reject Him. If men are "confounded," and yet are not convinced; if they cannot refute the proof, and yet in defiance of it will not admit the conclusion; if, though vanquished in argument, they withhold their faith, and fall back on prejudice, or wrap themselves in indifference—then surely theirs is the terrible condemnation of those who "love the darkness rather than the light," and, wilfully shrouding themselves in the gloom, gather it in thickening folds around them for ever. If this be the very Christ, let us hail His advent with rapture, contemplate His life in admiration, open our hearts to His words, strive to imbibe His spirit of untiring beneficence, prostrate ourselves in awful wonder round His cross, survey His empty tomb with sabbatic gladness, and follow Him with loud hosannahs as He ascends to His throne of Glory. Thou, the only-begotten Son of God and first-born Child of Mary—the living embodiment of Abraham's far-off visions and David's gladsome pæans; Thou, the Angel of the Covenant and the Man of sorrows; Thou, the Lord of the temple and the Infant of the manger—Blessed Jesus, Thou art the very Christ!

Saul's preaching during his second sojourn of "many days" at Damascus, so provoked his enemies that they resolved on his assassination—a miserable weapon of defence, and the token, too, of conscious defeat. The same spirit was rising against Saul as had risen in his own mind against Stephen. He saw his former self alive again in those adversaries, and by himself could measure their truculent ferocity. The tormentor became in turn the tormented—the knife he had whetted was pointed against himself. "I will show him how great things he must suffer for my name's sake," said the Lord to Ananias; and the neophyte soon began to learn the lesson, and he who was "in perils oft" never ceased to learn it. The Jews in many cities had a species of separate internal government, with a local magistrate of their own race, somewhat in the same way as British residents in a foreign port are under the protection of a British consul. When, therefore, "they took counsel to kill him," they obtained the assistance of the garrison, so as to seize him and prevent his flight. But his friends interfered: the ethnarch under Aretas missed his prey; and the sentinels at the gates found their vigilance ineffective. That life was too richly laden to be so prematurely cut off: "Through a window in a basket was I let down by the wall, and escaped." He who had entered Damascus a blind and stricken traveller, left it a fugitive in haste and by night, as if he had committed a crime, and sought in cowardice to avoid the penalty. His sincerity was tried, but he wavered not; the strength of his convictions was put to a hard and sudden test, but he stood it. Henceforth he might be used for any service the Master required —to do or to suffer; for the one or the other he was alike prepared, for into both he had been thus early initiated. Men may, by shifting sides, get greater popularity and a higher reputation for honesty. They may become leaders in the new warfare, or from a lower pinnacle they may be lifted to the summit, and the feeling that they are first may compensate them for any odium or satire which their change may have provoked. But Saul had no cheering prospect of this nature; for he was scorned by the Jews, then assaulted by the Judaizing Christians, and perhaps never fully trusted by the original apostles. His life was but a battle and a march, and a march and a battle, doing and suffering, suffering and doing. He was weak in every man's weakness, and burning with every man's offence; "in weariness and painfulness, in watchings often, in hunger and thirst, in cold and nakedness;" his heart oppressed and broken by "the care of all the churches." We who know the worth, wisdom, and devotedness of his life, are apt so to idealize him, that we cannot see these privations in their literal existence. We associate dignity and authority with the great preacher, and cannot picture the poor pinched stranger—insignificant, in "bodily presence," weary and footsore, ragged, hungry and shivering—coming into a city like a shiftless vagabond who had spent all, and was in want—the livid ring on his limbs so scantily clad, revealing his acquaintance with the stocks, and the scar of the whip on his back espied through his tattered mantle as he is seeking out a lodging in the meanest streets, where dwelt some pious Jews or proselytes amongst "the offscourings of all things." There he lived and fared, and thence he issued to preach "the unsearchable riches of Christ." And this was usual with him. Luther in knight's armour, Calvin in the garb of a vine-dresser, Tyndale in a blouse, or Bunyan in a smock—these were but disguises assumed for a brief period to escape peril, but the apostle's normal state was one of privation and suffering. Never, except in the instance of his Master, had appearance and reality been in such contrast. That mind had insight little less in clearness or in reach than that of "the living creatures full of eyes." That heart had more than man's firmness, and more than woman's softness; and that life was devoted to his species with an aim that never wavered, and a self-feeding ardour which was never damped, and which could not be extinguished save in the blood of him who felt and cherished it.

II.—SAUL AT JERUSALEM.

Acts ix. 26–30; xxii. 17–21. Gal. i. 18, 19.

The humble stratagem by which Saul had escaped those who were "desirous to apprehend" him, was neither a matter of shame to the inspired historian nor to the apostle himself, for both have referred to it. The wit of a woman had done a similar exploit in the olden time; Rahab let the spies "down by a cord through the window, for her house was upon the town wall." The apostle tells us that he had a special motive in going at this time to Jerusalem, for "he went up *to see Peter*," or make his acquaintance. He had formed this intention, but the conspiracy of his foes hastened his departure, and, when the basket touched the ground, he did not make for some safe and obscure retreat, but set his face toward the metropolis. It was night. It was in blindness that he had first entered Damascus—he "could not see for the glory of that light"—and now he is forced to flee from it under the friendly cover of darkness. As he left Damascus and proceeded to Jerusalem, he could not pass the scene of his conversion without a holy shudder. Every turn of the road during these hundred and twenty miles, must have reminded him of his eastward journey. But he hurries westward a changed man, dead to his former self, and to all previous impressions, aspirations, and hopes. And he must have sometimes wondered how he should meet the zealots of his nation, his instigators in his days of cruelty and ignorance, and he must also have surmised how they would shrink from his presence, or hurl against him the fierce curses which their eloquent fury could so copiously supply. But he was too brave to fear human opinion; he had "seen Christ Jesus the Lord," and heard His voice, and what cared he either for scowls or anathemas? And if he entered the city at the gate by which he had left it, or passed the place of Stephen's martyrdom, his soul must have trembled in its gratitude to sovereign mercy; for all such past things were severed by a great gulf from his present being. The bigot had become a Christian; the persecutor an apostle. His arrival at Jerusalem must have created as much doubt and wonder as it had done at Antioch, for we are told that "when Saul was come to Jerusalem, he assayed to join himself to the disciples: but they were all afraid of him, and believed not that he was a disciple." He had been a long time away from them; first rumours had subsided; he had been absent, too, from Damascus for a season, and tidings did not then travel very speedily from land to land. He *assayed* to join himself—made several earnest but ineffectual efforts. He did not attempt to take them by storm, and parade the glory of his conversion before them. "Less than the least of all saints," he humbly sought admission, but he was refused; his veracity was questioned—"they did not believe that he was a disciple." Indeed "they were afraid of him;" they deemed him to be a wolf in lamb's clothing, and would not credit him that his old heart was gone, and that he was a Nazarene who had been "a persecutor, and a blasphemer, and injurious." Yes, Saul was denied Christian fellowship—no small trial, in his present condition, for one who had done and suffered so much under his new convictions. His discipleship, gained by such a miracle, was disallowed, and, as he had left Damascus in haste, he had brought with him no credentials. But Barnabas kindly interfered and vouched for his sincerity, telling " how he had seen the Lord in the way" and had been converted, and how he had laboured so courageously on the very scene of his intended havoc. Then was he admitted to fellowship, and "he was with them coming in and going out at Jerusalem." He met at this time with only two of the apostles, James and Peter, and he resided with Peter. The apostle of the circumcision and the apostle of the Gentiles dwelt for "fifteen days" under one roof. What conversations, discussions, and projected enterprises from two minds so unlike in structure and discipline, and yet so very like in zeal and courage! The one flamed, but the other burned; the one was fitful and forward, the other was patient and uniform; the one was a creature of impulse, the other glowed with a steady enthusiasm. Peter loved Palestine, yet Paul loved it none the less that his heart embraced the world. The former felt at home in the sphere of the Old Testament, the other stretched beyond it while he did not forsake it. To the one, a Gentile was a man to be converted; to the other, a brother also to be won. Peter did what he knew to be his duty in repairing to the house of Cornelius, but he did not feel at perfect liberty to repeat such deeds; while the untrammelled Paul exclaims—"Inasmuch as I am the apostle of the Gentiles I magnify mine office." In a word, Peter was like the Jordan, the stream that belonged exclusively to his fatherland, though a foreigner, like Naaman, might once in its history wash and be healed in it; but Paul resembled the "great sea," which washes the shores of the three large continents.

Saul stayed only a fortnight in Jerusalem, but he was not and could not be idle. It is said of him briefly and emphatically, that "he spake boldly in the name of the Lord Jesus, and disputed against the Grecians: but they went about to slay him." Four features of his preaching come into view—

1. The class to whom he addressed himself were the *Grecians* or Hellenists, that is, Jews, but, like himself, born out of Palestine; Jews like Stephen, whom he had confronted in the Hellenistic synagogue, and to whose death he had "consented." He was most naturally drawn to them. The Jews born in Judæa were victims of narrowness and prejudice; the "genius of the place" overawed them, and held them in bondage. But the Hellenists born and brought up in other countries were less liable to these strong opinions, for they had mingled with other races, and their minds were expanded with literary and commercial intercourse. As one of them, Saul specially appealed to them, in the hope that, as he understood them and might expect them to sympathize with him, he might win them over to the gospel. For, there are certain ties of blood, education, and language which are to be recognized even in the advocacy of the truth, and which it would be

wrong in a public advocate or orator to overlook. Saul, therefore, "in the meekness of wisdom," laboured in a sphere where he imagined that he had most hopes of success. He did not fling the gospel in the face of the high priest, did not go to the temple and harangue the fanatical crowds, but prudently and earnestly he brought to bear upon the Hellenists the result of his training and experience in Damascus. "One of yourselves presents himself to you"—might be his preface as he began in the Greek tongue, more familiar to them than Hebrew, to advance and maintain the claims of Jesus as Messiah. Saul, therefore, as a preacher, was no unreasoning fanatic, unable to hold his tongue or control his temper; no agitator, reckless as to circumstances, and anxious only to obtrude his views, deeming still that he was doing his duty, though he only provoked without convincing, and excited dislike to himself and antipathy to his cause. He was indeed a man of one idea—the Messiahship—and that idea filled him; but it was not with him as with many men of one idea; it did not so overmaster him that he knew not when, how, and where to develope it. He might fail with the majority he spoke to, but his labours could not be wholly without fruit.

2. His preaching took the form of disputation. He spoke and *disputed against* the Grecians; for it was no studied oration which he had prepared and was able to deliver with fluency and power, but, during its recitation, would neither bear with interruption nor be annoyed with any impertinent questions or exclamations. He did not come forth simply with a "set speech," keen, argumentative,

and weighty; but after he spoke he allowed the free criticism of all his statements. He did not feel insulted when his conclusions were denied, and his interpretations were tossed aside. He met his opponents openly and fully, prepared to reply to their questions and to respond to their challenge. He was not afraid of close grappling, nor did he endeavour to elude the force of any objections or inferences that might be brought against him. The scene, though it began with preaching, became one of discussion, and Saul did not shrink from it, either as beneath his dignity or as unworthy of his commission. There would be in his audience some that sneered and some that scowled—some that simply liked a display of gladiatorial skill, others that were honestly seeking after righteousness. Each as he arraigned the sermon would get his answer as he merited — the preacher never off his guard or losing his temper at the folly or obstinacy which wrested his words, and never reduced to hide the weakness or inaptness of a reply by the sarcasm or bitterness of a personal retort. One opponent might question his interpretation of a portion of the law or the prophets, and try to set aside its reference to the Messiah; or another would affirm some base thing about our Lord's life, or some stupid and malignant thing about his religion, while to the one and the other Saul would speak with loving soul, reasoning out the validity of his interpretation from the words or connection of the paragraph, and teaching the truth as to the facts of the Master's career and the nature and purposes of his atoning death. And though another disputant, with a leer and a frown, should refer to his conversion, so strange and unexpected, the allusion could neither shame nor intimidate one who "had seen that Just One, and heard the voice of His mouth." Merely to silence and subdue them, and to gain an intellectual mastery over them, was no part of his aim; he loved them while he prostrated them, and his heart bled for them while he showed them the sophistry which entangled or the darkness which enveloped them.

3. His preaching was *bold*, for his convictions were thorough, and he uttered them without hesitation or fear. He was a stranger to faintheartedness. He believed, therefore he spake. Had he felt any secret doubts or misgivings; had the scene of his conversion recurred as some illusive phenomenon; had there been any suspicions within him that possibly after all he might be in error— then his preaching might have been timid and faltering. But Saul's mind could not admit the possibility of a doubt; as soon should he question his own existence as question that Jesus in glory had named him and spoken to him. It was no hallucination, for it was at midday that the voice had arrested him. The "light above the brightness of the sun" had blinded him, and some time had elapsed before he had recovered his vision—nay, probably at that moment he was labouring under defective eyesight. So assured and fortified, he could neither be reasoned nor terrified out of his belief. And the glorified Jesus being his shield, he was not alarmed at "what man shall do." The want of the age was the proclamation of the Messiahship, and Saul set himself bravely to the work—as in Damascus so in Jerusalem. He could not modify, and he would not

recant. Pressed on every side by the Grecians, while order and decorum were occasionally broken in upon by the " strife of tongues," he was unmoved—impervious alike to execration and ridicule—a mighty man of valour—a spiritual hero clad in " the whole armour of God."

4. And he was bold *in the name of the Lord Jesus*, that is, he not only preached Christ, but he claimed His express authority for so preaching Him. Christ had not only seized him and yoked him to the work, but commissioned him to do it. Whether, then, he looked to the authority under which he acted, or the momentous nature of the lessons proclaimed by him, or the pressing wants of men around him, he could not but be bold. Timidity would be treachery to his Master, cruelty to the world, and unfaithfulness to his own convictions. And all this brave outspokenness so early in his career, ere yet he had been taught to " endure hardness," was not the arrogance of a " novice," but the courage which one feels who has resolved at all hazards to be true to his beliefs, who has vowed fidelity both to God and to man, and who is supported by the grace which never fails in its sufficiency, and the strength which perfects itself in weakness.

That Saul's appearance should impress some needs not be doubted, but the multitude refused to believe. Nay, in their vengeful excitement *they went about to slay him*—tried various and repeated plans, but failed. His short sojourn had roused their passionate resentment, and they could not bear that he of all men should so boldly defy and confound them. In the meantime he had enjoyed a remarkable vision, which long afterwards he described to the

Jewish mob. In Jerusalem, in the temple, and when he was engaged in devotion, he fell into an ecstacy; the operation of sense being suspended, his higher spiritual nature was brought again into direct personal communication with Christ; so that he "saw Him," and heard Him utter these words—"Make haste, and get thee quickly out of Jerusalem, for they will not receive thy testimony concerning Me." As Saul had been only two weeks there, he wished to remain a little longer, and, probably with the advice of Peter, thought of selecting Jerusalem as a field of labour. It may have been one of the great feasts, and there might be in Jerusalem "Jews and proselytes from every nation under heaven." Another scene like Pentecost might be anticipated, and Peter might be hoping much from the ardour, erudition, and eloquence of his junior colleague; "James, the Lord's brother," being the only other apostle resident at the time in the city. Man proposes, but God disposes. Saul was at once ordered off the scene; for so long as he was there, he was out of the sphere which the Master intended for him. The outfield of heathenism was his place, and he was not to spend precious time among Hellenistic Jews in Jerusalem, since he would meet them in every city in the Gentile world, as he went about among the uncircumcised races. But as Saul did nothing without a reason, he honestly tells the Lord why he had come to labour in Jerusalem. He gives his own view thus: "I said, Lord, they know that I imprisoned and beat in every synagogue them that believed on thee: and when the blood of thy martyr Stephen was shed, I also was standing by, and consenting unto his death, and kept the raiment of them that slew him." The ground taken by Saul is very intelligible. The population of Jerusalem had known what he was, and he wished them to know what he had become. They could not but inquire into the nature and cause of the change which had come over him, and they could not doubt the honesty of one who by that change had so fully renounced all which the world covets—all the objects, indeed, of his own youthful ambition. Nay, he had been so furious that he *beat* the Christians savagely, or flayed them, as the word means; and at the martyrdom of Stephen he himself was standing over the scene, approving of the deed, and guarding the robes of them who acted the bloody part of executioners and dispatched the protomartyr. Therefore he thought, that on the spot where such points were notorious, and where he had been a ringleader in a fanatical murder, he had a special claim to be heard against himself and in favour of that system which he had adopted from the best of all reasons—autoptic evidence, the appearance and glory of the exalted Jesus. They could not imagine that he had been duped, for they were aware of his mental acuteness and vigour. Neither could they think that one of his austere honesty and straightforward disposition could deceive others; nor yet could they suppose that he had lightly or recklessly abandoned that faith for which he had so gallantly struggled. But his excuse is not even replied to by the Master. The only response to his argument is—"Depart, for I will send thee far hence unto the Gentiles"—a distinct and peremptory intimation that admitted neither of hesitation nor delay. Begone—the order of high authority—the majestic token of divine prerogative. Thus in Jerusalem, and in the temple, the very centre and citadel of Judaism, did he receive his express commission to be the apostle of the Gentiles. So commanded by Jesus, and so advised, at the same time, of danger by the brethren, Saul left Jerusalem, was "brought down" to Cæsarea, "came into the regions of Syria and Cilicia," and arrived at Tarsus. Three years had elapsed since he had been commissioned to the Gentiles by divine authority, and still he was reluctant to undertake the task for which his education and temperament so well fitted him. Moses, when summoned to go to Egypt and confront Pharaoh, pleaded want of eloquence; Gideon would not march till the fleece had been wetted, nay, till the omen had been reversed; Jeremiah urged his youth and inexperience when called to the prophetic office; Jonah set sail for Tarshish, instead of proceeding to Nineveh; Ananias, when bidden to seek out a stranger who had recently arrived at Damascus, demurred and said, "Lord, I have heard by many of this man how much evil he hath done to thy saints at Jerusalem;" and Saul, thinking himself possessed of special qualifications for a sphere of labour which he preferred, was backward toward that very work for which he had been born and called, and in which he so soon achieved signal success, and won imperishable renown. "Who art thou, O man, that repliest against God?" "The right man in the right place," has become a popular expression for mutual adaptation. Saul did not verify the saying either in Damascus or Jerusalem, but it might be truly predicated of him through his whole subsequent career, when he spoke, travelled, toiled, and suffered, as one " appointed a preacher, and an apostle, and a teacher of the Gentiles in faith and verity."

    Strange realms, wide waters o'er,
    The conquering Cross he bore;
In her own Isle the Love Queen he abash'd;
    Through Asian cities bright
    He poured the sweet strange light;
Diana in her Ephesus he dashed.
    Greece glowed beneath his golden tongue;
Full in Athenian ears their Unknown God he rung.

    Each rich Corinthian shrine
    Grew dim and undivine,
Philippi heard the captor-captive's song;
    O! ne'er from Grecian soul
    Such golden streams did roll;
No Roman hand e'er smote, e'er built so strong.
    Temples fell down where'er he trod,
And on from land to land stretched the one Church of God.

    O bearer of all shame!
    O Earth's most glorious name!
O weakling, by whom mightiest deeds were done!
    O prisoner, whose firm stroke
    Ten thousand fetters broke!
O outcast, by whose word the world was won;
    O bruised one, whose cheer ran o'er
To make divinely glad all souls for evermore!

III.—SAUL AT ANTIOCH IN SYRIA.

Acts xi. 22-26.

THREATENED assassination and divine command had sent Saul out of Jerusalem, and he went home to Tarsus. In that city, under the shadow of Mount Taurus, he might again recreate himself with Hellenic studies; and by intercourse with the philosophers who paced the gymnasium by the green banks of the cold and rapid Cydnus, he might learn what trains of thought were best adapted to work on the hearts of those who were "aliens from the commonwealth of Israel." The time was not lost, the apostle could not be idle—it was a season either of busy preparation, or of active missionary duty. He had hitherto come into conflict only with his own countrymen, whose prejudices he could instinctively comprehend, for he read them in his own past life. But he had been warned that another and very different field was to be occupied by him, and for which it behoved him, by every form of human discipline, to equip himself. Experiments upon the gentile population at Tarsus, either conducted by dialogue or more formal addresses, must have shown him how he could best serve the Master in making known His salvation to the pagan world. Though Saul was taught of the Spirit, he was also the pupil of experience; and what he saw and heard in his native province, either in its hilly regions or level shores—the feelings he encountered, the forms of antagonism he met with, the prevailing type of objection which the educated or uneducated heathen mind, Greek, Roman, and aboriginal, presented—must have been studied by him, and must have afforded guidance in his subsequent evangelical labours. He could afterwards anticipate hostile argument—trace its origin, detect its fallacy, ay, and counterwork it, ere it had time to express itself.

In the meantime, the gospel had been carried to different regions by those who had fled into exile after the martyrdom of Stephen. The blood of the martyr had already become the seed of the church. They who sped away for life carried with them the elements of a higher life. The first persecution of the church led to its first missionary enterprise. The death of Stephen occasioned obedience to the parting command of the Master—" Go ye into all the world, and preach the gospel to every creature." Not a few who "were scattered abroad," being probably Jews born in Palestine, " preached the word to none but unto the Jews only." But "men of Cyprus and Cyrene" had gone as far as Antioch, and their preaching " to the Grecians " had been attended with signal success. The inspired historian tells us that " the hand of the Lord was with them "—the power of Him who was upon the throne was sent down to crown and bless their labours. Throughout the Acts the primary agency of the Lord Jesus is uniformly recognized. What Christ did when among men, is told in the Gospels; what He still did when removed from men, is told in the Acts. How He governed when present, is described in the one group of narratives; how He governs when absent, is rehearsed in this book. The Christ of the Gospels is a present and tender friend—the Christ of the Acts still preserves the same character; is near, though He is away; loves, though He has left; and guides and controls, though the heavens retain Him. The scenes of this history, in which apostles preached, wrought miracles, or suffered, belong to Christ as really as the synagogue at Nazareth where He was rejected, the shores of Gennesaret where He wandered and strewed deeds of mercy on His path, the hamlet of Bethany where He enjoyed His friends, or the garden of Gethsemane where He met His agony.

News of the immense success of the gospel at Antioch had reached Jerusalem. The mother-church might not claim a formal jurisdiction, but it was startled and perplexed, as well as delighted, by the intelligence. If the heathen were admitted, it should like to know on what conditions, and by what authority? The zealots for the law desired to interfere, for they afterwards called Peter to account, and "contended" with him, because he had eaten with the uncircumcised. When the great results of Philip's preaching were known at Jerusalem, Peter and John were sent down to Samaria; and so Barnabas was commissioned as a deputy to the northern city, to ascertain from inspection how far the tidings were correct and what farther information might be gathered: and he cheerfully undertook the embassy. He must have been high in the confidence of the church in Jerusalem, for we have seen, too, that his introduction was the voucher of Saul's discipleship.

The benevolent and self-denied Cypriot came to Antioch,

and his mind, if it had been in any doubt, was at once relieved. There was neither disorder nor unwarranted innovation. When he had "seen the grace of God, he was glad." Every feeling of embarrassment left him. The noble spectacle filled his mind with unutterable gladness. He *saw the grace of God;* that is, overlooking the minor means and subordinate instrumentalities, he detected the workings of divine power. For whatever eloquence, zeal, and courage had been employed, God's grace had effected the change, as it alone reaches and renews the heart. The gospel is an embodiment of His grace, and they who believe the gospel, get that grace for their heritage. When Barnabas looked around on so many converts, and knew what their convictions were; when he saw the synagogue forsaken and the groves of Daphne deserted; when he beheld the sanctified intelligence and changed lives of the Christian multitudes—he could ascribe the phenomenon to nothing but the grace of God. It is true that the inner workings of grace are invisible, and that Barnabas could not see into the heart; but with the results before him, he at once recognized the cause. There was indeed no opening of the heavens—no "rushing mighty wind"—no "cloven tongues, like as of fire"—no scene of palpable visitation, such as at Pentecost; but the effect was not the less striking in the faith and devotedness, the purity and unity, of the Antiochean church. Were the grace of God implored, would it not still descend, reviving the church, and conquering the world? The exalted Lord will not deny it—He will bow His heaven, and pour it down in rich effusion. Lord, let

Thy grace come down in its majesty, so that Thy saints may rejoice in it, and that sinners may feel its sweep. Let the means of grace verify their name as vehicles of divine and saving influence. Lead sinners to Thy "throne of grace." Give "testimony to the word of Thy grace;" and bestow upon us "grace for grace," as Thou showest the "riches" of Thy grace. Help us who "believe through grace," by enabling us not only to "continue in the grace of God," but to "grow in grace." Make "all grace to abound toward us;" yea, let "great grace be upon us all."

When Barnabas saw the spectacle, he sympathized with it. Earth had nothing for him so rich in pleasure. The power in gracious operation was divine; the subjects wrought upon were the noblest — the souls of men — precious beyond computation; and the results, partially gained, and to be in the end fully realized, were the loftiest and best that God can achieve, or man can experience. Barnabas could look on neither with indifference nor envy. He rejoiced, for he saw the cause of Christ so prosperous after the dark season of persecution, and, after it had bled at Jerusalem, achieving such conquests in one of the prime strongholds of Eastern heathendom. That cause was endeared the more to them who had suffered for it; and while it lay at home under the frown of the priesthood and the ban of the Sanhedrim, it was rapidly and surely, and without molestation, planting and spreading itself in so renowned a spot as the third city of the empire. When the deputy of the metropolitan church had reflected on these circumstances, we may imagine what a glowing despatch he would transmit to Jerusalem.

But Barnabas felt that there was duty laid upon him. He was not only to report to the mother-church, but immediate obligation also pressed upon him. He must improve the opportunity, and preach; and the burden of his preaching was the duty or necessity of perseverance. "He exhorted them all, that with purpose of heart they would cleave unto the Lord." This was the one grand lesson for the time. He might be afraid that this outburst of enthusiasm might not last, that among a giddy and susceptible people such novel sensations might speedily subside. Therefore he addressed himself to the one remedy. For continuous faith alone is continuous safety. One must not only flee to the refuge, but abide in it, that he may escape the storm. The race must not only be begun, but the racer must hold on, for he must grasp the goal ere he get the garland. And the resolution to persevere was not to be taken laxly and vaguely, but with "*purpose of heart*"— with intelligent and cordial resolve. There needed such decision among the Gentiles. Society was pervaded with idolatrous usages, and the ordinary interchange of civilities was tainted with them. The heathen was reminded at every step of the religion which he had left—its altars, temples, and gods were on all hands. If he partook of a friend's hospitality, he would witness a libation poured out to Apollo; meats blessed in honour of an idol were found on every table; while urban pursuits and suburban recreation brought him into contact with objects and scenes of superstition and sensual indulgence. Nor was the Jew less powerfully surrounded with seductions. Hallowed associations mixed with all his memories of ancestral glory and worship. Great names were inwoven into the history of his ceremonial, and the archives of his country were, at the same time, the records of his faith. God had spoken to his fathers; the sea had been divided for them; angels' food had been, day after day, rained down upon them; the cloud and pillar of fire had been by turns the vanguard and rearguard of their march. They had possessed the rod of Moses and the sword of Joshua, the throne of David and the lyre of Isaiah. What Barnabas therefore impressed on the whole assembly was earnestness and tenacity, or resolution, at all hazards, to cleave to the Lord. What beauty and power in the thought—to *cleave* to the Lord; not simply to cling to their profession, or to adhere to an abstract or historical Christianity, but to cleave *to the Lord*—the living personal Redeemer—away from them, but yet with them—the one living source of blessing and object of fellowship. Theirs was to be a personal attachment to Him whom the gospel depicted as the centre of evangelical truth and the occupant of their hearts—Him to whom homage was paid as being of all others the most worthy of it, and to whom service was done as having a claim beyond all others upon it. For, alas! men may adhere to a denomination or to visible membership, and yet fall short of cleaving to the Lord. What folly—lingering by the fountain without tasting of its rill; lounging in the porches of Bethesda, but careless of the troubling of the waters!

One needs not to be surprised either at the joy of Barnabas, or the practical course he pursued, when an insight is gained into his character. The historian adds—He was a "good man." A noble eulogy, though a brief and uncommon one. The ordinary panegyric is a "great man," but the greatness of Barnabas was his goodness. His goodness had been already seen in his sale of his possession, when the first Christians kept free table in Jerusalem. The vulgar strife is to be great, but the Christian's ambition is to be good. Few can achieve greatness, but goodness is within the reach of all. Not to be first, but to be best—be this our heart's desire, for he who is best on earth shall be "greatest in the kingdom of heaven." The source of the goodness of Barnabas is laid open—"he was full of the Holy Ghost and of faith." *Full* of the Holy Ghost—so filled probably at Pentecost—not visited with occasional impulses, but like a vessel replete to overflowing. No wonder that Joses of Cyprus was surnamed "the Son of consolation." If he was so filled with the spirit of the promised Comforter, then surely words of consolation must have flowed from his lips. "Full of faith" was this companion of the apostles, and therefore full of the Spirit. A calm and uniform confidence possessed his soul, gave him the image of his Master, and won him his surname. When Stephen was stoned, and young Saul perpetrated these enormities, some of the brethren might wring their hands in dismay, and cry out in bitter lamentation, that it was all over with their cause—that the morning had been overcast, and the sun would never again shine through; but the faith of Barnabas, lifting him above such despondency, and fixing the assurance in his heart that Christ would ultimately triumph, enabled him to lift up "the hands which hang down, and the feeble knees," and so become in many ways and at many times a "Son of consolation." The labours of Barnabas were greatly blessed, and "much people was added to the Lord"—not simply to the church, but *to the Lord*—first to the Lord, and afterwards to the church, "by the will of God."

But Barnabas felt the work growing upon his hands. Unaided and alone, he was not a match for the crisis. He longed that during the bright hour the harvest should be gathered. He had none of that littleness of mind which, in order to monopolize the praise, could not bear the presence and labours of a rival, and he took a step which immediately brought him into a secondary position. He who had introduced Saul to the church at Jerusalem, and been his good genius, soon became his subordinate colleague, and is overshadowed by the greater soul, as Melancthon by Luther, and Beza by Calvin. The Holy Ghost says once "Barnabas and Saul;" but soon the order is reversed, and it is afterwards "Paul and Barnabas." Feeling that Saul was quite the man for the occasion, Barnabas left Antioch in quest of him. He had gone from Jerusalem to Tarsus, and thither Barnabas went in search of him. Barnabas must have known him somewhat intimately, and it may be had been associated with him in academic study. Saul may have been absent from Tarsus, labouring in some quarter of the province of Cilicia, but Barnabas at length found him—pointed out this sphere of labour as one specially adapted to him; and Saul consented, and accompanied his patron to Antioch. The eager spirit of Saul would need no urgent solicitation. It would spring to the scene in anticipation of earnest labours among the Hellenes and Hellenists—the renewal of the work of Damascus and Jerusalem. And they twain laboured for a whole year with uninterrupted energy, and drew large assemblies round about them. Saul displayed his former intrepidity, while his past experience must have made his dialectics more skilful, and his own growth in the divine life must have deepened his yearning for men's salvation.

Our object in this volume is to illustrate the oral addresses of the apostle. Now, though the topic of his sermons at Antioch is not formally given us, we are at no loss to infer what it was. It must, indeed, have been the same as at Damascus and Jerusalem, for the one kind of preaching alone could enlighten and save. The preacher did not vary in his themes. Christ and Christ alone, and in Him salvation, only and fully, and of universal offer and adaptation, was his unvarying subject. Speculation and hypothesis, ingenuity and rhetoric, had no place in his addresses, but the plain, direct, and vivid exhibition of Christ. It was the story of salvation by the cross—the life and death of the Son of God. It was not opinion about Him, but what He really had been. It was not what conclusions might be formed of Him, but what He was, and what He did to redeem the world. With this lesson Saul "taught much people." For the population that filled the four great wards of Antioch was numerous and motley, and gathered from every nation under heaven.

But the twenty-sixth verse supplies us with another and distinct proof of our statement, that Saul preached Christ, and nothing but Christ, at Antioch. The disciples, we are told, "were first called Christians at Antioch"—not in the holy city that reclined on the slopes of Mount Zion, but in the pagan town that lay on the northern sides of Mount Sylphius; not by the Jordan, which had parted its waters at the presence of the ark, but by the Orontes, the banks of which were disgraced by the legends and polluted by the scenes of the vilest lusts; not on the spot where three thousand on one day had been converted, but where impurity was hallowed with religious obligation, and luxury and dissipation held perpetual carnival. They got a distinctive epithet from the name Christ. And why? Simply because that name was so often on their lips; because Saul preached Christ, and Christ was the burden of all his addresses, and they believed Christ, and so often spoke of Christ; because Christ was the word that of all others marked them out as a class, from their fond and familiar use of it—they were naturally named Christians. So effectually and repeatedly did Saul preach Christ, so thoroughly did his preaching identify his party with Christ, that the name was imposed upon it as a new and distinct religious class. The "disciples" did not voluntarily assume it; the Jews could not give it to the "sect of the Nazarenes;" but the heathen population catching the sound so frequently, coined the epithet as a true and happy designation. Because they so often called "upon His name," His name was called upon them. And though it does not hold a place in the nomenclature of the New Testament, yet it was well bestowed.

The name originated among non-Christians, and was used by them. Thus Agrippa addressed Paul—"Almost thou persuadest me to be a Christian;" and Peter says to the elect strangers of the dispersion—" Yet if any man suffer as a Christian, let him not be ashamed;" the term being that employed by the persecutors, and constituting the principal element of accusation. "Christ came into the world to save sinners," even the chief, and among the chief sinners grew up this name given to His followers, and derived from His own. What, indeed, more appropriate than to name after Christ that body of men of whose creed Christ was the core; of whose prayers Christ was the plea; of whose praises Christ was the burden; of whose preaching Christ was the theme; of whose life Christ was the pattern; of whose actions Christ was the law; of whose hopes Christ was the foundation; of whose hearts, indeed, Christ was the one occupant? What more natural than to term Christians the people who learned from Christ as prophet, and bowed to Christ as king; who looked up to Christ as advocate, and forward to Christ as Judge; who enjoyed pardon through Christ's blood, and sanctification through Christ's Spirit; whose weekly holy day was Christ's or the Lord's day; who "named the name of Christ" in their sacred rites of baptism and the Lord's Supper; who regarded the presence of Christ as the glory of their assemblies, and anticipated fellowship with Christ as the crown and consummation of spiritual bliss? Thus the name arose as a matter of public convenience or necessity, in consequence of the numerous accessions to the church at Antioch, and the special prominence which the name Christ had in all their own services, and in their intercourse with the population swarming around them, in those theatres and baths, or thronging those magnificent colonnades—the resorts alike of business and gaiety.

And is not the title appropriate still? He was Christ—the anointed One; they, too, have "an unction from the Holy One." O that those who bear it verified it in everything—so living, speaking, and acting in the spirit of Christ, as to compel the world still to "take knowledge of them," and to name them after Him whom they so strikingly resemble—Christians, because of their avowed and visible connection with Christ. Are not they rightly called Christians whose life springs from their being in Christ, whose ambition is to be like Christ, whose work is for Christ, and whose hope is to be with Christ for ever? Who then of those who "call on this name" would say "I am of Paul," or "I of Apollos," or "I of Cephas?" let every one say—I am of Christ, and never forget that he has said it. Let the coinage of other titles cease—

> Let names and sects and parties fall,
> And Jesus Christ be all in all.

May we not anticipate the time when names assumed from leaders, or taken from forms of government and ritual, or drawn from points of history or from local origin and predominance, shall merge in this grand catholic designation?

Yet strange it is that the other name of the Redeemer should give title to a class of men whose history has been notorious for audacious intrigue and villany; that those who have named themselves from Jesus, should have been distinguished by unparalleled chicanery and the most subtle and delusive casuistry, so that Christians called after Christ shrink from Jesuits who have so vilely appropriated the name of Jesus—nay, who style themselves the Society of Jesus, as if they were bound to Him by a closer tie, or were self-devoted by a deeper consecration. Strange it is to use this pure and loving name as identified with men whose arts and ambition have so often troubled Europe; who have wielded the highest and most dangerous power without being suspected; whose versatile genius has had innumerable modes of action and forms of diplomacy; sometimes editing learned tomes, and sometimes compiling disgusting and prurient directories; equally at home in drawing a will and penning an erudite and ponderous preface; as well skilled in negotiating an expedient marriage as in contriving an opportune death; holding the royal stirrup while they are grasping and giving away the crown; creeping when they dare not walk; now the wriggle of the snake, and now the spring of the panther; ready at any moment to obey orders to betake themselves to any region, no matter how distant, and carry out any policy, no matter what peril and labour it involve; drudging in the kitchen when they may not discourse in the library; assuming the livery of a menial, if it is not convenient to wear the robe of a confessor; making a wife their tool or a concubine their decoy; controlling education with a witching devotedness to youth; outwitting the sharpest and defeating the boldest; spreading a net whose invisible meshes catch and hold the stoutest and most wary; most charming when they are most malignant; smiling the most serenely when their purpose is most deadly; "which devour widows' houses, and for a pretence make long prayers;" banished from every country, and yet found at home in each of them; persecuted, and still thriving when to all appearance extinct; detected, but never disconcerted; often counterworked, though always in the end unbaffled; permitting a defeat in one quarter, to secure a greater triumph in another; furnished with a hundred eyes, and putting forth a hundred arms; all things to all men; possessed, in short, of a craft and might which kings could not cope with, and before which popes themselves have helplessly trembled. Luther and Loyola represent progress and check, action and reaction, in the same epoch of the ecclesiastical world.

IV.—SAUL IN CYPRUS.

Acts xiii. 1—12.

The world was yet in the shadow of death, though light had shone upon Judæa. Idolatry and polytheism were everywhere—vice and misery—life without peace, and death without hope. A thousand altars smoked in honour of a thousand divinities, and the richest fruits of genius were images and temples. There were gods of the hills, and gods of the valleys; gods of the streams, and gods of the groves; gods of the earth, and gods of the ocean; gods of the sky, and gods of the underworld of death. The sacred sculptures bore upon them the oak of Jupiter and the myrtle of Venus; the eagle of Juno and the owl of Minerva; the trident of Neptune and the bow of Apollo; the lance of Mars and the wand of Hermes. There were erroneous and conflicting notions of duty—dubious and degrading ideas of destiny. How shall a sinner be just with God, was a question which could not be solved, and the relationship of man to futurity was unbrightened by life and immortality. That there is no God at all, but highest nature working divinely and impersonally, was the thought of some; that everything is God, or a necessary evolution of his nature and a portion of him, was the dream of others. That the present system is bound up in fate, was the conjecture of one class; that it is the offspring of chance, and without superintendence, was the vanity of another class. Grecian tastes and studies, Roman roads and conquests, arts and laws, commerce and literature, could not impart the requisite spiritual benefit. "The world by wisdom knew not God;" its population "became vain in their imaginations, and their foolish heart was darkened." Shall not, therefore, the glorious gospel take a step westward towards Europe, and at length fix itself in its heart and capital? Glorious promises were nearing their fulfilment—"the isles shall wait for His law."

After Antioch, Cyprus is formally visited. Antioch had indeed become the metropolis of Gentile Christendom, and it was faithful to its position when it organized the first formal missionary enterprise. It had in it certain *prophets*, or living depositaries of sacred truth. The prophets in the New Testament stood to the early churches nearly in the same relation as do our printed Bibles to our modern churches. They spoke by authority and without error, and gave to their audiences such details as occur in the gospels, and such illustrations and precepts as are found in the epistles. They were the "men of their counsel"—present oracles, whose "lips keep knowledge." It would seem as if missionary labour had been occupying their attention, and had been the theme of their earnest and united service and fasting. These religious exercises might have had such an end in view—perhaps the inquiry who shall go for us, and where shall the first experiment be made? At this crisis the Divine Spirit, who fills and informs the church, said—"Separate me Barnabas and Saul for the work whereunto I have called them." The two teachers were at once designated by the imposition of hands; not ordained simply as ministers, for they had ministered already; nor yet elevated to the apostolate—a promotion not within human power, nor could the prophets impart an office higher than that held by themselves: the river cannot rise above its source. The call of the Holy Spirit was a separation from their brethren and their settled labour. The work to which they were set apart was that missionary tour recorded in the following chapters—from Antioch to Cyprus; thence to Perga and Antioch in Pisidia; thence to Iconium, Lystra, and Derbe, and back through these towns; then by Pamphylia, Perga, and Attalia to Antioch, where they gave the church which had sent them a report of their labours. Barnabas and Saul were sent of the church, and they were sent of the Spirit: the Spirit nominated, but the church installed them. Their qualification was the gift of the Spirit; but money to defray necessary expenditure was the contribution of the church. The church prayed for them, too, ere they left. The missionaries were to do His work, and they prayed Him to bless it; to speak His truth, and they prayed Him to seal it; to build up His church, and they prayed Him to prosper it; and to fill up His reward, and they prayed that His beauty might rest upon his servants.

Evangelistic work hitherto had been sporadic in nature, the mere result of circumstances, or the prompting of spiritual instinct. The church had made no direct effort to carry the truth abroad; it thought more of conserving it than of spreading it. The spirit of Judaism still reigned. It did not go in quest of proselytes, but proselytes might come to it. No ship left Judæa carrying Bibles to Tarshish, or missionaries to the ends of the earth. It might accept such as sought it—it did not go out and seek them. But Antioch has the signal honour of sending out the first heralds of the cross. It felt what were the wants of the world, and sought to supply them. The Spirit selected Barnabas and Saul, and the church cheerfully separated them for the work. The two preachers, so commissioned, and so well furnished too, left the city, passed down to its seaport Seleucia, nigh the mouth of the river, and set sail for Cyprus, an island about a hundred miles distant to the south-west, and the summit of whose hills might be seen by them from the moment they embarked. The vessel which carried them bore in the highest sense the fortune of the world. As she flew through the waves, and the opposing current sent the white spray over her, the two strangers felt that her course was not fleet enough for their earnest anticipations. They were inagurating a new era, and commencing a work which should be repeated in many an age and in many a country, until every people shall have its sanctuary, and every tongue be enriched by its version of the scriptures, and the world bow to the happy and universal reign of the Lord Jesus. Cyprus was chosen for good reasons. It was the birthplace of Barnabas, and the gospel had already got a footing in it, being carried out to it as to Antioch by them "who were scattered abroad upon the persecution that arose about Stephen." Barnabas must have known something of the manners and characters of its population; and, judging that his native isle was somewhat similar in these respects to Antioch, he might anticipate as great success in the work of the Lord. It was as natural for Barnabas to visit Cyprus, as for Saul to go to Tarsus, or labour in Cilicia. Besides, it was "men of Cyprus" who had brought the word to Antioch, and they would love their island home, and long to see the faith of Christ proclaimed in it.

The evangelists landed at the nearest port, that of Salamis, on the east of the island, and commenced operations. There were many Jews in Cyprus—it was close upon their own country, and was a garden of rare fertility and beauty; and when Augustus leased its copper-mines to Herod, crowds from Palestine had settled in it. Salamis had a number of synagogues, while other towns usually had but one. There Barnabas and Saul preached *the word* —the revelation of Jesus Christ, the doctrine of salvation by the cross of Christ. It is also to be borne in mind that numerous proselytes must have been in those synagogues, for paganism had greatly lost its hold, and the unsatisfied spirit of many sought refuge in Judaism. While there was profound indifference on the part of the majority, there was also with others a restless searching after some other and higher object of confidence and homage. Thousands were powerfully attracted by the purity and simplicity of the Mosaic faith and worship, for it presented so noble and striking a contrast to the crude idolatries and licentious indulgences round about them. Such minds were the more easily impressed by the gospel, for they would find in it a history without parallel, doctrine that spoke to their inmost longings, and ethics that realized the loftiest ideal of human obligation and destiny. Preaching in the synagogues reached this class of the community, besides bringing truth into contact with the Jewish mind. A preference was given to the Jews in the delivery of the message—the ancient heritage of the Lord is first saluted with the gracious offer. How could it have been otherwise? It was impossible even in the apostle of the Gentiles to throw off the attachments of blood and kindred; and when he remembered what he had felt against Christ, and knew from himself what so many of his brethren must feel, too, his spirit kindled at the thought, and his life's labour, as well as his "heart's desire and prayer to God for Israel, was that they might be saved." John was "their minister" —the relative of Barnabas—in a variety of ways serving them and making arrangements for them; their pioneer, assistant, and subordinate colleague.

Barnabas and Saul visited many places, and went through the whole isle as far as Paphos on its western shore, and above a hundred miles from Salamis. The Roman proconsul was at Paphos, a place infamous for its temple and dissolute worship. It has been remarked that Luke employs the proper term for this officer—one, indeed, that would not have been applicable many years previously, when the island was governed by an imperial legate or proprætor. But Cyprus, originally an imperial province, had before this period been handed over to the senate. At Paphos the gospel came again into contact with the magic of the East. Already it had confronted Simon at Samaria, who professed himself a convert for the sake of initiation into a knowledge or possession of what he deemed its occult powers; and here it met Bar-Jesus, who sought to oppose it with selfish and quick-witted hostility. Such Jewish impostors, false prophets by old Hebrew statute, abounded in the empire; trading in imposture, pandering to the wily or to the weak-minded. Through that superior religious knowledge which every Jew possessed, or by that quackery which esoteric associates kept secret among themselves, or even by mere trickery and vulgar fortune-telling, they often contrived to obtain both secret and open influence over ignorant, inquisitive, or superstitious minds. Many of the higher classes among the Jews practised these arts, as is shown by the abundant references of the Talmud. The nation which refused Christ's miracles was imposed on by jugglery. It would not have the sun, as he rose upon it—and it chased the meteor, flitting through the marshes. It listened not to the divine oracle, and it now crouched to those "that peep and mutter." It spurned away the truth, and there fell upon it a "strong delusion to believe a lie," to give heed "to profane babblings," and occupy itself with "foolish and unlearned questions." The religious instinct sought gratification; and having rejected its appropriate pabulum, but still hungering and clamouring for bread, it got a stone. Throughout the Roman empire religious conviction was shaken; the state-worship no longer impressed; spiritual delusions were breaking up, and in this transitional state impostors found ample scope for the exercise of their ingenuity, and profited by it.

The "deputy of the country" was in these circumstances, and Bar-Jesus—son of Jesus or Joshua, "*was with him,*"—had attached himself to his court, and probably exercised no little sway over him as a confidential adviser. The proconsul was a "*prudent*"—or intelligent man, one that thought for himself; he had apparently thrown off the religion of his country, but had adopted none other. He had seen the folly of idolatry, and may have revolted at the filthy Paphian worship, consecrated lust. He had ceased to adore "gods many, and lords many," but had not done homage to the one Jehovah; the altar of Venus no longer charmed him, and yet was he haunted with the inquiry—"Wherewith shall I come before the Lord?" The old faith was gone, but it had not been succeeded by a newer and better creed. His soul was groping in darkness, scarce knowing what it yearned after, and uncertain where and how to find the object of its desires. To a mind under such painful and distracting apprehensions, any doctrine claiming divine authority is welcome, and the theology of this Jewish magician must have to some extent commended itself. It brought with it the great truths of the unity and spirituality of the Divine Being—a refreshing doctrine to a mind wearied out with the very names of numberless divinities. But he was not satisfied, and the same desire that brought him under the power of Elymas, and upon which Elymas had traded, led him to send for the preachers of a new religion—to learn what other novelties they introduced, or what deeper mysteries they might expound. He could not be supposed to know much of the gospel, yet he seems to style it "the word of God," for it was in its character of a divine revelation that he wished to hear it. It was not speculation or philosophy that his soul thirsted after, but an oracular intimation of duty and destiny. He would not be chilled with Stoicism, nor lulled into Epicurean indifference. His anxiety was not to hear hypotheses, or be amused with reverie, but to have something said to him of his religious interests, something which referred itself to a divine source, and brought with it supreme authority.

The addresses or conversations of the evangelists produced a deep impression on the mind of the proconsul. The sorcerer who had arrogated to himself the Arabic term Elymas, or wise man—wizard—a term still applied to the Mahometan doctors in the Turkish empire, could not suffer those impressions to be deepened, but sought by every means to disturb and remove them. His selfish schemes would all vanish if his patron should yield to the teaching of the two strangers. Such an issue must at all hazards be prevented, and therefore the impostor withstood the apostle, and sought to prejudice the mind of the governor against him. He sought "to turn away the deputy from the faith;" he was loath to lose his victim, and struggled hard to retain him in bondage. How he strove to keep his ground is not known; but, perhaps, if the rebuke of Saul have any special reference to the mode of his antagonism, it points to sophistry and malignant insinuation; perversion of facts, and wilful misinterpretation of doctrines and motives; an attempt so to picture the faith in its proofs, precepts, experiences, or results, as to induce the deputy to dislike it, suspect its teachers, and refuse their message. So pertinacious was he and dexterous, that an example must be made of him; and Saul's first miracle must be one of judgment on a spiteful and irreclaimable adversary. The contest was, whether Elymas the sorcerer or the truth of Christ was to have the ascendancy over the mind of the insular governor. The new power was about to dash and confound the old and cunning errors, and to show its superiority to all that kind of hidden deceit, charms, and " curious arts " with which it might be ignorantly and popularly identified. It was to disentangle itself from all those superstitions which, from Syria and Judea, had overspread the empire. Just as Bar-Jesus was with Sergius Paulus, so had a Syrian seeress been with Marius in his campaigns; so had oriental astrologers been occasionally with Pompey, Cæsar, and Crassus; so had Thrasyllus been with the emperor Tiberius; and Josephus speaks of a Cypriot named Simon who rose into high favour with the governor Felix. The apostle Peter had already unmasked another Simon, and a few years later the Ephesian converts burned their costly books. Banished from Rome again and again, those spiritualists maintained a place in it, for they were feared, and yet courted; and while they were frowned upon, they could not be dispensed with. Thus Saul, the king of Israel, had put down all that had "familiar spirits," and yet, in his extremity, he resorted to a woman reported to have one of them.

Saul, henceforth to be named Paul, has been during this mission rising to a full conception of his apostolical dignity and prerogative. " The Spirit of God came upon him " to do a mightier act than Samson ever did by the same influence. Intensely conscious of his position and what it involved at that awful moment, and looking on the wizard with an eye that read his soul, the anathema burst from his lips. It was no idle rebuke—his word came with power. The magician might be appalled at the fulmination, but could scarce expect such an instant retribution. *Filled with the Holy Ghost*—armed with a supernatural power to chastise the incorrigible—Paul said: "O full of all subtilty and all mischief, thou child of the devil, thou enemy of all righteousness, wilt thou not cease to pervert the right ways of the Lord?" What a concentration of scorn and wrath! every word withers and denounces. *O full of all subtilty!*—a master of low cunning and ingenious retort; so that he easily turned the edge of the apostle's arguments. He understood the weak points in the character of Sergius Paulus, and knowingly plied him with such objections as should most powerfully tell upon him. Such subtilty is not penetration, and such casuistic ingenuity soon imposes on its possessor, and he comes to have faith in his own coinage. *And all mischief*—facility of evil-working; he was clever in his mischief. Highest mischief, not to enter into the kingdom himself, nor yet to suffer the proconsul to enter either; infinite harm so to trade on man's spiritual instincts, and tamper with his eternal destiny!

Thou child of the devil—the devil's own; not a child of Jesus the Blessed, as thy name is, but a child of the devil—proving thy lineage by showing thy father's spirit and doing thy father's work, the very work he did in Eden when by hellish craft and falsehood he seduced the first pair to their ruin. He tempted Eve by the tree of knowledge, insinuated into her mind doubts of God's disinterestedness, as if He were jealous lest she should rise to an equality with

Himself by her eating of that fruit; so that under this delusion she felt it to be a duty to eat, become a goddess, and be wise. Elymas, in a similar spirit, had persuaded the proconsul that highest wisdom dwelt with him—the knowledge of God and of the way of life. And surely error in the guise of truth, or death wearing a mask of life, is the devil, or the child of the devil. " Thou enemy of all righteousness, wilt thou not cease to pervert the right ways of the Lord?" This terrible interrogation was a solemn command to desist, and it tells his crime. "*The right ways of the Lord*" is a phrase which may be employed to characterize not only the gospel as the true path, but also the old dispensation. He might pervert it so as by it to oppose Christianity, or use it as a principal engine to perplex the mind of his victim, so that it might repel Christianity. He contrived either to give a crooked turn to the right way, that it might lead in an opposite direction, or he hoped to make it such a labyrinth that none could find their way in it save such as paid him for the clue to guide them. Wicked and wilful cleverness —dexterity in the devil's own likeness—so to "pervert the right ways of the Lord," so to misrepresent Judaism or Christianity, as that in either case poison should be plucked from the tree of life!

The apostle adds the terrible words — " And now, behold, the hand of the Lord is upon thee, and thou shalt be blind, not seeing the sun for a season." This challenge, so far as we know, was Paul's first conscious putting forth of supernatural power. Strange that his earliest miracle should be one of doom—the infliction of such a blindness as in the moment of his conversion had come upon himself. He could not but compassionate the guilty wretch, as he saw him gradually losing the power of vision, gazing around him with wild eyeballs, and groping in dismay. The miracle is described with awful precision. "And immediately there fell on him a mist and a darkness; and he went about seeking some to lead him by the hand." A mist gathered over his eyes, so that he saw indistinctly, but it soon thickened into total obscurity. The haze that for a moment floated before him darkened into midnight; and his frantic gesticulations indicated his desire for "some to lead him by the hand." That blindness was a symbol of his own spirit and work. His moral sense was blunted, and in attempting to sway Sergius Paulus, it was the blind leading the blind, while he needed to be led himself. He might profess to work by the finger of God, but the heavy hand of God fell upon him, and its shadow extinguished his vision. His sin might be read in his judgment. His boast was of insight, but he was taught that he saw nothing.

Infliction coming direct from God's hand, often takes its shape from the crime. Ham mocked his father, and his doom was one of servitude, under which a father's claims are ignored, and he is valued but as the producer of living marketable tools. Abimelech wished to add Sarah to his harem, and sterility was the penalty of his household. Israel, God's first-born, are kept in bondage, and Pharaoh's first-born fall before the destroying angel. Korah, Dathan, Abiram, and On conspired to undermine the authority of Moses, but a mine was sprung under themselves—"they went down alone into the pit, and the earth closed upon them." Miriam murmured that the alien wife of her brother should be naturalized, and she was smitten with a loathsome distemper, which instantly excluded her from the camp. Jeroboam put forth his hand against "the man of God which had cried against the altar in Bethel," "and his hand which he had put forth against him dried up, so that he could not pull it in again to him." When Uzziah "was strong, his heart was lifted up to his destruction;" and when he intruded into the temple to burn incense, "the leprosy rose up in his forehead," and he durst not afterwards pass beyond his own dwelling; "and he was cut off from the house of the Lord." Those that exhausted the flesh of Israel by labour and slavery, shall be fed "with their own flesh," according to the menace of Jehovah. "They have shed the blood of saints and prophets, and Thou hast given them blood to drink." In the hour of his impious exultation, when he thought himself a "mortal God," Nebuchadnezzar was smitten with a strange mania, and herded with the beasts of the field. The tongue which had spoken proud words imitated the lowings of the oxen; the fingers which had grasped the sceptre carried the green provender to the royal lips; and all this "till his hair was grown like eagles' feathers, and his nails like birds' claws." Zechariah saw the vision, but spoke to Gabriel in incredulity; therefore he was struck dumb, and was "not able to speak" till the promise was fulfilled. When Herod accepted homage as a god, his godship—set upon by the lowest vermin —"was eaten of worms, and gave up the ghost."

Paul had risen to the dignity and authority of his apostolate. He had a "power to edification," though it now assumed a terrific aspect; and the deputy, awed and overcome, believed, *being astonished at the doctrine of the Lord*—at the way in which the Lord taught, and so strikingly authenticated His doctrine. The blindness inflicted on his evil genius for endeavouring so malignantly to prevent the true light from entering into his heart, proved to him that Paul was no pretender, and that the doctrine which could take so sudden and signal vengeance on its opponent, was armed with a power that betokened its supernatural origin. He was awe-struck, and was unable to refuse his assent. He could not allow the sorcerer to trifle with him any longer, nor durst he longer "halt between two opinions;" but he bowed to the truth proclaimed by the Hebrew missionaries. Thus judgment and mercy have been often associated. The acceptance of Abel led to the banishment of Cain; the water that bore up Noah's ark drowned the old world; the escape of Lot was the signal for the fire-shower upon Sodom; the exodus of Israel was preceded by the doom of Egypt; the possession of Canaan is the expulsion of the Canaanites; the child Jesus is "set for the fall and rising again of many;" the life of the world springs from the murder of Calvary; men live to righteousness in proportion as they die to sin; the casting away of the chosen race was the "reconciling of the world;" and the enlightenment of Sergius Paulus has by its side the blinding of Elymas the sorcerer. "Behold, therefore, the goodness and severity of God!"

V.—PAUL AT ANTIOCH IN PISIDIA.

Acts xiii. 13—52.

BARNABAS and Saul had gone to Cyprus, but their relative position was changed during their residence in the island; and in the record of their departure from it, Paul occupies the place of honour and prominence. The conversion of Sergius Paulus seems to remind the historian that he of Tarsus then assumed, and afterwards bore, the similar name of Paul; and that with the proper commencement of his labours as the apostle of the Gentiles, the native Hebrew name of Saul is for ever dropped. The subsidence of Barnabas into a subordinate position may have offended his nephew Mark, and been one of the reasons which induced him to desert the enterprise and return to his mother at Jerusalem. At length "Paul and his company loosed from Paphos," passed over to Asia Minor, skirting the western confines of Cilicia, and sailed up the Cestrus, landing at Perga in Pamphylia. Then crossing the great table-land of the country, they entered Antioch of Pisidia—a city, the ruins of which have been only recently discovered. What induced them to make this visit we know not; perhaps they anticipated that this second Antioch would be as rich in its spiritual harvest as the first Antioch on the Orontes. They took an early opportunity of worshipping on Sabbath in the synagogue;

and "after the reading of the law and the prophets," an appeal was made to the two strangers, or rather a message was sent to them by the presiding elders. Paul at once rose, and, waving his hand, solicited the attention of the audience. It has been asserted with some show of probability, that on this sacred day the portion of the law read was the first chapter of Deuteronomy, and the corresponding section of the prophets, the first chapter of Isaiah. The discourse of the apostle grew out of the scripture which had been repeated, and he takes from it some of his historical allusions. In the synagogue of Nazareth Jesus read the scripture for the day, and proceeded to expound and apply it; but the apostle speaks after it had been chanted by the appropriate officer, and introduces such ideas and associations as the word which they had heard must have stirred up within them. His audience was composed of Jews and proselytes—*men of Israel* by birth, and *those that fear God*—those of other nations who had renounced idolatry for the spiritual worship of Jehovah. This discourse, the first of Paul's discourses reported at any length, dwells on three points—the prior history of the people, and its connection with the advent; then the Messiahship of Jesus, and its proofs; and lastly, the solemn application of the truth to themselves.

The historical exordium of the apostle is brief but pointed. "Men of Israel, and those fearing God, listen. The God of this people chose for Himself our fathers, and the people He exalted during their sojourn as strangers in the land of Egypt, and with a high arm did He lead them out of it, and for about forty years did He nurse them in the wilderness; and, having destroyed seven nations in the land of Canaan, he assigned by lot their land to them; and after these things, for about four hundred and fifty years he gave them judges, until Samuel the prophet; and thereafter they desired for themselves a king, and God gave them Saul, the son of Kish—a man of the tribe of Benjamin—for forty years; and, having deposed him, he raised up David to them for a king, to whom he spoke, giving this testimony—' I have found David, the son of Jesse, a man according to my own heart, who shall perform all my will (all the expressions of my will).' Of this man's seed has God, according to promise, brought to Israel a Saviour—Jesus; John having preached beforehand, before His entrance (on His public ministry) the baptism of repentance to all the people of Israel. And as John was fulfilling his course, he was wont to say — 'Whom do ye suppose me to be? (the Messiah?) I am not. But, behold, there cometh one after me, whose footstrap I am not worthy to loose.' Men—brethren, children of the stock of Abraham, and those among you fearing God, to you was the word of this salvation sent."

And first, be it remarked, the leading feature of this portion of the address is—what God had done for the nation. A series of divine benefactions is detailed, culminating in the gift of a Saviour—Jesus. Each of these divine interpositions was a salvation for the time; each hero and legislator had been a saviour; but this great salvation was now finally sent. Each crisis in Israel's history proclaimed—"this is the Lord's doing;" but the last was the most glorious of all. Every period was preparatory to this great end—the election, the emancipation, the settlement, the judges, the monarchy, Saul's elevation and deposition, the choice of David, and the baptism of John. Christ's mission was the crowning act, to which all these acts of God had pointed, and for which they all prepared.

"The God of this people chose our fathers"—*this people*, in contradistinction to the worshipping proselytes, or, for the sake of emphasis, a people so special in origin and history. Israel did not choose God, but God chose them, and chose them neither for their numbers, intelligence, civilization, nor piety. It was by no spirit of independence or heroism that they formed themselves into a nation; but God organized them. Their origin was of His sovereign choice, without aspiration or effort of their own.

The same God who had chosen them "exalted the people when they dwelt as strangers in the land of Egypt" —*exalted them*, perhaps brought them up, or perhaps gave them numbers and strength. Nay more, the same God's "high arm brought them out" of Egypt. They did not take up arms and beat back their oppressors. Their own courage did not secure their independence, as Scotland did at Bannockburn, or as when the Swiss peasantry repelled the legions of Austria. They departed from Egypt without so much as striking a blow for liberty. The common motto—

"Who would be free, themselves must strike the blow,"

was in their case reversed. When they left they did not sharpen their swords, but they buckled on their kneading troughs; they did not carry a spear, but only a staff in their hand; for plagues in succession smote Pharaoh and his people, and in their panic they let Israel go. The Lord brought them out—another divine interposition. Their leader was not a conqueror with a sword, but a shepherd with a crook. Their prowess did not break the yoke, nor did Pharaoh emancipate them; but Jehovah "brought forth His people with joy, and His chosen with gladness."

And, being brought out, they were utterly helpless. They could not sustain themselves, and they had only provisions for a few days' march. But the Lord "nursed them," as the proper reading is. They did not sow, they did not plunder sown fields. The sands of Arabia could supply nothing more than a scanty herbage for their cattle. For *about* forty years, that is, thirty-eight years, were they in this predicament. But the manna fell around them, the water gushed from the rocks, and quails flew into their camp. The cloud by day and pillar of fire by night protected them. The divine oracle was with them, and the divine hand was round them. One day of their own will would have brought them into jeopardy. Like a nurse with a weak and wayward child, so was Jehovah with them in their wanderings.

They marched at length to the eastern bank of the Jordan, and under Joshua, crossing it, took possession of the country. The Canaanitish heptarchy was subdued, and the land divided equitably and by lot. They fought, indeed, against the aborigines, but their own bow and sword did not gain them the victory. Priests, and not warriors, marched round Jericho; nor was the assault made with engines of war; but at the blast of the rams' horns the walls fell unstruck by human hand—a symbol of the entire conquest. In such an army idolatry was as fatal as cowardice, and disobedience to God as bad as treason to the general. The Lord " destroyed seven nations in the land of Canaan." According to Josh. iii. 10, these seven nations, so steeped in odious sins that they had forfeited all right to their territory, were the Canaanites, used there in a restricted sense to denote the tribes that dwelt on the western bank of the Jordan and the coasts of the Mediterranean, and which, from their numbers and influence, gave their name to the entire population; the Hittites, from Hebron to Beersheba; the Hivites, near Gibeon and toward the north as far as Baalhermon; the Perizzites, in the villages of Jezreel; the Girgashites, the smallest of the septs; the Amorites, occupying the mountains in the south, and stretching to the hills of Gilead; and the Jebusites, possessing the central territory of Jerusalem. In the promise given to Abraham ten nations are mentioned as then existing, but some of those earlier aborigines had been dispossessed by the Canaanites. He divided their land by lot, as recorded in Joshua, the old Doomsday-book of the nation, and the charter of their inheritance. The lot was a direct appeal to God, and was so sanctioned by Himself. Joshua died, and the nation again and again sank into anarchy. Each tribe had its separate and independent jurisdiction, and the principle of federal unity was not fully recognized nor acted out. Judges or dictators were occasionally raised up as exigency required, but they seldom had power over the entire country. And even that form of provisional government was of God, not the result of their own political sagacity. This period lasted four hundred and fifty years, as may be computed from the book of Judges; and it was also the popular chronology, as may be seen in Josephus.

Samuel was the last of the judges, and toward the close of his life, and from a combination of circumstances, the nation "desired a king." Samuel's sons did not walk in their father's steps; and there was no reason why they should succeed him, the hereditary principle not being recognized in the succession of the judges. The nation had ceased to feel the power of faith. Jehovah was their first magistrate and their general-in-chief, but they could not endure "as seeing Him who is invisible." They clamoured for a visible leader, one who, mailed and helmeted, should marshal them to battle and victory. On a similar principle they had already taken the ark out into the camp, as a palpable token of the divine presence. They, therefore, in demanding a king, rejected not Samuel, but God. And "God gave unto them Saul, the son of Cis," who reigned in Samuel's lifetime eighteen years, and twenty-two years after his death. The Hebrew king was virtually God's lieutenant or representative, raised up to act out or defend the principles of the theocracy. Saul, whose heart was spoiled by his elevation, in course of time did his own will, not God's—forgot his peculiar function, became disloyal to his divine Head, and, therefore, He "removed him," and "raised up" the son of Jesse in his room. This shepherd-king was the most illustrious occupant of the Hebrew throne. The divine eulogy is, "a man after mine own heart"—no formal quotation, but rather the spirit of several passages. No little wit and malicious ingenuity have been expended upon this saying, as if it threw a covering over David's sins. Primarily, it refers more to his official than to his personal character—that he should vindicate the theocracy, put down idolatry, make no political compromise at variance with the Mosaic law, and confer on the nation the possession of the whole territory which God had given Abraham in charter. That this is the meaning of the phrase may be learned from the language of the book of Kings. Any future sovereign who patronized idolatry or wicked superstitions, is spoken of as not walking "with a perfect heart, like David his father." His successors are indeed judged of and praised or censured according as they resembled their ancestor, or did not resemble him, in the royal care he took of the spirituality and purity of God's worship. And when you look at David as a hero, king, or saint, and analyse the various features of his character, and dwell on his generosity and prowess, his forbearance toward Saul, and his love toward Jonathan; when you reflect that though he sinned, and sinned so grievously, he repented, and mourned and wept in the bitterness of his heart; when you think that but for his fall and his penitence those psalms had never been composed—those sighs and moans of a broken heart, which have been the voice of every age in the church, the language of its sorrow, and faith, and hopes; when, in short, you judge the son of Jesse by his age and position—the true standard of judgment: who would hesitate to pronounce him a man after God's own heart?

Now, Christ was "the root and branch of David"—his branch as He descended from him in human lineage, and his root, too; for, had it not been for the coming Messiah, he had never been enthroned. His family became a dynasty in order that Jesus might spring out of it—"Of this man's seed hath God raised unto Israel a Saviour, Jesus." Moses had been raised up a saviour; Joshua's very name implied his being one; each judge in turn was a saviour to his country; so Saul had been in his best days, and so was David. But a Saviour more worthy of the name had recently been raised—Jesus—who, himself a nobler personage, had achieved a mightier deliverance, and at a more awful cost.

Nor did He come without a prior announcement. His herald prepared the way for Him, according to ancient prediction. The son of Elisabeth went before Him "in the spirit and power of Elias." In dress, manner, and tone, he resembled the great demigod of the olden time, whose brow was clothed with thunder. The nation was shaken at his voice; it came like a whirlwind from the desert where he had been reared; and as men's hearts quaked and hoped, they flocked to his baptism. Few ventured to challenge his divine commission, and therefore the apostle introduces his testimony. His was a *baptism of repentance*—it accompanied a profession of repentance, and also of faith in a coming Messiah—repentance being at once its condition and its lesson. The persons baptized vowed to prepare themselves for the great advent. John, with all his popularity, maintained his humility, solemnly disclaimed being the Messiah, asserted the high dignity of his successor, and that he was unworthy to stoop to unstrap His sandals. And then Jesus came and wrought out salvation—a salvation not confined to the age in which it was secured, or the territory on which it was achieved. For the apostle thus announces his first application—" To you is the word of this salvation sent "—*this salvation*—as the work of this Jesus; and the word of it *was sent* by God and through Christ; the past tense of the original verb referring to the earlier period. The previous salvations were confined in their efficacy. They affected but the generation who enjoyed them, and the exploits of Gideon, the feats of Samson, or the equitable administration of Samuel could not be transplanted to distant regions. If men wished to receive Jewish benefits, they must travel to Jewry; there alone could such blessings be of old enjoyed, and not in Cyprus or Asia Minor. But to Jew and Gentile the word of this best and last salvation had been sent; it could be enjoyed in Pisidia not less than in Palestine. It came to them; they needed not to go to it. And to every one of them was it sent—Jew and proselyte, without exception, without discrimination. It had been wrought out in Israel, by a son of Israel, and for Israel—but for the world also, yet first for Israel. Their duty, then, was to receive the message, and give welcome to the glorious Deliverer. He had come in God's name to save them: Hosanna to the Son of David! To us, too, the message was sent, and is still offered. Though He was a Jew, the Gentiles are not neglected. That blood, though it flowed from Jewish veins, "cleanseth from all sin." This salvation is for thee, whoever thou art—man or woman, whatever thy character or position, thy age or country, it is for thee.

Salvation for thee! Burst into singing at the intelligence; clasp it to thee, keep it, "let it not go, for it is thy life." If not saved, thou art yet in danger, and that danger is becoming more and more imminent. The longer the vessel sails, the nearer she approaches the sunken reef, unless her course be changed. Every step which the blind wanderer takes, brings him nearer the precipice, unless he accept the friendly warning and turn away. If salvation has been provided, and be offered, and be within reach, surely it becomes us to respond and lay hold on it, and by faith make it our own. Britain owes its superiority to Madagascar, because to its inhabitants these words have been verified—"To you is the word of this salvation sent." More earnest improvement of the privilege is yet demanded of us. If the word of salvation be sent and not received, sent and only scorned, sent and made a theme of curious inquiry, and not an object of faith; shall not God feel that it has been missent, and may He not withdraw it? Already, and in other lands, He has done this work of judgment; and may He not be provoked to repeat it? If we are guilty—

> "What better can we do than prostrate fall
> Before Him, reverent, and there confess
> Humbly our faults, and pardon beg with tears
> Watering the ground?"

The next portion of the address demonstrates the Messiahship from Old Testament proofs. The apostle thus proceeds—

" For they that dwell in Jerusalem, and their rulers, not having recognized Him, and having condemned Him, fulfilled the voices of the prophets read every Sabbath. And having found (when they found) against Him no cause of death, they asked Pilate that he should be slain; and when they had accomplished all the things written concerning Him, having taken Him down from the tree, they laid Him in a tomb. But God raised Him from the dead. And He was seen for many days by them who came up with Him from Galilee to Jerusalem, who at this moment are His witnesses before the people. And we declare unto you the glad tidings, to wit, the promise made to the fathers, that God hath fulfilled it to us their children, in that He hath raised up Jesus again; as it is also written in the first psalm—'Thou art my Son, this day I have begotten thee.' And that He raised Him from the dead, as one who should no more return to corruption, He thus said—'I will give you the promises, holy and sure, made to David.' Wherefore also he saith in another psalm—'Thou shalt not suffer Thine Holy One to see corruption.' For David after he had served the will of God for his own generation, fell on sleep, and was laid unto his fathers, and saw corruption; but He whom God raised up again, did not see corruption."

The word of that salvation was sent to the Jews and proselytes of Pisidia, for this reason among others, that Jerusalem, both rulers and population, had rejected it. It was offered to them, and they would not have it. The Sanhedrim had set it at nought; the metropolis had refused it. Thus the apostle explains his anomalous position; how he a stranger to them had travelled so far to make them such an offer—an offer of a deliverance not confined to

Israel in Palestine, but extending to the children of the covenant in every region. And lest they should contract any suspicions against his message, from the fact that the central spiritual authority of their nation had refused it, the apostle shows them how, even in this unbelief, their own oracles had been fulfilled. To the wisdom of their high council they might be apt to bow, and its decision in a matter of supreme importance they would be inclined to take, for it was upon the spot; and having all the evidence in its hands, would, as they fondly imagined, examine it without prejudice, and come to a conclusion that courted scrutiny and defied appeal. The apostle therefore asserts, that in doing what they did, in acting out their pleasure and condemning Jesus, they fulfilled the prophecies.

The *rulers*, or the majority of the Sanhedrim, condemned Jesus, and the populace was at one with them. "Hosanna" they shouted to-day, and with equal sincerity, "Crucify Him" to-morrow. Strange it is that He should be thus condemned; this prince of preachers, who "spake as never man spake;" this greatest of wonder-workers, who did as never man did; this purest of saints, who lived as never man lived; and this noblest of benefactors, who gave as never man gave—blessings in freest form, and for highest ends, in crowded succession. But they sat in trial upon Him, and they condemned Him. It was but a mockery of judgment. Not only was the spirit of law violated, but its forms were set at nought; the safeguards which protect justice and liberty were broken through. Caiaphas had arrived at a foregone conclusion, which no amount of opposing evidence could shake. "It is expedient that one man should die," said the crafty placeholder, and Jesus was sacrificed to that expediency. Blood must be shed to propitiate the jealous Roman power, and His was selected as the political libation. The people acquiesced in the decision of the rulers. They *knew Him not*—in His origin, claims, and mission, recognized Him not as the Messiah. They could not discover the promised Deliverer in Jesus of Nazareth. He did not correspond to their anticipations. He disappointed them, and so the Saviour of men became the rejected of men. As our version reads, the apostle says that they also knew not *the voices of the prophets ;* that is, they misinterpreted their own oracles, applying them to political liberation and national blessing. Had only a solitary voice been heard on this theme in Jerusalem, and its echo borne to Galilee; or had the sacred roll been opened but once in a century, leaving the intervening years to the faint and yet fainter record of tradition—there might have been some excuse. But the prophets were read in the synagogues *every Sabbath day ;* the prophetical books being so divided that week after week their voice was heard, and in a year all of them were gone through. But they were misinterpreted. This version, however, is somewhat cumbrous and involved, and demands the repetition of an object for the verb "fulfilled." We regard the apostle as saying, "For they who dwell in Jerusalem and their rulers, not recognizing Him, and having condemned Him, fulfilled the declarations of the prophets read every Sabbath day." Still, the meaning is not very different. They fulfilled the prophecies because they were in ignorance of them. They were working out their own unhallowed inclinations when they were embodying in action these ancient sayings. When they knew Him not, they realized the prediction—"There is no form nor comeliness that we should desire Him." In their condemning Him was verified the oracle—"He was oppressed and he was afflicted." Their placing His cross between those of the two thieves brought to pass that "voice"— "And he was numbered among transgressors." When He was laid in Joseph's grave, the divine declaration was confirmed—"And he was with a rich man in His death." Thus, the apostle alleges that, in condemning Jesus, his enemies fulfilled the prophecies—acted as unwitting instruments in giving reality to inspired oracle—so that the Pisidian synagogue was not to be swayed by the metropolitan bench; rather were the results of their enmity so many proofs of the divine origin and truth of Christianity. They did simply as it had been foretold, though they did not intend it. For, it is one thing to read the scriptures, but a different thing to understand them. One may apprehend their general historical contents, and yet fail to perceive their spiritual import and beauty. They can only be understood in their relationship to Christ the Saviour, and they produce spiritual benefit just in so far as they reveal to the heart the glory and power of Christ; His infinite love to move it, and His atoning death on which it can securely rely. One may admire the gospels as a biography of rare simplicity and tenderness, but more is needed than delight in the composition—faith must be added to the gratification of taste. The pen of the evangelist may fascinate, but the Redeemer's cross must be the one object of an adoring confidence. "Search the scriptures, for in them ye think ye have eternal life, and they are they which testify of Me."

The apostle does not enter on the question of their criminality, nor take up the theory of their responsibility. He would not discuss a metaphysical problem as to man's moral freedom when he acts in a path predicted for him, and engages in actions the time, mode, and results of which have been already portrayed. The scene was one of necessity—the mouth of the Lord had spoken it—but it was a necessity consistent with most perfect liberty. The rulers and people were in no way constrained; they had no sense of compulsion; they were in no form led or lured by a controlling power. They had their own motives, motives springing out of their associations and judgments, and these they allowed freely and fully to sway them. Never is prophecy the rule of duty; ethics are a present obligation, wholly disconnected with the divine prescience and its foreshadowings. My duty is not sketched by the Spirit's pencillings, but prescribed by the Spirit's words. It is with injunction, not with prediction, that I have to do. God will take care of His own plans, but I am charged with the purity of my own motives and actions. What I should be, is my question, apart from what shall be in the drama acting around me. The men who condemned Jesus cannot be assoilzied because through them prophecy was fulfilled, and life brought to the world. No, the Pharisees writhed under exposure, the Sadducees hated religious stir, Judas grasped the money, Pilate loved his place, the crowd raged in chagrin and disappointment; and the result of these combined and opposite causes was, that Jesus was condemned and put to death, in fulfilment of "all that was written of Him."

Nay, their criminality was of deepest dye. They found *no cause of death* in Him—nothing worthy of capital punishment, and therefore they desired Pilate to have him taken off. Could they have so arraigned Him as by a common judicial process to have condemned Him, then they would not have resorted to clamour for His death, or asked it as a favour from a heathen governor. They tried Him on a charge of blasphemy, and, though bolstered up by false witnesses, it failed on cross-examination—"their witness did not agree." They laboured to induce Him to inculpate Himself, and from one of His declarations they professed to recoil in horror, and to convict Him of blasphemy. But they had lost what is technically called the power of life and death, and though they might pronounce a capital sentence, they could not inflict it. It must be ratified by the procurator ere it could be executed. Honest judges on going to him would have shown him what the evidence was, and how it supported the conclusion at which they had arrived. But the Sanhedrim, on approaching Pilate, did not venture to substantiate the charge of blasphemy before him; they cuningly shifted their ground, and accused Him of political crime. But the accusation of treason could not be at all brought home to Him. They then stooped to clamour and vociferation, and by influencing the selfish and timid mind of Pilate, they obtained their end. On every appeal that he made to them, they cried out the more "crucify Him." They would not have deigned to do this if other and more plausible means could have secured their purpose. But, in spite of His innocence, they were resolved on His death, their tumultuous cry prevailed, and Pilate, against his own conviction, gave way. But prophecy was coming into act, as Jesus was condemned, scourged, mocked, crucified, and buried. His death, in itself and its concomitants, was a signal fulfilment of prediction, verifying the "things concerning Him" in the law, the prophets, and the psalms.

Jesus was taken down from the tree after there remained no doubt that He was dead. *They*—that is, the rulers and dwellers in Jerusalem—took Him down; the burial as well as the death is, in the popular construction of the sentence, ascribed to them. The same persons that crucified our Lord did not, indeed, entomb Him; though, certainly, the Jewish rulers took care that, if they did not bury Him, His grave should be jealously watched. They thought, indeed, that His cause and claims were buried along with Him, and they did not expect a resuscitation. The burial was also an indispensable step to the resurrection; a proof of the reality of His death, and necessary as a palpable evidence of His being brought back to life. His second life on earth was not simply a revival—as with the daughter of Jairus— for its reality might have been impugned, but it was a resurrection, for He was openly laid in the sepulchre, and His grave guarded by sentinels. Thus did men act toward Him: condemn Him, slay Him, and bury Him. It was a dark period, that of His abode in the tomb. Enemies rejoiced and friends desponded, "trusting it had been He who should have redeemed Israel." That was a mysterious Sabbath during which He lay under the power of death—the light of men in the gloom of the sepulchre, the life of the world a lifeless corpse; He who promised that any one believing on Him should never die, had Himself died and gone to the grave. The sun was under eclipse, and a deep shadow fell on the earth.

On the other hand, " *God* raised Him from the dead," men buried Him, but God raised Him: and the best proof that He did rise is His being seen, and seen "many days," of them that had been familiar with Him, and who could not be mistaken in His appearance and identity. The apostle here probably refers to the eleven, and the early band of believers, those who accompanied Him from Galilee to Jerusalem on His last journey. He appeared often to the apostles, and also to above five hundred brethren at once. Peter has the same line of proof—He appeared "not to all the people, but unto witnesses chosen before of God, even to us who did eat and drink with Him after He rose from the dead." To have appeared in a crowd who could not identify Him would have been no proof, and therefore the eleven were signally honoured. And they were not concealing their testimony. The Pisidian Jews might ask whether, in the very focus of these wonders, the same word of salvation was proclaimed, and the apostle tells them that the chosen people in Palestine were amply supplied with eye-witnesses of these awful realities. They could not but speak the things they "had seen and heard," and while they were "His witnesses unto the people" in Palestine, the apostle says for himself and his colleague—

" We declare unto you glad tidings, how that the promise

which was made unto the fathers, the same God hath fulfilled unto us their children, in that He hath raised up Jesus again." That gospel should be no novelty to the Hebrew mind, it was but the fulfilment of a promise long ago made—a promise the Hebrew nation had for centuries clung to, and fondly prayed over. That a Deliverer should come to them and of them, was the voice of their prophets and the song of their bards; the testimony of Jesus was the spirit of prophecy; and if the promise was in itself of such moment, as being God's highest gift; if it was the text of inspired men for more than two thousand years; if they were raised up from time to time to repeat, confirm, and illustrate it; if the nation lived by the hope of it, and anxiously longed for the period when it should be realized, now, when it had come to pass, they were surely to hail its fulfilment as glad tidings. Israel had lived on promise—the Christian church is sustained by facts. The world was never left without hope, but it was long "hope deferred." The first promise was made in Eden, but Adam died, and yet the "Seed of the woman" had not bruised the Serpent's head. Abraham and the patriarchs passed away, and still the Blessing of all nations had not appeared. Moses and his successors in judgment left the world, but the Prophet like unto him had given no utterance. David and his royal sons were carried to the tomb of the kings, and yet his throne was not filled by his Son and Lord. Isaiah sang, but his melody was inspired by the future; the tears of Jeremiah fell on unrepaired desolations; the thunders of Habbakkuk died away in the distance; Daniel pictured revolutions, but they were only shakings preparatory to the era of universal peace; Haggai portrayed the glory of the second temple, but its courts had not been trodden by "the Desire of all nations." No wonder that, when a promise so often made, on which so much depended, and which was so deeply cherished as the hearts' life of the nation, was fulfilled, the news should be styled "THE GLAD TIDINGS." The suspense of four thousand years was removed when the babe was born in Bethlehem. The children reaped what the fathers had sowed—glad tidings truly; news such as had never before been proclaimed; not political deliverance, nor triumph over oppressors—good news for a downtrodden people; not the mission of Joshua to settle, of Gideon to smite, or of Samuel to rule, but salvation—freedom from the worst of evils, sin and death; restoration to the divine favour and image, fully provided, freely offered, and certainly enjoyed by every one who believes the blessed intelligence.

What emotions should not such tidings stir up within us! Speak to Poland of resuscitation, and it surges into armed fury; whisper to Hungary of independence, and its valleys burst into a warlike song; inform the patriot of his country's danger, and his eyes flash out his nobleness of soul; proclaim to-night the discovery of a gold field to a city, and the news empties it of all its able-bodied men before the sunrise of to-morrow; let the warder, as he walks the ramparts, tell the blockaded town, stricken with hunger and pestilence, and the living scarce sufficing to bury the dead, that he sees the glittering banners of a relieving army drawn on the distant evening sky, and the populace cannot sleep for joy. Were we really alive to our state, did we turn our gaze within, and did we, as we survey that spiritual havoc which sin has wrought, shudder at the danger which it has entailed; did we feel that no hand can rectify those disorders but His who made us, and did we remember that all depends on such a change produced by Him, and that the moral wreck untouched is hell begun and to gather in fierceness—O would we not cheerfully accept, as glad tidings, the advent of One who knows and pities us; who blesses and saves us; whose blood pardons, and whose Spirit transforms; who produces a mighty revolution within us, bringing with it the germ, as it reveals the certainty, of everlasting life? And yet, alas, how often are such tidings received with indifference or contempt, scarcely exciting attention, as if they were indifferent trifles, or were melancholy in their contents. Let those who hear them receive them as true tidings, and welcome them as glad tidings: that the peace and joy of the gospel may fill their hearts; and that they may learn to "joy in God through our Lord Jesus Christ." Comprehend the good news and their adaptation to you. Bless God for them, and walk in the spirit of them. Beyond the tomb there is no such message. No herald there makes proclamation of respite, or pardon, or amelioration, or end.

The apostle is addressing Jews, and he gives point and pith to his appeal by references to the Old Testament, not for illustration, but for argument. Christianity is regarded by him as the crown and realization of Judaism. The career of Christ was but the fulfilment of an old promise. The speaker then refers to some elements of that promise, and his first quotation is taken from the first psalm, which is reckoned the second in our notation—"Thou art my Son; this day have I begotten Thee." The words have been variously understood, both in their dogmatic and historical reference. Not a few regard them as distinctly pointing to the resurrection, giving the verb the sense of "raised up again," and verifying the interpretation by what Paul elsewhere says—" Declared to be the son of God . . . by the resurrection from the dead." But we apprehend that the apostle comes not to any argument about the resurrection of Jesus till the following verse. He appears in this verse to look upon the quotation as proving His sonship, by showing Christ's exaltation to universal sovereignty.

Let us revert to the second psalm, and contemplate for a moment its occasion and scope. The point of view which the inspired bard assumes, is the period of the crucifixion—when the city of Jerusalem is in uproar, and foreigners and natives are seen to be in unnatural league against Messiah. The poet's eye surveys the tumult in which Jew and heathen so strangely unite, and he exclaims in wonder—

"Why do the heathen rage, and the people imagine a vain thing;
The kings of the earth set themselves, and the rulers take counsel together,
Against Jehovah and against His Messiah."

At an early period in the history of the church those words were thus interpreted—" Of a truth, against Thy Holy child Jesus both Herod and Pontius Pilate, with the Gentiles and the people of Israel, were gathered together." The description is thus literally correct; the "heathen" or Roman power; "the people" or Jews; "kings" and "rulers" or Herod and Pilate—were combined against the Son of

God, and resolved to triumph over Him. And the watch-cry of the conspirators is—

"Let us break His bands asunder, and cast away His cords from us."

But their machinations are so utterly futile, that Jehovah only smiles at them, for they are but as the child's hand spread out to stem the rising tide:—

"He that sits in heaven shall laugh,
Jehovah shall have them in scorn."

And the reason is, that the Messiah's government is founded by Jehovah, and therefore cannot be shaken:—

"I have set my king upon my holy hill of Zion."

And He who has been enthroned beyond the reach of revolution, avouches His confidence thus:—

"I will declare the decree: Jehovah hath said to me,
Thou art My Son, this day I have begotten Thee."

In spite of every opposition He has been enthroned on the holy hill of God, and in that inauguration an earlier decree has been fulfilled, as some think; while in their opinion the term "to-day" does not specify the time when the decree is now declared, but when it was first promulgated; that it does not mean that the birth and the investiture of royalty are in any sense contemporary events, or that the Messiah was begotten on the day He was crowned; but that the sonship is eternal. The meaning, however, seems to be that the Father owned Jesus for His Son, and that this sonship was openly and publicly evinced when He rose to the throne. It was true at the incarnation, when the infant lay in the manger; but its reality was not fully and finally manifested till God made Him His King over His holy hill of Zion. Solomon's sonship was always a fact, but it was formally avowed when David set him apart as his royal successor. The incarnate Jesus is the Son of God, and that sonship is solemnly proclaimed in His exaltation by the Father to His own right hand. According to a common Hebrew usage, to do a thing is to declare it to be done. Thus in Peter's vision it is said, What God has cleansed, that do not thou pollute; that is, do not call or reckon it unclean. Thou art my Son, to-day have I declared Thee begotten of Me—evinced Thy sonship by raising Thee to the kingdom, co-enthroned with Myself.

The relation of the Messiah to God is that of Son, "firstborn," and "only-begotten." As Son He always recognized His Father—again and again referred to Him under that appellation. "My Father worketh hitherto;" "the Father loveth the Son;" "I am in the Father;" "I came forth from the Father;" "I leave the world and go to the Father;" "I speak that which I have seen with My Father;" "I and My Father are one;" "O, Father, glorify thou Me with Thine own self;" "I thank thee, O Father, Lord of heaven and earth;" "no man knoweth the Father but the Son;" "even so, Father;" "Father, if it be possible, let this cup pass from me;" "Father, glorify thy name;" "Father, forgive them;" and "Father, into thy hands I commend My spirit;" In the words spoken, deeds done, prayers offered, and sufferings endured by Him, he ever recognized his relation to the Father as

His Son, His only-begotten Son, so loved by Him as to be the Son of His bosom, and so like Him that he could say —" He who hath seen Me hath seen the Father." His work being over, having done His Father's will, he enjoyed His reward. The Father "raised him up from the dead and gave Him glory;" and as the Son of that Father He sits upon the throne. The Son of God incarnate and suffering, the Son of God exalted and reigning in token of God's approval of His work, are the doctrine of this quotation. The promise given to the fathers had been fulfilled to the children in the life and royalty of Christ Jesus. Infinite truth has kept its pledge; the Son of His bosom is now His Regent; Christ is Governor, because He has been Saviour.

The orator now proceeds formally to the resurrection—not to prove it, since he had done that already in the thirty-first verse, but to demonstrate from it Christ's superiority to death; for He was "no more *to return to corruption*"— to be entombed. Christ died once, but He shall not die again. He lay in the grave once, but shall no more descend to it. When the apostle uses the words—"no more to return to corruption," he speaks popularly, and does not mean that Christ had already been in corruption; for he proceeds to affirm that He did not see corruption. The meaning is, that Jesus will never again be in a place where corruption might be anticipated of Him, or where He might be exposed to it. The point of the argument here is not that He rose, but that He rose never again to die. The son of the widow of Nain might die, and again be carried by mourners to his long home, and Lazarus might be a second time interred;

but Christ, being once raised from the dead, "dieth no more: death hath no more dominion over Him." He is endowed with "an endless life." His work on earth being over, He rose to immortal reward. And, to prove this truth, the apostle reverts to quotation—"I will give you the *sure mercies* of David;" literally, sure holy things; that is, holy promises of perfect security. The adjective rendered "mercies" signifies rather things sacred from their connection with God. The promise made to David was sure, trusty, or inviolable; it was sacred, as being divine in origin, and relating to a divine person. What, then, is the meaning of the quotation, and what the proof it affords of the apostle's statement?

The quotation, with only as much variation as serves to introduce it, is taken from Isaiah lv. 3; and the phrase "sure mercies" is narrowed to a personal reference in the next verse—"Behold, I have given Him for a witness to the people." The sure and sacred pledge is connected with the gift and appointment of Messiah, or is identical with it; and it is the "sure mercies of David," because it was solemnly promised to him, and realized in connection with his family—his "house and lineage." Isaiah's allusion is to the oracle of Nathan, as recorded in 2 Sam. vii. 13—16: "He shall build an house for my name; and I will stablish the throne of his kingdom for ever. I will be his father, and he shall be my son. If he commit iniquity, I will chasten him with the rod of men, and with the stripes of the children of men: but my mercy shall not depart away from him, as I took it from Saul, whom I put away before thee. And thine house and thy kingdom shall be established for ever before thee: thy throne shall be established for ever."

The spirit of this prediction is, that David's dynasty shall continue—that his throne shall be filled, and filled for ever, by the last and most illustrious of his sons. The eye of the seer did not regard David's seed only for a few generations, or as ending with Zedekiah whom Nebuchadnezzar carried captive to Babylon; but it comprised in one vast perspective all his sons, till the line was seen to end in Jesus, to whom " the Lord God shall give the throne of His father David, and He shall reign over the house of Jacob for ever." The throne so filled is never to be vacated, but to be established for ever. The 89th psalm is a poem on this old covenant:—"I will sing of the mercies of the Lord for ever; with my mouth will I make known thy faithfulness to all generations. For I have said, Mercy shall be built up for ever; thy faithfulness shalt thou establish in the very heavens. I have made a covenant with my chosen, I have sworn unto David my servant—Thy seed will I establish for ever, and build up thy throne to all generations. Selah. And the heavens shall praise thy wonders, O Lord; thy faithfulness also in the congregation of the saints." Such, then, are "the sure mercies of David"—the promise of an unfailing line, which terminates in his Son and Lord, who shall occupy the throne without pause and without successor. Christ on the throne, and for ever on the throne, of His father David, constitutes the sure and sacred promise of David. But if death were to strike one so exalted—if there were to be any interregnum—if the head wearing David's diadem were to be discrowned, and again be covered with a "napkin"—if the occupant of his throne were to vacate it at the summons of the King of terrors; then the sure mercies of David would disappear, and the promise would be falsified. These sure mercies thus guarantee that David's Son, once upon his throne, shall always sit there; and if He always sit there, He must be superior to death, for it empties all thrones but His. He is in no hazard of that corruption which follows death, and has received into it in succession every other inheritor of royalty. The citation, therefore, proved the apostle's position; and such a proof had a charm and power to a Hebrew mind which it can scarcely have upon ours.

The apostle now rises higher, and affirms that though Christ died and even was buried, He did not see corruption. The proof is taken from the 16th psalm: "Thou shalt not suffer thine Holy One to see corruption"—the same epithet being here applied to Christ as characterizes the promise made about him to David. The argument is, that the words have no reference at all to David, but solely and singly to Christ. They were not and could not be fulfilled in David; for there happened to him the very change which, as the quotation vouches, should not take place on the Holy One. Having mentioned David, the preacher pronounces a brief eulogy on him. He does not barely say that he lived or reigned, but that he *served*—did not simply enjoy the luxuries of royalty, but he ministered for the good of his own generation; and that in a variety of ways. With his finger on his harp he composed a psalm; or sword in hand he gained a victory; or seated on the tribunal he dispensed justice to the tribes. "*His own generation*" or his contemporaries were benefited by him, and through them all ages are under obligation to the "sweet singer of Israel." David lived a life of usefulness. His was not mere existence and selfish enjoyment; but, having got good, he did good. His powers did not lie fallow; cultivation was cheered by blessing, and followed by increase. And the "will of God" was his rule. There were, alas! many aberrations; but, when he fell, he prayed and sobbed and rose again, and God helped him. " So he fed them according to the integrity of his heart, and guided them by the skilfulness of his hands."

The doing of present duty is serving the will of God, and in acting as it prescribes, you bless your contemporaries. Blessed yourself, you become a blessing. But service due to one age is not exhausted in it; it may descend to other generations and reach to distant lands. There lived last century in England an obscure woman with an only son. When he was but seven years old she died. But her image and her prayers for him haunted him by land and by sea—in the ports of Britain, and on the beaches of Africa—when shipping manacled negroes, or carousing on shore with a seaman's zest. His heart was at length touched, and that sailor became a minister, renowned for his impressive conversations and correspondence. His words reached Claudius Buchanan and sent him to India, where he preached and translated; and the recital of his labours so attracted Judson, that he sailed from the far West for Burmah, and found it a sphere of eminent usefulness. The same gift to a mother's asking threw light on the benighted soul of Thomas Scott, and he became the popular and voluminous commentator. It strengthened the feeble and clouded soul of Cowper, and when the poet cried—"O, magnify the Lord with me, and let us exalt His name together," the Olney hymns sprang into existence. Wilberforce was greatly indebted to the same source; and his "Practical View of Christianity" brought truth into the mind of Legh Richmond, who wrote that holy, homely tale—the "Dairyman's Daughter." What an interlaced and unexhausted influence did this pious praying woman produce!—in sermons, letters, translations, commentary, and song; work at home, and work among the heathen—among the polished, and among the rustic—in the senate of England, and on the lowly hearths of Hindostan. What her name was, we know not; where her tomb is, we cannot tell. She was the mother of John Newton.

David's period of service being over, he was released. Wearied out with age and with the burdens of government, he *fell on sleep*—exhausted nature sank into repose. He was immortal till his work was done. The image of sleep, so pleasing and tender, suggests the notion of rest and subsequent awakening. "When I awake, I shall be satisfied with Thy likeness." The king was "laid unto his fathers," was buried in the city of David—the phraseology being borrowed from the custom, that each family had its burial-place in its own garden or grounds. The parents of David were probably buried at Bethlehem with their "rude forefathers of the hamlet;" but the phrase is well enough understood. The royal corpse experienced decay, decomposed in its narrow vault, as do other dead bodies; it "saw corruption"—fell into "dust and ashes;" so that very soon the form of its skeleton could no longer be distinguished. But He of whom Psalm xvi. speaks—this Jesus of David's seed—was buried, and yet saw no corruption. The ordinary process of decay and putrefaction did not take place on Him, though His body was mangled and pierced. He rose on the third day in health and freshness, a victor over death. In the very place of death, He obtained a triumph over death. On its field of victory—the realm of corruption, where the dead moulder away, and the dust returns to the earth as it was—did He signally vanquish mortality. He who won such a victory is surely above death, and lives for ever. Ours is an immortal Saviour, the first and the last, and the living One. Our life is secure, for it springs from His. There was once a dead Christ, but the spectacle shall be seen no more. He lives, and He gives life; nay, He shall open the tombs and summon His people to immortal existence. They see corruption, but "this corruptible shall put on incorruption." The living Jesus shall do it, and He is coming to do it—" Amen, even so, come, Lord Jesus." The conclusion of the apostle, then, is— that the Saviour, David's Son, was the promised Messiah —the great hope of the nation—who had died, indeed, but was now the immortal Governor. These quotations show that the Old Testament, though its imagery and costume be national, is a message of salvation by a coming Redeemer. Then it was hope, but now it is faith; then was the age of prophecy, now is the age of history. There was then a longing that He should come, but now there is rejoicing that He has come. What was latent in the prophets, is now patent in the evangelists and apostles. Christianity was the core of Judaism; and, if not so old as the creation, it is, at least, as ancient as the fall.

One may remark the great similarity between this first recorded discourse of the apostle Paul, and that delivered by Peter on the day of Pentecost. Both dwell on the same theme, and both refer to Ps. xvi. Peter's proof is, This old ode cannot refer to David; for David still lies in his tomb, and "his sepulchre is with us unto this day." Nor has David ascended into the heavens; therefore, what he sang in Ps. cx. does not refer to himself, but to the same Jesus who was crucified, and who is now "Lord and Christ." These early preachers could scarcely avoid this track of argument; and as the Old Testament was common ground with them and their audience, they allowed the cross lights of prophecy to play over their addresses. Those to whom they spoke admitted the truth of such predictions, and might not quarrel on all points of interpretation, and therefore they strove to show that their fulfilment in Jesus was a matter of ocular demonstration. Men saw the living Jesus in a great variety of situations after He rose, and affirmed that they did eat and drink with Him—affirmed it without hesitation and at all hazards.

The apostle proceeds to apply his discourse—"Be it therefore known to you, men-brethren, that through this One (this divine immortal Jesus) to you is forgiveness of sins proclaimed, and from all things from which ye could not in the law of Moses be justified, in Him every one who believes is justified; Beware lest there come upon you what is spoken of in the prophets—'Behold, ye despisers, and wonder, and be wasted, for I work a work in your days, a work which ye would not believe, even though one should describe it to you.'" In this quotation, which is taken from the Septuagint, there is a remarkable variation from the Hebrew, which reads—" Behold ye among the heathen." The apostle adopted the ancient Hellenistic version in a Hellenistic synagogue, though that clause in the original text specified the geographical position of his hearers, and would have been a very significant appeal.

In this third and last portion of his address, the apostle announces the distinctive blessing of the gospel—forgiveness of sins through this Saviour who had died and risen again, and was beyond the power of corruption. *Therefore*—such is the inference, such being His career and character; such His relation to prophecy and the Jewish people; and such now His exalted position, as the immortal Son of David on His Father's throne: therefore is this announcement made—" Be it known to you "—a solemn preamble, and one also employed by Peter—" Be it known unto you, that through this man is preached unto you the forgiveness of sins." That proclamation reaches the depths of man's spiritual nature, for it speaks to his sense of guilt; to that profound agony which ever haunts him, and has shown itself so often in sacrifices so costly as that of his first-born for his transgression, and in pains and tortures, even to suicide. A consciousness of guilt oppresses and stings him, and what are his altars and victims, but its dark and terrible outlet? He struggles for peace with God; and to gain the assurance that God will regard him with favour, he resorts to every form and means of propitiation. The apostle probed the hearts of his audience when he announced forgiveness—uttered the word which every thoughtful spirit had longed to hear. Did we feel what guilt is, or what the frequent confession of such guilt implies; did we but know what it is to fall into the "hands of an angry God;" could we faintly shadow out the picture of "weeping and wailing and gnashing of teeth;" had we any conception of what is involved in death as the wages of sin—O then, how would our heart glow at the mention of forgiveness; what an immediate grasp should we lay upon it, and how we should cherish it as the charter of our freedom and hopes!

The apostle exclaimed—"Through this man to you forgiveness of sin is proclaimed," laying special emphasis on the medium—"through *this one*"—this one I have described and proved to be an immortal Saviour. When had a Jewish synagogue listened to such an announcement? It dealt not with such external blessings as peace and plenty—it amused them not with national glory or conquest. Neither did it chain them with the things of sense or time. It spoke not of a leader to break the yoke of Rome, nor of a legislator to give freedom and security, but of Jesus—the Saviour. There was no promise of the dew of Hermon or the balm of Gilead; no picture of plenty—the olives on Carmel, the vineyards of Eschol, the barns of Hebron, or the nets of Gennesaret. The announcement was meant neither to equip a camp nor convoke a senate, but to form a church. It might leave man's civil relations as they were, but it gave him a new and blessed relationship to his Maker. He might remain at Antioch; but he became a citizen of the New Jerusalem, the partaker of a circumcision not made with hands, and the guest at a richer and more frequent feast than the national passover. He might not return to his fatherland, but he was enfranchised in a "better country," and should "come to Zion with songs and everlasting joy upon his head." The waves of the Jordan might never meet his vision, but he shall recline on the bank of the river of "water of life." Forgiveness—yes, forgiveness through this Saviour, is the apostle's message. This Saviour had died, but had risen again no more to die. The fact of such immortality is proof that His enterprise had been completed, and pardon through "this one" is the news brought by His herald, since it is in consequence of what He has done and suffered, that the blessing has been provided, and is now promulgated. According to this brief report of his address, the apostle does not fully develop the connection between the death of Christ, and the pardon secured by it. He alludes to the leading facts, appealing at once to the experience of his audience, and treating the subject more as matter of history than doctrine. In many of his epistles, the apostle gives special prominence to the forgiveness of sins. And no wonder. It is the first blessing which a sinner enjoys—the curse is taken off him, and he enjoys peace with God. It comes directly and at once from the cross of Christ; for He bore our guilt, that we might not bear it ourselves. It is connected, too, with every other gift; forgiveness first, and all other things shall be added unto us—purity, spiritual strength and progress, all that fits for living and prepares for dying.

And he does not leave the subject without a farther illustration and contrast. The contrast gave a vividness to his meaning, and may have startled his audience—" And by Him, all that believe are justified from all things, from which ye could not be justified by the law of Moses." The apostle throws his ideas into an antithesis—justification in the law of Moses opposed to justification in Him, for the words—" in Him"—belong to the whole clause, and not simply to the phrase—"all who believe." Our common version reverses entirely the order of the apostle's words, and so far obscures the sense. *In Him*, not "by Him," is in union with Him; and *in the law*, is in connection with it. The apostle's favourite term is now introduced —justified; *justified from all things*—absolved from all charges, or all elements and results of guilt. And not only there is absolution from guilt, but the absolved is treated as righteous, or is reinstated in the Divine favour. Blessed truth! not acquitted only, and left with a brand upon him, but regarded as if sin had never been committed; freed from the penalty, and also accepted by the righteous Judge. This justification is in Him, and through what He has done, the righteousness He has brought in, and the sufferings He has endured. But it is not a blessing thrown upon the world at large, like the gifts of Providence of which all are partakers. It is possessed only by "all who believe." Every citizen of Israel had it not, though a Saviour had been raised up in Israel. In former times of deliverance, when the sword had been uplifted to smite the oppressor, or a wise edict had been promulgated, the entire community had felt the advantage without individual effort or concern. But now only he who believed was justified. There must be personal recognition of the Saviour, and the conscious reception of His claims.

The apostle does not stay to describe what belief is, nor tell his audience what things were to be believed. They were well aware of what they were summoned to believe—to wit, the address now delivered to them. Justification is promised to belief in the apostolic statement as to Messiah, who was the Son of David, the embodiment of ancient oracle, the fulfilment of divine promise, and the realization of the nation's prayers and hopes. "Believe in the Lord Jesus Christ, and thou shalt be saved." "He that believeth is saved." All spiritual blessing depends on faith, for "with the heart man believeth unto righteousness." How can any one who rejects Christ, receive of Christ's; how can he who spurns the provider, expect to enjoy the provision? He comes with gifts, but the unbelieving heart retorts—"Thy gifts be to thyself." It opens not to admit the Saviour, and excluding Him, it of necessity shuts itself out from His salvation. It cannot be otherwise. Sinners are not saved against their will—are not rapt upward in a fiery chariot from earth to heaven. Their own consent is asked, and is given by the exercise of faith. But any one may have this faith, and every one who has it is justified—every one in that assembly—whatever his rank or character—without distinction of sins or classification of sinners. So broad is the apostle's statement—"all who believe are justified" in Jesus; nay, more—"justified from all things, from which ye could not be justified by the law of Moses." Not as if there were some things from which the law of Moses could justify, and others to secure justification from which it was inadequate. The phrase is *all things*—all elements of charge or indictment; but from none of these could the law of Moses secure acquittal. Christ justifies from all things— the law of Moses could justify from nothing. The ceremonial law was a shadowy picture of things to come; it prefigured this justification, but figure is not substance. It might absolve from the charge of ceremonial impurity, yet "the blood of bulls and of goats" could not take away sin. And the moral law, since it condemned fallen man, did not and could not justify him; for though "ordained unto life, it was found to be unto death." "What things soever the law saith, it saith to them who are under the law, that every mouth may be stopped, and all the world may become guilty before God." "Cursed is every one that continueth not in all things that are written in the book of the law to do them." Only he who should obey it perfectly, could hope to be justified by it; but "all have sinned." The law discovers man's sinfulness, and the more its spirituality is understood, the more awful will his guilt appear. Yet the Jewish nation vainly hoped for justification by works; in its folly it sought life from a law which had wrought its death.

The apostle thus brought his illustration to a point, at which either faith or rejection would be developed. This declaration of the incapability of the Mosaic law for justification, must have rasped across the mind of his hearers. They gloried in the law, for it was their pride and ornament; and in obedience to it, they not only observed the Sabbath, and had that day assembled in the synagogue, but they also kept themselves distinct from heathen nations. How they must have gazed when this bold stranger so addressed them! His conclusion must have been a sad disappointment. They had listened with delight, as he recounted their ancestral glories and spoke of their great heroes; they must have marvelled, as he told them of a last Saviour—nay, one of David's lineage, who had died, but now lives and lives for ever; and they would eagerly stretch forward to learn what deliverance eclipsing all others was to be ascribed to Him. Their awakened fancy may have painted a national resuscitation, before which the scenes of the Exodus and of the return from Babylon should be shorn of their lustre. What shall David's Son —God's Son—the immortal Redeemer, achieve for them? —victory, when they should have the honour of binding "kings in chains, and nobles in fetters of iron"—redistribution of power and territory, when judgment should be given "to the saints of the Most High," and they should "possess the kingdom"—royal pre-eminence, when "the forces of the Gentiles should come unto them"—or equitable and benignant jurisdiction, when "the mountains shall bring peace to the people, and the little hills by righteousness?" Such a picture may have been gradually gathering before the mind of the synagogue, and assuming consistency and colour, as they listened to the words—"Be it known unto you, men-brethren," when suddenly it was dashed by the announcement, that the issue of the whole was forgiveness of sins, and not only so, but their own law was underrated and set aside. And has it come to this? Is this really the whole result after so glorious a prologue? They could not bear it: chagrin and unbelief were too plainly seen on numerous countenances. The speaker well knew what emotions and conflict his words would create. He knew it from himself, when, some time before, he heard Stephen "speak blasphemous words against Moses," and soon after consented to his death. And therefore, so warned, he concluded with an awful fulmination. He did not implore or argue; he did not dissolve in tears; he saw the impression already produced on not a few of them, and he hurled against them this tremendous menace—" Beware therefore, lest that come upon you which is spoken of in the prophets; Behold, ye despisers, and wonder, and perish : for I work a work in your days, a work which ye shall in no wise believe, though a man declare it unto you."

The quotation referred originally to the invasion of Palestine by the Chaldean armies. Such a devastation appeared impossible to the men of that day; nor could they for a moment imagine that the fane of Solomon could or would be laid in ruin. Though they had been repeatedly warned of that "work," they refused to credit it. But God did work the work when the troops of Nebuchadnezzar sacked the city, and burned the "holy and beautiful house." A similar doom was impending over Judea; the Romans were about to come and take away their "place and nation." This destruction, though told them, they would not believe. The Jews would not see their guilt in crucifying Jesus, and therefore could not forsee their punishment. National sins bring national penalty, and history is but a series of such retributions. The God of nations is even now on His tribunal, and as nations have no hereafter, and their organic existence is so brief and uncertain, therefore are they judged and punished in the present life. While the apostle warned his hearers that the rejection of Messiah would assuredly bring upon the nation its last and most terrible catastrophe, his present audience might imagine that they should escape the national havoc, bloodshed, and captivity, because, resident in Antioch, they were so far from the scene. But these ancient words had at the same time a personal reference to them. If they were despisers, and a smile of derision might be seen on the faces of some—if they were wondering, and it were the surprise of incredulity—if they did not appreciate the apostle's message, and accept the forgiveness by faith in Christ which he had announced—they must perish. His message was strange, but true; their refusal to receive it was fatal; and, "knowing the terror of the Lord," he endeavoured to persuade them. For, it is either forgiveness or endless misery—awful alternatives. "He that believeth is saved; he that believeth not is condemned already." The character man dies with is irreversible, lasts for ever. What he is when he leaves the world, he is for eternity. What an inducement now to believe! Despise not, wonder not, but believe and live. Threatenings of wrath are no idle fulminations. "How shall we escape, if we neglect so great salvation?" And may not our nation take the warning to itself? What has been done to other people may fall on it—not, perhaps, physical evil, flood, or earthquake, but spiritual visitation.

> "What, then! were they the wicked above all,
> And we the righteous, whose fast-anchored isle
> Moved not, while their's was rocked like a light skiff—
> The sport of every wave? No, none are clear,
> And none than we more guilty. But, where all
> Stand chargeable with guilt, and to the shafts
> Of wrath obnoxious, God may choose his mark—
> May punish, if he please, the less, to warn
> The more malignant. If he spared not them,
> Tremble and be amazed at thine escape,
> O guilty England, lest he spare not thee."

We may now for a moment glance at the result.

According to the correct reading of the next verse, the sense is—" And they (that is, the apostles) having gone out, they (that is, the rulers who had asked them to speak) besought that these words might be preached to them the next Sabbath;" or it may be, as the people were going out they besought—a request complied with, as is stated in verse 44. More fully are we told in the next verse. "Now, when the congregation was broken up, many of the Jews and religious proselytes followed Paul and Barnabas: who, speaking to them, persuaded them to continue in the grace of God." The sequence of events seems to be, that Paul and Barnabas withdrew first, leaving the congregation still assembled, though on the eve of breaking up; and that as soon as the meeting was formally dissolved, many groups of Jews and proselytes made up to the speakers, had an interview with them, and received an earnest exhortation to *continue* in the grace of God—to persevere in cherishing present convictions as to the truth of the gospel and its being the spiritual fulfilment of the old economy. "If ye continue in my word," Christ had said, "then are ye my disciples."

During the week the excitement was great; the novel oration was the universal topic of reference and discussion; the two strangers would neither be silent nor inactive in the interval; and the consequence was that when the Sabbath came round, "almost the whole city" was gathered to hear *the word of God*—that new revelation which he had vouchsafed to the world. The Jews could not bear the spectacle; indignation and jealousy filled them at the apparent popularity of the new faith, as it supplanted theirs; and, true to their bigotry, they were found *contradicting and blaspheming*—opposing in a spirit of impious scorn. They had a recognized superiority among the Gentile races from their possession of a true and spiritual belief, and had won over many converts. They could not tolerate the loss of this prestige, and they must have been cut to the heart that many of their own people and of the proselytes seemed to be captivated. Their rage could not be vented in a simple denial; that denial must be barbed with vituperation of the apostles, or a profane caricature of Him whom they proclaimed. The scene kindled Paul and Barnabas, and they spoke in holy boldness—offered no apology, dealt in no personalities, uttered no words of vindictive surprise or impetuous recrimination. They solemnly declare that what they had been doing, and were going to do more fully, was warranted by the conduct of their Jewish antagonists, and was in harmony also with God's own revealed purpose and prediction. The Jews *put away*—spurned the divine message, or in the more awful phrase of the apostle, "Ye judge yourselves unworthy of everlasting life." They pronounced a fatal verdict upon themselves, since, by refusing to accept salvation, they declared themselves not worthy of it. Why, then, should it be longer held out to them? It was not ignorance, which might be excused; it was not doubt, which might be enlightened; it was not hesitation, which might be quickened: but it was decided, violent, and defamatory refusal, which would not profit by discussion, and put an end to all hope of a happy change. This being your character and self-pronounced doom, "lo, we turn to the Gentiles"—not in other countries still to be visited, but in this very city. They began with the synagogue: two Sabbaths had they been in it, but they felt at perfect liberty now to go to the forum; to apply themselves at once to the gentile conscience, and offer the gospel without respect of race or blood. Their meaning is, not that they were to turn to the Gentiles for the first time, nor was it a vow never to labour again for the conversion of the Jews. Their conduct was in harmony with the inspired oracles—"For so hath the Lord commanded us, saying, I have set thee to be a light of the Gentiles, that thou shouldest be for salvation unto the ends of the earth." The words are originally applicable to the Messiah, but He and His are identified, and an injunction laid upon the Head thrills in its power to all the members. The light was to flash first upon the Jews, but it was also to be carried to the Gentiles, bringing the knowledge of salvation and life. No wonder that the poor heathen were glad when they heard that they were not to be excluded, but were formally embraced in the divine plan—no wonder that they "glorified the word of the Lord."

And the result was, that "as many as were ordained to eternal life believed." The gospel spread with rapidity in the district. But the enmity of the Jews could not be appeased; the more the gospel prospered, the more rancorous grew their rage. They would not reason, nor yet condescend to toleration; but their ingenuity helped them. They enlisted proselytesses of high rank, who employed their influence over "the chief men of the city" to effect the expulsion of the agitators. Women are rarely ranged against the gospel. In its introduction high honour had been conferred upon them. "Blessed art thou among women," was Gabriel's salutation to the mother-maid; "she hath done what she could," was the Lord's eulogy on another Mary; and to a third, as she stood by his tomb, and did not recognize her risen friend in the dim light of the morning, he simply said "Mary," and the familiar tone at once excited the joyous response, "Rabboni." Last at the cross, they were first at the sepulchre. This attachment to Jesus was no temporary outburst; it remained after the ascension, and its influence has not yet subsided. But these *devout women*—heathen women gained over to Judaism, formed an exception, and wrought with female art against the preachers. A storm of persecution burst upon them, and on being driven out "they shook off the dust of their feet against them"—in obedience to a solemn ceremonial which the Master had prescribed. But the disciples left behind were not depressed; suffering and menace failed to overawe them; a divine source of gladness, which no earthly influence could shut, had been opened within them—they " were filled with joy and with the Holy Ghost." The Divine Spirit was the source of this joy. It might have been expected under such a crisis, that they should be " cast down," even though they adhered to their profession; it might have been thought that fortitude and resignation was the highest that could be anticipated of them. But they rose far above this negative attitude, and were filled with joy. It was not like a few scanty pools on a rocky beach after the surge had retired; the tide overflowed the entire channel. This emotion is independent of circumstances; it is influenced not by what is without us, but by what is within us. Thus Jesus, on the eve of His own death, over its sacred emblems, and in a scene of sorrow and sad farewells, said to the eleven, " These things have I spoken unto you, that My joy might remain in you, and that your joy might be full."

When shall such spiritual gladness fill the churches? Why should our joy be so tardy and dull—at best like a gleam of sunshine through the clouds of a winter's day? Has not our privilege been continued without pause, and is not the Spirit still promised? Or is it that the world intervenes and the heart is distracted, and that its joys are feeble because they are dissipated? The early church rejoiced under persecution, for it brought them so close to Jesus that no stranger intermeddled. In the midst of surrounding gloom, they blessed and welcomed the radiance which cheered them. The Spirit filled them, for there was no rival; He had their hearts all to Himself, and He took complete and undisturbed possession. Shall not our prayer be—Come down, Divine Gladdener, and enter our souls? Without Thee we are weary and languid. Others are usurping Thy place, or labouring to share it with Thee; dispossess them, we entreat Thee, and fill us wholly and always with Thyself. Let Thy presence lighten our burdens and dispel our glooms. Lift us to rapture, as the "power of the Highest" overshadows us. Open our hearts to Thy genial influences, and let no night fall on them and close them again. Let Thy absence be our moan, and may we never grieve Thee so that Thou shalt depart. Let there be in us no darkness to scare Thee; no sensuality to withstand and provoke Thee; no worldliness to compete with Thee; no sullenness which will not yield at Thy touch: so that we may sing the hallelujah in no cold and constrained melody as we come into the possession of "joy unspeakable and full of glory."

VI.—PAUL AT ICONIUM.

Acts xiv. 1—5; 2 Tim. iii. 11.

ICONIUM was forty-five miles southeast from Antioch, and was reckoned sometimes to Phrygia and sometimes to Lycaonia. It was a city filled with a miscellaneous population, like all the Greek cities of the east. Jews were there, and, indeed, where were they not? Greeks, too, were numerous, and there might be some remnants of its earlier or native people; but all were placed under the controlling power of Rome. The mode of evangelical operation was the same here as at the city from which they had just been so ungraciously expelled. They did not seek out new devices, that they might incur less enmity; or so modify their message as to mitigate the repugnance which it might create. But as usual, and without hesitation, they entered the synagogue together, and addressed the assembled audience. They would not fling off the Jews, though the Jews had flung off them. They would not usurp God's part, and judge them before the time; for they had drunk into the spirit of Him who had shed tears, the last He shed for others, over doomed Jerusalem. They would yet wrestle with Jewish obstinacy, though it so often repelled and scorned them. They would try it again and again, still again and yet once more, with unexhausted attachment and patience. They, therefore, repaired to the Jewish meeting; and, though the substance of the address is not given, its result is briefly stated.

In this section the character and effect of the apostle's eloquence are presented to us, and these we may briefly consider. "They so spake, that a great multitude, both of the Jews and also of the Greeks, believed." From the effect produced, we can argue as to the oration delivered. These persons credited what the apostles uttered. It is belief of evangelical truth which is ascribed to them, and therefore we infer that evangelical truth had been proclaimed to them. The address might be much the same as that at Antioch, already recorded. They *so* spoke —in such a manner, that many believed. Therefore they proclaimed the gospel as truth, and surrounded it with such evidences that it commanded assent. The persons addressed were not summoned to believe a romance or a story without a voucher; but the truth, armed with proof, produced conviction and faith within them. And they proclaimed the gospel as saving truth; not as idle speculation, or as common truth, which, though credited, has no power over heart or life. No, they held it up as the only means of safety, and pressed it on the conscience so tenderly and pointedly that "a great multitude" were brought under its influence. Their minds accepted it on evidence, and their hearts took it home as "the power of God and the wisdom of God." Many of the Jews believed, therefore the gospel must have been preached as the fulfilment of the Old Testament; for the Jew would only receive it as in unison with his scriptures, as verifying the oracle of the prophet, and proving itself that reality which the priest and altar had so long foreshadowed. Many also of the Greeks believed, and therefore the gospel must have been held out to them as a divine testimony, and as the means of a sure and immediate deliverance from sin and death.

And this belief was the end contemplated, the end for which Paul and Barnabas spoke and suffered. To create and sustain it was the one object of their oratory, and no other effect would satisfy them. Every result coming short of it disappointed and vexed them, for, without faith, salvation was not secured, and on this their hearts were set. To create a commotion, and be the observed of all observers; to excite wonder, and set the crowd on talking about their addresses; to be stared at, while they moved from place to place, as tellers of the marvellous, as wandering rhapsodists—to such an unworthy motive they were strangers. But even to impart information on their high themes, to bring men's attention to God and his Son, to stir up the careless to think of the soul and eternity, simply to communicate knowledge or impart impression—such a result did not of itself suffice them. O, no; they longed to give that instruction which, appreciated by the intellect, should also be grasped by the heart, and to lodge such convictions as should ripen into saving belief.

So soon as such an effect was produced, a sharp distinction between two parties was at once apparent. The Jews might not be able to disprove the new religion, but they could bring it and its adherents into disrepute. They therefore so misrepresented the teachers in their motives or actings, in their opinions or purposes, as to make the "Gentiles evil-affected against" them. It might be easily done—by a bold caricature, satirical ingenuity, or direct and unblushing falsehood. Whatever might be the process, the result was that the unbelieving Jews "made their minds evil-affected against the brethren"—literally, "made bad their souls"—the *brethren* being the new converts, whether of heathen or Hebrew extraction. This unprincipled opposition detained the missionaries to confront it, and therefore "long time they abode" in Iconium. Such was the amount of their success, and such the enmity it had provoked, that they resolved to remain, to live down the calumnies uttered against themselves, and to confirm the disciples. And they spake *boldly*—undismayed by the danger. It was no cowardly and private interview that they held, they did not crouch because threatening assailed them. Nor did they exchange a verity for a perhaps, descending from certainty to probability. Neither did they so mutilate the gospel as to win over opposition, explaining away or modifying what was most unpalatable to their antagonists. No; the same truths they openly and undauntedly proclaimed, and their boldness rested on a true foundation—*in the Lord*—as its source or sphere; in Him whom they preached, and whom they served, the story of whose career filled their sermons, and whose Spirit accompanied their ministrations.

Nor was their trust unwarranted, for the Lord supported them, as He "gave testimony to the word of His grace, and granted signs and wonders to be done by their hands." He *gave testimony* to the word of His grace,—bore witness to its heavenly origin and its truth; by *wonders* in themselves, and which, as being out of the usual course of nature, were *signs*—tokens of divine interposition. These the Lord *granted to be done* by their hands — the privilege of being His instruments was conferred upon them. His power alone can work a miracle—all created power is unable to the task. He works in His ordinary form, and in unison with His own established order, and we call it nature: He works in an unusual way, apparently in opposition to His ordinary methods, but yet in harmony with some higher law, and we call it miracle. The apostles had no discretionary power of working miracles; only when the Lord granted it, and they were filled with Him—were *en rapport* with Him—could they do signs and wonders. The city was rent into two factions, some taking part with, and as many, or perhaps more, taking part against the preachers, here both termed " apostles," though only one of them possessed apostolical commission. A conspiracy was formed, Jews and Gentiles sinking their mutual antipathies in their common hatred of Christianity. The rulers of the Jews, as well as the common mob, were concerned in it. The resolution to " stone " the missionaries shows that the Jews were the ringleaders, stoning being a special penalty under Jewish law. But intelligence of it reached the apostles ere the plot was ripe. They therefore left the city and fled the province, crossing the desert into Lystra and Derbe, and making occasional tours into the surrounding country.

But their work was the same; whether in city or country, in garden or desert, " there they *preached*—were preaching the gospel "—told the same good news to all with whom they came in contact; did not invent another gospel, but proclaimed the glad tidings which had brought persecution on them both in Antioch and Iconium. The *gospel*—well named it is, for it is "good news from a far country"—the happy news that God's Son has appeared in our nature and died to save us. Such a visit as that of the Son of God to the world; such a mystery as that of the incarnation, the babe in the manger; such a tragedy as that of the cross, the Lord of glory hanged on a tree; such a salvation in richness as that offered in His name without stint, and in freeness as that proclaimed on His authority without reserve; the assurance of pardon, purity, peace, and glory, suspended neither on previous qualification nor on subsequent merit, but patent to every humble and believing recipient—are not these the substance of the gospel? And if all men are in immediate need of these blessings, and if they are revealed, provided, sealed, and applied nowhere else, need we wonder that Paul and Barnabas persisted in preaching the gospel? Noble benefactors, we honour your services; we admire your heroism as we weep over your trials. They were the seal of your sincerity, the libation poured out upon your faith. Blessings rest "on the head" of the man, "on the crown of the head of him separate from his brethren" for the purpose of carrying the same gospel to distant countries. He is a true successor of the apostles, who in their spirit does their work. Far rather be Paul than Cæsar; far rather be the apostle of China than the hero of Waterloo, the originator of a new translation of the scriptures than the author of "Waverley;" far rather carry the scrip of a missionary than the sword of a conqueror; far rather be Neff than

Nimrod. Evangelical labours win a crown which cannot fade away in heaven, and the time is fast approaching when it shall be true of such a labourer on earth that—

> " The might
> Of the whole world's good wishes with him goes;
> Blessings and prayers, in nobler retinue
> Than sceptred king or laurelled conqueror knows,
> Follow this wondrous potentate."

VII.—PAUL AT LYSTRA.

ACTS xiv. 8-21; 2 TIMOTHY iii. 11.

THE apostle had come to Lystra, about twenty miles south from Iconium. The road traversed a bleak and exposed country, and a large portion of the province—" the region that lyeth round about "—partook of the same character. It was so remote and uninviting, that the population seems to have remained unaffected by the great changes which Grecian literature and Roman subjugation had wrought in western Asia. In the same way Dr. Samuel Johnson saw many extensive tracts in the north of Scotland, which were out of the sweep and circuit of revolutionizing influences —wild, moorish districts, the sparse population of which adhered to the languages, superstitions, and costumes of their fathers; understanding English, but not caring to speak it; or, when able to use it, yet, under any sudden impulse, breaking out into a Celtic exclamation.

At Lystra the apostle Paul wrought a miracle. The object of it was a cripple; not lame from an accident, not suffering from a temporary disability, but one who, from some congenital defect, " never had walked." As he *sat*— probably in some thoroughfare, and asked alms, the words of the stranger arrested his attention; and as he eagerly gazed up into his face, Paul perceived that he had *faith to be healed*—such faith as made him the fitting subject of a miracle, or that state of mind which disposed him to receive that salvation of which the act of healing was the symbol and proof. Perhaps the apostle was speaking of the Lord's miracles of healing as the evidence of His mission and outgrowth of His sympathy, and the cripple might be musing within himself that, if he had been in Judea, Christ could and would have healed him. As he listened, those inner cogitations pictured themselves on his countenance, and might be read there by an onlooker, even though he had not the gift of " discerning of spirits "—

> His eloquent blood
> Spoke in his face, and so distinctly wrought,
> That one would say his body thought.

The apostle, "steadfastly beholding him," with a loud voice uttered the words of power—" Stand upright on thy feet." There was no manipulation of his limbs—no application of an electric current to stimulate dormant energy. The command being given, the cripple did not slowly and painfully gather up and adjust his limbs, and try to balance himself, but at once he " leaped " to his feet " and walked." The spectators were amazed—they could not account for it. It was a cure far beyond the reach of human surgery, and they could ascribe it only to divine power. And as they knew nothing of a miracle—of a work done by a man through power lent to him by God—they came to the natural conclusion, that he who had done it was a god in human disguise. Therefore they exclaimed, in their own vernacular, " The gods are come down in the likeness of men." Their own legends had told them of a similar visit at a former epoch, and surely what had happened once might occur again. The deed was one of such power and benevolence, so plainly superhuman in its style, that they supposed it to be the feat of a god.

And so it was, though not as they imagined. For God had indeed come in man's likeness—"Immanuel, God with us," had verified the appellation in word and deed—had walked on the waves, and had raised the dead. In consequence of this manifestation of God in flesh, Paul had received the commission under which he now acted, and was endowed with the healing power which he had just put forth. A proud philosophy would have laboured to explain the miracle, or, perhaps, to impugn it; would have prated of the occult powers of nature, or suggested something about the effect of a sudden surprise, or the secret sympathy of magnetic influence. But the untutored pagans dipped not into such mysteries, did not do violence to their first convictions, and came far nearer the truth when they exclaimed in awe and wonder, "The gods are come down to us in the likeness of men." There are few nations that refuse a belief in such theophanies, whether it spring from instinctive suggestion, or be the lingering lesson of old tradition. Humanity rejoices to believe that it is not uncared for by Him who is good as well as great; that He who made the world is not so high and distant that He may not visit it; and is not so far removed beyond us, or so alien to us, that He may not clothe Himself with our nature as He descends to bless us. The notion is a wide one, spreading from India to Peru, however it may vary in different creeds or mythologies—that God has stooped to the senses, and spoken to the hearts of His creatures as He walked among them, and left traces and tokens of His presence behind Him. Homer, representing the popular belief, sings of the gods—

> "They, curious oft of mortal actions, deign
> In forms like these to round the earth and main."

A Latin poet, telling a legend connected with Lycaonia and Lycaon its mythical sovereign, represents Jupiter as saying, when rumours of wickedness had reached him—

> "I will descend, said I,
> In hope to prove the loud complaint a lie;
> Disguised in human shape, I travelled round
> The world, and more than what I heard I found."

The god came into this province; the people worshipped; but the tyrant, laughing outright at their stupidity, resolved to put the divine stranger to the test, and served up human flesh for his repast. The indignant Jove overturned the table and fired the palace, while the profane scoffer, on fleeing to the woods, was transformed into a wolf, whence, as was popularly supposed, the name of the kingdom. Jupiter and Mercury were often associated, and it was believed that both had visited a neighbouring province, or rather a province of which Lycaonia was one of the districts—

> "Jove with Hermes came, but in disguise
> Of mortal men concealed their deities."

When the rest of the people refused to receive them, both had been kindly entertained by Philemon and Baucis, a worthy couple who for their piety were saved from that inundation which the enraged divinities sent upon the country. Now, might these scenes of their mythology be re-enacted? Barnabas, from his more august appearance, they took to be Jupiter, and Paul Hermes, as "the chief speaker." Grant them their premises, and you cannot withhold their conclusion. If the gods in human shape had honoured their city, and favoured them with such a token of their benignant power, if they had left Olympus and come to Lycaonia, surely it became the citizens of Lystra to honour their illustrious guests—to do homage and sacrifice to the propitious divinities. The priest only acted as became him, when he would bring a victim to the god he served, and to whose temple he was attached. Jupiter's image—or rather his temple—was "before their city," and he was its divine patron and guardian. His priest brought "oxen and garlands," the one to be sacrificed, and the other to ornament the residence of Zeus and Hermes. Such was a common ceremonial: and thus the Twin-gods speak in a well-known lay—

> "Our house in gay Tarentum,
> Is hung each morn with flowers."

Is not such conduct on the part of the priest and populace a rebuke to those who, admitting that God came down in man's nature, and laid aside the splendours of His Godhead, neglect or refuse to render to Him the homage and service to which He is entitled? These unsophisticated heathens acted faithfully up to their light; but men with the Bible in their hands, the great portrait in which is God incarnate, are strangely indifferent to its lessons and untrue to themselves. That priest who "would have done sacrifice with the people" is a "swift witness" against such inconsistency.

The historian tells us that the crowd made their strange exclamation in the speech of Lycaonia. What it was we know not, as no remains of it have been preserved. Some philologists have thought it a Shemitic or Assyrian dialect, and some a Pelasgic or Greek one; a dispute not unlike that about the old Pictish tongue in Scotland, whether it were a Celtic or a Gothic speech. Two words of Lycaonian and only one of Pictish have been accidentally preserved. But the remark seems to be introduced for the purpose of explaining how the preachers did not sooner interpose, and put an end to the idolatrous project. They had been speaking in Greek, which the Lystrians quite well understood, but in a moment of sudden excitement they cried in their mother tongue. "Barnabas and Paul"—Barnabas occupying his old place once more, as the Lycaonians had styled him Jupiter—did not understand it; could not interpret the Lycaonian exclamation, and never, therefore, dreamed that they were taken for gods. The possession of the gift of tongues is not inconsistent with this supposition. The working of miracles was, with the apostles, neither a perpetual nor a discretionary power, but only granted when occasion required. He who said, "I thank my God, I speak with tongues more than ye all," might not understand the dialect of Lycaonia, for he needed not to preach in it, and thus had not at the moment the ability either of utterance or of interpretation. Therefore it was not till they beheld the overt act, and saw the procession— the priest and the axe, the bulls and the crowns—that they comprehended the meaning of the scene, rent their clothes in dismay and sorrow, and, springing into the heart of the excited crowd, laboured with no little difficulty to dissuade them from their sinful and preposterous design. They were struck with grief and terror that they should be supposed to be gods—heathen deities; they who were only humble instruments in the Saviour's hands. Peter had said, on a similar occasion—"Why look ye so earnestly on us, as though by our own power or holiness we had made this man to walk?" The evangelists were honest men, and would not impose upon the people, or be guilty of a pious fraud. Nor would they lodge themselves in the temple, and obtain possession of that wealth which was often stowed away in such edifices.

The "chief speaker" raised his voice, and delivered the following rebuke and argument against idolatry, either the worship of men or dead and dumb idols—"Sirs, why are ye doing these things? We, too, are of like constitution as you—but men; and we are offering you as glad tidings that from these vanities ye turn away to the living God, who made the heaven, and the earth, and the sea, and all in them; who in generations gone by suffered all the nations to walk in their own ways, though, indeed, He did not leave Himself unwitnessed, as He was doing good, sending rains from heaven and fruitful seasons, filling your hearts with food and gladness." "*Sirs*-men"—not different from our "gentlemen" in the opening clause of an address to a promiscuous assembly—"why do ye these things?" This is the first sentence of his expostulation. What an absurd and frantic step! Why not assure yourselves by some other proofs? We are not gods; we have not descended from the skies. We have no claim to any rank higher than that of mere humanity. We are simply what we seem. "We are men," not men of special lineage or walking on some higher platform, but *of like passion with you*—literally "homœopathic with you." Our nature is yours; with the same functions and susceptibilities, the same appetites and instincts. When we hunger we eat; when we are thirsty we drink; when we toil we are fatigued; we weep under grief; we smile in our joy; and when mortal disease comes upon us we shall die. Why then attempt to invest us with divinity, and offer sacrifice to us? No sin is so heinous or so provoking to God. We did not claim to be gods, nor did we lead you by any words of ours into such a delusion. Nay more, one special object of our mission, and our preaching of the gospel, is to induce you to abandon such idolatrous follies. Our teaching is designed to induce you to forsake them, and turn from them to the *living God*—who has a real existence, as shown by His creative acts and providential bounties. The gospel proclaims one God "above all, through all, and in us all"—one tri-personal Essence; Life, and the source of all life in the universe. The apostle, in arguing against idolatry, does not appeal to scripture, and to its many striking assertions, for the people did not know it, and could not recognize its authority. He takes common ground—lower ground—that which is furnished by natural theology. We have here the germ of the fuller argument against atheism and polytheism elaborated in the first chapter of the epistle to the Romans.

There are two proofs adduced by the apostle of God's real and sole existence. There is, first, proof of God's existence as Creator; and secondly, the proof of His continued existence as Provider. God was, for He created the universe. God still is, for He supports us in being by His goodness. God reared this stately fabric, and filled earth with its appropriate population; but He has not retired from it, left it to itself, or placed it under the operation of impersonal law. He still presides over it, and in His uniform kindness, care, and government, presents a perpetual monument of His being and beneficence. Creation testifies that He did exist; providence is a witness that He still exists; and the movements of providence are successive acts of creation. "We preach unto you," says the expostulator, or rather "we bring the gospel to you" in order to supersede those delusions. The object of the apostle was to overthrow, but also to build up. Argument might show the fallacy of idolatry, and satire like Isaiah's might expose it; but the heart meanwhile was not to be left without some object of worship. The true was to displace the fictitious, for faith in a Saviour-God, expels all false theology. It speaks of one God, and bids us adore Him. It describes His throne of majesty, but assures us it is one of grace. The idol in that temple "which was before the city," and all others, were but "vanities." They have no being, they cannot stir; a nail holds them in their place, and they need to be carried should their place be changed. Though they have the semblance of humanity, they are inferior to man who makes them. "They have mouths, but they speak not; eyes have they, but they see not; they have ears, but they hear not; noses have they, but they smell not; they have hands, but they handle not; feet have they, but they walk not; neither speak they through their throats." Jupiter and Mercury are but vanities—nonentities; "an idol is nothing in the world," there are no such things. Mahomet could call the idols of his country "bits of black wood." When an image of the Virgin was brought to Knox in the French gallies, and he was asked to adore it, he called out that it was no goddess, only a "pented bredd" (painted board), and tossed it into the Loire. But God is the living God—a spirit and everywhere—the one God—the one Will that guides and controls. The idols are dead, are but inert matter, having no more divinity in them than the rock out of which they were hewn, the metal with which they were moulded, or the tree which got its deified shape from axe, saw, and chisel. But the living God is Creator, and the one Creator; ay, Creator of the very materials out of which these false gods are framed. "He made heaven, and earth, and the sea, and all things that are therein." The three terms describe the universe. There are not more Gods than one, each claiming a separate jurisdiction and jealous of intrusion, such as Jupiter, Neptune, and Pluto. The one living God brought all into being, and governs all by indefeasible right.

He "made heaven"—the sky with its orbs, the sun in his splendour, rising, ascending, sinking, and setting; the moon "walking in brightness," planets and constellations rejoicing in their courses, "the sweet influence of the

Pleiades, Mazzaroth in his season, and Arcturus with his sons." Not the heaven only, but "all things therein"—the fowls that "fly in the face" of it, armies of bright-coloured butterflies, myriads of gnats, the gathering clouds and the refreshing shower, the light of day and the darkness of night. The earth, too, and all that is in it—its green carpet enamelled with flowers of every hue, and scented with herbs of every fragrance; its trees, "from the cedar which is in Lebanon to the hyssop that springeth out of the wall;" its "pastures clothed with flocks," and "its valleys also covered over with corn;" its mountains bearing on their brow the snows of ages; its forests vocal with birds of every note and plumage, "singing among its branches;" its animals, fierce and tame; "all sheep and oxen, yea, and the beasts of the field." The sea, too, and all that is in it—river, lake, and ocean—smooth as a floor or heaving in fury, when "the waters thereof roar and be troubled"—with the monster in its depths, and the minnow in its shallows—"this great and wide sea, wherein are things creeping innumerable, both small and great beasts; there go the ships; there is that leviathan whom thou hast made to play therein." The universe, with its furniture and population, is the work of God—a condemnation of atheism; of the one living God—a protest against polytheism; and the fact that He made it shows that it is no necessary emanation or co-eternal phenomenon—a warning against pantheism. The apostle employs no metaphysical argument as to the nature and connection of cause and effect; discusses not the question, whether a finite effect can warrant the conclusion of an infinite cause; dwells not upon the notion of the eternity of matter so current in Greek philosophy; enters into no speculations on the relation which physical or ethical law has to a lawgiver, or power has to a person; speaks neither of necessary intuitions nor of formal logical processes; puts not the truth as either a theorem to be proved, or a problem to be solved, but at once asserts God's sole existence. In the first chapter of the epistle to the Romans, the apostle writes the argument; and, before the Athenian sages on Mars-hill, he spoke it with vivid energy.

The crowd so challenged might wonder why, if idolatry was such sin and folly, it was not sooner checked. The apostle adds, that "God in times past suffered all nations to walk in their own ways." Not that idolatry, as displacing Him, was not offensive to Him, but that He took no active measures to check it. Only one people had divine instructors, and their oracles are full of fulminations against idolatry. The nations walking in *their own ways*—not in paths presented by God, could never rise above polytheism, nor reason themselves out of it. "Hath a nation changed their gods, which are yet no gods?" And still, though the nations were tolerated in their gross absurdities, and no special herald was sent to proclaim the nullity of "gods many and lords many," yet those nations were guilty of disloyalty, for God "never left Himself without witness." "They were without excuse, because that which may be known of God is manifest in them, for God hath showed it unto them." This is the second branch of the apostle's argument. The providence of God is a perpetual witness for Him. Had there been no such continuous and mighty evidence pressing upon all sides, and ever multiplying its force as men gave themselves to the contemplation of it, the culpability of the idolatrous nations would have been proportionably diminished, and the aggravations of their crime exceedingly modified. But they were "without excuse." God "never left Himself without witness." There were hosts of monitors ever pointing to Him, as they ceaselessly reminded men of His being and goodness. He was ever doing good. Such benefaction should have led men to the divine Benefactor. That good was too uniform to have come from chance; too rich in itself, and involving the exercise of too vast a power, to have sprung from any created source; and too skilfully adapted to human wants, yea, too surely promotive of human happiness, to have been the result of inert and mindless mechanism. The good done and daily done, often elaborated by secret processes, and enjoyed by men in its ultimate maturity, should have been traced to the one source.

The preacher now particularizes—"Giving us rain from heaven, and fruitful seasons"—the cause and the results. Rain in those countries is more marked in its periods and its beneficial influence, than with us. Every eye there beholds the blessed change which the shower produces. The earth is covered with verdure, and nature assumes a mantle of living freshness. The grain rises in the blade and the trees burst into foliage. There is heard on all sides the music of a thousand rills. "Are there any among the vanities of the Gentiles that can cause rain?" is the challenge of a Hebrew prophet. Their Jupiter could not create the dark cloud, and bid it distil its blessing. One

Being of power and wisdom and goodness can alone give *rain* —rains, as the apostle phrases it—at the appointed seasons, and by the laws which He has established. The vapour ascending and floating invisibly in the upper regions of the atmosphere, forming, as Moses describes it, " waters above the firmament," waits the period when it shall descend and fertilize the ground. The rain connects the three regions, heaven, earth, and sea, which the apostle has mentioned. Ascending from the sea and gathering into a secret reservoir in the heavens, thence to fall upon the earth, it returns to the sea—" into the place from whence the rivers come, thither they return again."

And rain indicates sovereign power and goodness—" it tarrieth not for man, nor waiteth for the sons of men." In seasons of eastern drought, when the earth is parched, when " the field is wasted, and the land mourneth, and the new wine is dried up," when the dread of hunger appals every one, and even the dumb brutes are looking up to heaven in stupid despair; then it is felt that man cannot help himself, that he must only wait and long and pray till the clouds begin to gather, for he is conscious of being wholly in the power of a higher Will. Day after day passes, and the sun looks down on burnt pasture, dry channels, and a cracked and dusty soil. At evening there are hopeful symptoms, but they are vanished before the morning. The heavens are anxiously scanned if the smallest speck may be discovered, and the imagination often creates it. It is hoped that the wind may veer, and every breath excites, and then belies such an expectation. Spirit and energy are gone—" dimness of anguish" is seen on every countenance. Men dream of floods, and waken to more disappointment. They can do nothing, and devise nothing, to better themselves. No wonder, then, that the giving of rain was associated with divinity. It is pointedly asked in a Greek drama, when the existence of Jupiter is denied—"And who then giveth rain?" as if this were proof beyond all doubt. In southern Africa, where the idea of God is nearly effaced, there is still a belief in a Supreme Power, whose awful prerogative is, not to create men or govern them, but simply to give rain—a gift which is felt to be so necessary, and withal is conferred or withheld in such precarious and variable times and quantities; the dreaded Deity is He who brings them what they so much want, and on the gift of which they can never count—He is the rain-maker. Nay, in that dry upland region of Lycaonia water was often scarce; the heaven as iron, and the earth as brass, and water fetched up from deep wells was so precious as to be sold for money. It was with peculiar point, therefore, that the apostle turned his audience to God—who is doing good—giving rain from heaven. This was the special token of His goodness.

And the result is, that He who gives rain, gives "fruitful seasons." The seasons, as they revolve, tell the same lesson. They come with perfect regularity, as the earth moves round its orbit. And they are "fruitful seasons"—crops ripening for the sickle—the vine bowed down with ruddy clusters—the tree covered with its fruits—all the benefactions of Him who is ever doing good, and "filling our," or rather "your, hearts with food and gladness." This clause is a compacted form of speech, the sense being that, when men are filled with food, and life is sustained and prolonged, their hearts are also filled with gladness—their existence is cheered and blessed. "The eyes of all wait on Thee, and Thou givest them their meat in due season; Thou openest thine hand, and satisfiest the desire of every living thing." The apostle's earnest protestation scarcely restrained the people, "that they had not done sacrifice unto them"—so convinced were they that it was a real epiphany, and so delighted were they with the honour of it.

We may pause for a moment and look at the contrast which Jerusalem presents to Lystra. Upon "a man lame from his mother's womb," and now forty years of age, a similar miracle had been " showed " at the word of Peter. But the result was not his deification, but his imprisonment. His judges admit that a "notable miracle" had been done; indeed, " beholding the man which was healed standing with them, they could say nothing against it;" but enraged by it, they "straitly threatened" the apostles that they speak no more in Christ's name. They would not listen to the teaching, nor bow to the wonder by which its truth was confirmed. Their minds were hardened and beyond conviction, and by various theories they might try to account for the phenomenon. But the Lycaonians did not reason, and came at once to a conclusion, which, though wrong in its immediate application, had yet such truth in it as shames the boasted enlightenment of the Jewish council. Thus there is more hope of the untutored than of the proudly civilized; more hope of the Samoan than of the Brahmin who must first unlearn all his subtleties, and strip off his traditionary prejudices, before he can "receive the kingdom of God as a little child." It was nature at Lystra "feeling after the Lord"—it was Sadducean philosophy in the spiritual court of Jerusalem. The one was open to proof, the other was shut up in cold and supercilious negation. The one might blunder in its eagerness, but the other was wrapped in continuous and immovable falsehood. The one deified two men for a moment—men who had displayed the mercy and power of God, and the error was soon rectified; but the other humanized divinity, looked upon the "healing"—God's own work and witness, simply as done by man; and, instead of adoring God in it, were only annoyed at the craft and success of a Galilean fisherman.

But a reaction soon occurred at Lystra. The enemies of the apostle pursued him; " certain Jews from Antioch and Iconium" maligned and misrepresented him, and, gaining the people over to their views, proceeded to wreak their vengeance on him. These Jews seem to have been both instigators, and also principal actors—they stoned the apostle, as their law enjoined for crimes of impiety. In the city itself, they fell upon him; a heathen country town could not be, as they thought, polluted by such a murder. It was not like holy Jerusalem, out of which Stephen must be hurried before he was put to death; but they dragged Paul out of Lystra, " supposing he had been dead." He who had been taken for a god was stoned as a malefactor—apotheosis followed by martyrdom. The Lystrians must have been sorely affronted at their mistake, and they hated him who had so honestly undeceived them. The Jews must have told them too, that so far from being a god, Paul was the foe of the gods and detested by them, that he was in league with the dark powers, and deserved not to live. Such revulsions are not uncommon with uneducated and impulsive people. The islanders of Crete took Paul, first for a murderer, and then for a deity. When the Gauls, nigh four hundred years before Christ, invaded Italy, and entered Rome, they found the city deserted; but as they entered the forum, they were met with the strange spectacle of fourscore aged and white-bearded priests and patricians ranged in order, each in his robes of state and seated on his curule chair of ivory. At first they were awed, as if the sires had been gods; but no sooner did one of them resent an act of familiarity, than the spell was suddenly broken, and the whole body were at once set upon and dispatched. It is said, too, that it was not till the natives of that South Sea island where Captain Cook was slain, discovered, by his wincing under an accidental blow, that he was a man "of like passions" with themselves, that they ventured to surround and stab him.

"As the disciples stood round him" in grief and consternation, the apostle was resuscitated; a miracle was wrought upon him, for at once "he rose up and came into the city." His enemies, terrified at seeing him whom they had stoned, drawn along the street, and left for dead, would not venture again to assault him: their labour was fruitless, stones were hurled at him in vain, he could not as yet be killed. "Once was I stoned," says the apostle, referring to this outrage; and he reminds Timothy, who, as a native of Lystra, may have witnessed the scene of "persecutions and afflictions which came unto me at

Antioch, at Iconium, at Lystra," adding—" Out of them all the Lord delivered me." Next day the apostle " departed with Barnabas for Derbe." Barnabas, as being less prominent in speech and action, had escaped injury. This was the farthest point of the journey, and, having preached there and *taught many*—made many converts or disciples —they retraced their steps to Lystra, to Iconium, and Antioch, preaching words of comfort and confirmation, organizing the churches by ordaining elders over them, and fortifying them against coming persecutions. Then " they passed throughout Pisidia" and came to Pamphylia, and preaching in Perga, descended to Attalia, where they embarked, and sailed to the Syrian Antioch. From that city had they commenced their travels—" being recommended to the grace of God for the work which they fulfilled;" and, to the assembled church which had sent them out, they gave a report of their labours, " rehearsed all that God had done with them, and how He had opened the door of faith unto the gentiles." They rested now for a season in Antioch — " abode long time with the disciples." And thus ends the first great missionary tour of the apostle—probably in A.D. 47 or the following year.

VIII.—PAUL AT PHILIPPI.

Acts xvi. 6–40.   1 Thess. ii. 2.   Phil. i. 30; iv. 15.

The peace of the church at Antioch was soon disturbed by Judaists, who taught the pernicious dogma—"Except ye be circumcised after the manner of Moses, ye cannot be saved." To quell the controversy, Paul and Barnabas were sent as deputies to Jerusalem, and Paul "went up by revelation." A circular was issued from the assembly which discussed the question, and carried to Antioch by special delegates. The deputies returned also to that city, and "continued in it, teaching and preaching the word of the Lord." Prior to their departure from Jerusalem, the mission of Paul and Barnabas to the heathen was specially recognized "by James, Cephas, and John, who seemed to be pillars." But Paul soon longed to revisit the scenes of his previous tour, and "see the brethren in every city." Such anxiety uniformly characterized him—"the care of all the churches" came upon him. To live and labour in Antioch was not his vocation. Barnabas on this occasion wished his relation Mark to accompany them, as he had previously done to Cyprus. Paul opposed such a resolution, for the young man had deserted the enterprise, "departed from them from Pamphylia, and went not with them to the work." The contention was sharp, and keen feelings sprang up. Perhaps the tergiversation of Barnabas when he had been carried away with the dissimulation of Peter and the other Jews, was not forgotten. Probably Paul judged by too high a standard, was too resolute in carrying every point, and allowed not for the inexperience of Mark—a mother-sick youth, who, however, had now returned, and was ready to undertake what he had previously shrunk from. Alas, for human frailty! Strange is the record that Paul and Barnabas, who had toiled, travelled, taught, and suffered in company, should " depart asunder one from the other "—twin stars, that had revolved round each other, shooting off at once and for ever into different orbits. The first journey had begun with Cyprus, and Barnabas for obvious reasons chose it—it was his native island. It rejoices us to hear afterwards from Paul that Barnabas was still prosecuting the missionary enterprise, " or I only and Barnabas, have not we power to forbear working?" He who had been the cause of the dispute had also fully redeemed his character, nay, had risen high in the apostle's favour, for he says of Mark, " he is profitable to me for the ministry." Paul chose as a new partner, Silas, a prophet who had come to Antioch with the decree. Shall we say that the church sympathized with Paul rather than Barnabas, when we read of him on his departure " being recommended by the brethren unto the grace of God," or did this recommendation happen only because he was formally leaving Antioch for a prolonged period?

Thus commenced the preacher's second missionary journey.

From Antioch " he went through Syria and Cilicia, confirming the churches." In these regions he had preached already, when he left Jerusalem after his first visit, as he tells the Galatians. Taking a different direction from his first journey, he passed from Cilicia, through the great gorge or mountain pass called the "Cilician gates," to Derbe and Lystra, the extreme points of the former circuit, and in the latter town he met with Timothy, his "own son in the faith." But the apostle had no anticipation at this period of entering Europe, his thoughts were concentrated on Asia Minor. He accordingly "went throughout Phrygia and the region of Galatia" doing the Master's work, and forming churches in towns like Pessinus and Ancyra. On proposing an evangelical journey, he does not seem to have mapped out the minor details, but left them, not, as the modern phrase is, to the chapter of accidents, but to the will of God, and to enlightened deliberation on the spot. He was led by providence, and by the Divine Spirit. On this occasion God had a special errand for him in the West, and therefore the Holy Ghost forbade him "to preach the word in Asia;" the "set time" to visit Ephesus had not yet come. Paul and his party arrived in Mysia, but the "Spirit of Jesus," for such is the genuine reading, did not suffer them to go north-east into Bithynia. The apostle was thus checked and checked again, and brought through Mysia down to Troas, the point of embarkation. The waves of the narrow Ægean now lay between him and Europe, which might be dimly discerned under the setting sun. Did he wonder why he had been guided to this sea-port, when he would have wandered far inland, or gone down at length to some more distant maritime city? Did he not now perceive the reason why on this side and on that side his path had been hedged in, till he was brought step by step to the harbour of Troas, the scene of so many classical legends?

If there was any doubt upon his mind, a vision dispelled it. "A vision appeared to Paul in the night; there stood a man of Macedonia and prayed him, saying, Come over and help us." The apostle could not refuse such an appeal: "immediately we endeavoured to go into Macedonia, assuredly gathering that the Lord had called us for to preach the gospel unto them." That man was the representative of Europe, and of its confessed helplessness. He appeared, not clad in mail as one of the invincible phalanx, nor yet draped in the stole of the academy. He stood " a man," a sinner seeking help, and that help which the apostle was privileged to carry with him. The valour of Macedonia, the wisdom of Athens, and the power of Rome were of admitted impotence. The weary heart sought repose, the guilty conscience longed for peace. Altars smoked and victims bled in vain. Temples were dedicated, monuments erected, friezes carved, and statues sculptured in vain. Help was needed from a foreign source, and this Asiatic wanderer was employed to bring it. He had no external pretensions—his "bodily presence was weak "—and once he had been stoned to apparent death. He spoke not in the language or " audacious eloquence " of the schools, but he brought help. He had a simple story to tell of " one Jesus;" no ingenious allegory or gorgeous fiction, but a plain narrative of one who had lived in privation and died in ignominy. Yet it was help; the one effective help which neither philosophy nor civilization could provide. The apostle at once obeyed the vision, set sail, and reached

Samothracia "with a straight course." The errand was urgent; there was no beating up against adverse winds, no tacking to secure the breeze, no idle flapping of the sails in a calm. The next day the vessel dropped her anchor in the harbour of Neapolis, which stood in the same relation to Philippi as Seleucia to Antioch, Cenchrea to Corinth, and Ostia to Rome. The voyage was speedy, for the man of Macedonia was very earnest, and God "by His power brought in the south wind." The apostle then journeyed up from the coast and along the Egnatian road to Philippi, and there commenced his European enterprise. On the Jewish sabbath he went to the oratory "without the gate," and "spoke to the women which resorted thither," either proselytesses, or Jewesses whose husbands were perhaps heathens, perhaps indifferent to religious service. This oratory or place of worship was a mere inclosure, and was, as was common, by the side of a stream, probably in this case the Gangites, though rivulets were numerous, and the city itself was anciently called the "Springs." The Jews were so few that they do not seem to have had a synagogue.

What the "things spoken of Paul were" may be learned from the result. It was no fiction or romance which "the Lord opened the heart of Lydia to attend to." She was a native of Thyatira, but was pursuing business in Philippi as a seller of purple, Thyatira being famed for its dyes, and indeed inscriptions have been discovered relating to its corporation of dyers. She was a proselyte, and therefore a lover of truth, and that feeling which had made her an anxious inquirer, and introduced her to the synagogue, prepared her to be a Christian, and to pass over into the church. The divine blessing sealed the divine truth.

The Lord opened Lydia's heart while she "heard." And where? In the scene of duty and privilege. Had she not shut her place of business, had she expected some wealthy customer and waited for him to buy her vestments, that blessing would not have been enjoyed. But she left the city and went to the oratory, where alone the words of truth were to be heard. And she *heard*—was listening —did not frown at the intrusion of a stranger, or deem his address impertinent and incredible. Neither did she weary of it, and wonder when he should conclude. His oration arrested her attention, and she greedily drank it in. As she listened, she understood, glimpses of the meaning were caught by her, and this partial perception of the truth only increased her eagerness to catch every syllable, that she might lose no incident in the narrative or step in the argument. As she understood, her heart was opened. The novelty which Paul expounded rose in power above that Judaism to which she had conformed. It spoke home to her conscience, and brought a message neither vailed in the dimness of type, nor arrayed in the cumbrous attire of ceremonial. In it God had become man to win man to himself. In it there was an actual expiation for guilty humanity—blood shed, mediation based upon it, and a Spirit to apply it. Mosaism was noted for its anticipations —a religion of hope; but Christianity is based on faith—a religion of present and palpable blessing. Lydia was convinced as she "attended." What she heard was what she was feeling after, and to obtain which she had renounced paganism. Judaism brought her 'nearer it, she saw it pictured, but did not possess it; now it was presented in reality, and she at once embraced it.

And the heart needs still to be opened by a divine hand. The Spirit alone can so reveal a man to himself that he shrieks in alarm, and flees to the cross, and He alone can so present Jesus, that the heart bounds for joy at the vision, and surrenders itself to His grace. The things spoken may be true and evangelical, and may be spoken with earnestness and power, yet the presence of the Lord alone can impart the blessing. The sinful heart is impervious to human eloquence. Only He who made it and claims to know it, can unlock it. Were there with attendance earnest prayer for divine influence, attention, impression, and faith would follow in order; and if there were better preparation for the sanctuary, there would be more benefit from it. If there were previous and hearty invocation of the Spirit, would He not rejoice in coming down? Then would the "things spoken" find a ready entrance, and the opened heart would receive the love of the truth, grow "wise unto salvation," and be moulded into the image of the Blessed. No sooner did Lydia possess faith than, professing it, she was baptized, and then, as a sister, she pressed her generous hospitality on the instruments of her conversion. Paul wrought with his own hands in other Grecian towns, in Thessalonica and Corinth, but the kindness of Lydia forbade such a necessity in Philippi.

May we not, in fine, conclude that one needs not retire from his ordinary secular occupation in order to be called of God? The divine vocation has often been enjoyed on the scene, or at the post of worldly duty. Moses was feeding Jethro's flock, when the sight of the Burning Bush, and the voice out of the midst of it, arrested him. Gideon was threshing wheat by the wine-press when the Lord called him to be military dictator. The youngest son of Jesse was keeping the sheep when Samuel asked for him and anointed him. Elisha was ploughing when Elijah cast his mantle over him. "The Lord took me," says Amos, "as I followed the flock, and the Lord said unto me, Go, prophesy unto my people Israel." Peter and Andrew were "casting a net;" James and John were "mending their nets;" and Matthew was "sitting at the receipt of custom," when they were summoned by Jesus to the apostleship. Nay, as Lydia found the pearl of great price in a distant country from her own, so many have had similar experience in the British colonies. The Negroes, themselves or their fathers torn from Africa, have been brought into contact with the missionaries in Jamaica—have heard and believed, have been washed and made white in the blood of the Lamb.

As the conversion of Lydia shows the result of the apostle's preaching, that of the jailor points out its substance. A pythoness, owned by a wicked and greedy copartnery, who brought "her masters much gain" by fortune-telling, followed the apostle again and again "many days," and was ever crying—"These men are the servants of the Most High God, who show unto us the way of salvation." Either the evil spirit, like those in the demoniac of Gadara, was so sensitive, that he felt the vicinity of a power higher than himself, and must make a confession; or the girl had heard some of the apostle's sermons, and picked out the word salvation as their most frequent and distinctive term. That sound was so often upon the apostle's lips, that she characterized his addresses by it. Salvation, and the way of salvation, formed the refrain of his oratory. Yes! it was "the way of salvation" which the apostle proclaimed—not the road to wealth, or health, or greatness, but the path to peace and heaven. Blessed work—to exhibit to a lost world, not how God made it, but how He redeems it; not how it travels in its orbit, or how its winds and waters are governed, but how it may be recovered from its moral apostacy; not how its countries should be ruled, their laws enacted, their battles fought, their freedom maintained, and their capabilities developed, but how its population may be brought out of guilt and misery, fitted for serving God in time, and enjoying Him through eternity. It was this message that the apostle brought. And he spoke it so fully and so often, dwelt upon it with such intense reiteration, that no one could mistake its substance; and he stood in such a pure and lofty relation to it, as to appear in tone, gesture, and conduct, a "servant of the Most High God." Such was the impression made on the fortune-teller, with whose nervous and superhuman excitement and visions her masters were working to such advantage. Her clamour *grieved*—wearied the apostle, and he disenchanted her, commanding the spirit to be gone. Her power of divination being gone, her owners saw that their hope of gain "was gone" too. The same word is used three times—in Paul's command to the spirit to "come out," in recording the fact that he "came out," and in describing the result that in his exit the owners' hope of gain came out

-too. Her nervous susceptibility had subsided, and all that eagerness and frantic clairvoyance on which they had traded was gone. The capital which they had invested in her, and which had yielded a handsome return, was rendered suddenly unproductive. Their avaricious rage at once vented itself on Paul and Silas. The sickly and possessed slave's restoration excited no sympathy, they would rather have her again under the mastery of the python or serpent —the prince of deluders; for her value must have greatly fallen in the market. They hurried Paul and Silas to the forum, raised a tumult against them, first as Jews, and then as religious innovators. Toleration was not known to the Roman law, though it was sometimes practised. Thus Judaism was allowed, but proselytism forbidden. It was, as Livy tells us, one of the laws of the Twelve Tables—the great Roman Charter—" Let none have gods apart, neither let new or strange gods be privately worshipped unless publicly received."

The "masters" had become suddenly conscientious in defence of the old established faith. Not that they cared in truth for any altar; their motive was pelf and not piety; and having so strangely lost one source of wealth, under the plea of religion they thirsted for vengeance. The bench yielded to the clamour, and the clothes of the preachers being torn off them by the lictors, they were scourged, not as under Jewish law, by which the castigation was inflicted by thongs, and limited to stripes "forty save one," but "many stripes" inflicted by rods were laid upon them. With their backs unwashed, and their wounds bleeding, were they thrust "into the inner prison;" and, to augment the torture, the raw and quivering flesh was further bruised, jagged, and irritated by the friction and the unnatural posture, for " their feet were made fast in the stocks." But their courage did not fail them. On losing a battle in that neighbourhood, Cassius, " the last of the Romans," hid himself in his tent, and bade his freedman strike, while Brutus, in his sullen desperation, fell upon his sword. But, so far from drooping and murmuring, and calling God to account, who had beckoned them to Europe, and yet had permitted them to be so " shamefully entreated;" so far from resolving to desert a Master who had not protected them, or deeming the vision at Troas a lure to draw them on to stripes and a dungeon, " Paul and Silas" prayed, and not only poured out their hearts in supplication, but " sang praises unto God," and that in no whispered melody, for " the prisoners heard them." Peter slept soundly in prison " between two soldiers, bound with two chains," and that on the eve of expected martyrdom; for Herod was " intending after Easter to bring him forth to the people." There was more peace in Paul's heart than in that of the damsel's masters who were cursing their loss; more than in the hearts of the prætors who had caused him to be scourged, for it is plain by their conduct on the following day, that their minds were uneasy as to their rash and cruel procedure. A Hebrew melody was chanted in that inner prison at the dead hour of night. The sleep of the prisoners had been often broken by oaths, groans, and terrible noises; but that hymn, falling and swelling with its strange music and foreign words, produced a profound sensation.

And as the prisoners *heard*—were listening, to the song as its dying cadence was echoing through the vaults and corridors, the edifice was shaken, the massive doors were opened, and "everyone's bands were loosed." The concussion awoke the jailor, who staring around him in consternation, and guessing the result, would have committed suicide—a miserable but common Roman refuge. Paul prevented so insane an act, and the keeper, with a light in his hand, "sprang in" to the cell of the apostle, and, in an agony of alarm, cried—"What must I do to be saved?" Self-murder was often eulogized by Roman sages, and had been practised by not a few of them. The jailor would have reckoned it a less disgrace to die by his own hand than by a military execution. But his hand was arrested by the apostle's abrupt command—"the life that now is" was prolonged, that he might be soon put in possession of the life "that is to come."

"What must I do to be saved?" was his exclamation; and it shows that he was no stranger to the general lesson of the apostle's preaching. Like the fortune-telling demoniac, he had heard the word "salvation." He knew that Paul proclaimed this, and, terror-stricken by the phenomenon which had happened—ay, and convinced by it, that a supernatural power guarded the two prisoners, he eagerly demanded how it could be got by him. It was the best thing for him as he now imagined, but how was he to attain it? He might previously have laughed at the term, but he had caught some idea of what it meant. It was a blessing which he had not, and now his soul was on fire to have it. Did he deem that he was unworthy of it

—that his conduct yesterday to its preachers excluded him from it? Must there be some other path for him than that which the Jewish stranger ordinarily pointed out? I know what is presented to others, but as for me, so cruel and guilty—as for me, who have acted savagely to the strangers—"What must I do to be saved?"

"What must I do to be saved?" The response—the immediate and unhesitating response—was—"Believe on the Lord Jesus Christ, and thou shalt be saved." A true reply. If a man wishes salvation, let him accept the Saviour. If he will have the gift, let him confide in the giver. Can he have redemption, and yet reject Him who wrought it out? Can he be taken out of the pit, and yet spurn from him the arm that alone can lift him?

"What must I do to be saved?" Believe on Him who provided and who bestows this salvation. This is the only effectual process. He is able and He is willing. The lash on the back of Paul and Silas may have cut their skin into ribands, and the jailor did not dress their wounds; he put them in the inner prison, and by a refinement of cruelty locked them in the stocks; his office in a Roman jail was one which few could discharge without misgiving, for torture and outrage were often resorted to; and yet let him, even him, but believe, and the coveted blessing would without doubt be conferred upon him. Yes, let a man's station be what it may, his position what it may, his past life what it may, he is not placed beyond the pale of this salvation. He is welcome, and he is warranted to believe on the Lord Jesus Christ. It is not the idea of belief, nor the desire of it, nor the hope of it, but actual belief itself, which secures salvation. One may not be able to analyze it, far less to define it; he may not discover its adaptation, nor understand why it should be selected as the means of safety; yet he may possess it, and enjoy all the fruits of the possession. The Lord Jesus Christ is so exhibited in power, truth, and love, that they who see Him may be attracted to believe on Him; the *Lord*—Governor—on the throne, because He died on the cross; *Jesus*—the Saviour, His name taken from his work; *Christ*—the Anointed One, commissioned to redeem humanity, and qualified for the great enterprise by the unction of the Holy Spirit. What can keep us back from faith in Him? Has not He the arm of God and the sympathy of a brother? Has He not given Himself to death, and what higher of attachment could He tender? Is He not anxious that His salvation be dispensed? He that provided it in His blood, He it is that rejoices to confer it. Are not all those invitations and promises sealed in His blood? Are they true, then, or are they false? Yea or nay? Let there be no ambiguity—decide. Is God duping you, that you refuse to trust him? Did anyone ever find it so? Why, then, be "slow of heart" to believe? "Be not faithless, but believing;" yea, let the individual response be—"Lord, I believe, help thou mine unbelief."

"What must I do to be saved?" Believe, and salvation is obtained in its fulness—not a segment of it, as if its perfect fruition depended on some other grace. The state of salvation is attached to faith and every blessing connected with it. There is pardon—we are "justified by faith;" there is acceptance, for "faith is counted for righteousness;" and there is also perseverance, for we are "kept by the power of God through faith unto salvation." Belief gives sweep and power to prayer. "Whatsoever ye ask, believing, ye shall receive;" and He is "able to do exceeding abundantly above all that we ask or think." The possessor of faith enters into God's family; for "as many as received Him, to them gave He power to become the sons of God." He has tranquillity of soul; for "we which believe do enter into rest;" and he has a growing purity; for he is "among them which are sanctified by faith that is in Christ." There is guidance, for "we walk by faith;" and life, too, "for the just live by faith;" and triumph also, "for this is the victory that overcometh the world, even our faith." There is, in conclusion, a chartered fulness of gift—"Blessed is she that believed, for there shall be a performance of those things which were told her from the Lord." And thus it is that "the end of your faith is the salvation of your souls."

"What must I do to be saved?" Believe, and salvation is certain. It is not believe and you may be saved, or there is a chance or even a probability of salvation. The result is immediate. Not at some distant day, or when you come to die; but at this moment faith possessed is safety enjoyed. To say, Believe, and thou shalt be saved, is equivalent to saying, Take it and you have it. Guilt is cancelled, and the Spirit descends into the soul. "He that believeth on the Son hath everlasting life"— " is passed from death into life." Not only do believers possess salvation, but they are conscious of it: " being justified by faith, we have peace with God "—" by faith ye stand." "He that believeth on the Son of God hath the witness in himself." He is not told about safety only, but he enjoys it — he has experience of it. Tell the mother that her strayed child is safe, and she credits the statement; but let her clasp it to her bosom, and she has the witness in her rapture. Show a man the electric machine and describe its results to him, he does not deny them so far as he comprehends them; but let him feel the shock, and then he has the witness in every nerve as it tingles and vibrates. He that feels what peace is, what a changed heart is, what the spirit of adoption in prayer is, what advancing purity is, and what the hope of glory is; feels as well as knows, rejoices in the record, but also has experience of its truth and power.

If all depend on faith, it is a truism to say that the want of it must be fatal. Nay, to disbelieve God, is to call him a liar. Devils do not commit so insulting and flagrant a crime. They believe, and they tremble through their belief; they cannot sink into unbelief. But, alas! if a man wants faith, he wants every spiritual blessing; for God does not thrust His salvation on an insulting heart. O, then, give Him credit for what He has done, and take Him at His word for what He has said. And your faith rests on decisive evidence. There needs no great trial of it; it is not beset with obstacles. Abel believed, and acted out his belief, when the testimony was scanty and the ceremonial not very transparent. Enoch believed and maintained his faith, when faith seems to have fled the earth, and all around were "ungodly men," full of "ungodly deeds" and "hard speeches" against God. Noah believed, and persisted in building the huge fabric from keel to deck, under a cloudless sky, and in a country which gave no token of earthquake and inundation. Abraham became an emigrant through faith, yea, went out under this lodestar, "not knowing whither he went." Moses, with the eye of faith, saw "the reproach of Christ to be greater riches than the treasure of Egypt," when the crown of the country might have devolved on him as the son of Pharaoh's daughter. Joseph believed that his mummy should not lie in Egypt though laid up there, and "gave commandment concerning his bones," at a time when Pharaoh was strong and his own people were but a handful. Job was smitten with terrible calamities, but his faith did not waver; and even when he contemplated the worst, he would not renounce it—"Though He slay me, yet will I trust in Him." In Christ's days there were many external barriers to faith in the carpenter's son, and yet many believed. The woman of Samaria accepted as Messiah the way-worn Jew who sat upon the well and asked for a draught of water. And though it was a Jew, one of a despised and obnoxious race, one who had been scourged and thrown into the inner prison by himself; though it was a poor, defenceless stranger, bruised, bleeding, pale, hungry, and ragged, who preached unto him Jesus—the jailor "believed, with all his house." And if we have clearer evidence—no ambiguity or mystery; not types, but facts; not prophecies, but annals; if we are not summoned to do battle against appearances, and soar on strong pinions above what seems dark and hostile, as it mocks our heroism and brands our confidence as a mere romance at variance with all reality; if we have the gospels and the epistles, the church and the Spirit, all attesting our faith, the lives of so many to illustrate its powers, and the deaths of so many to show its triumphs—then, if we be faithless, we are surely without excuse, and our doom must be that of those of whom it is written—" They could not enter in because of unbelief." " He that believeth not is condemned already "—" shall not see life, but the wrath of God abideth on him."

Paul's further exposition is called speaking " *the word of the Lord* "—delivering the message of Jesus. It was a strange locality and an unusual hour; but the gospel triumphed. The terror of the night passed away, and joy came in the morning. The jailor was a new man; he led the apostles to his house, washed their stripes with all tenderness, was himself baptized, " set meat before them," for evidently none had been given them previously; hunger, fasting, and cold had embittered their imprisonment. The prætors send the *serjeants*—lictors—with an order to the jailor to dismiss them—a curt and contemptuous message—" let these fellows out." But Paul and Silas refused to take such a dismissal. No doubt the jailor thought that Paul would gladly listen to such a message; but the apostle at once demurred, and avowed himself a Roman citizen— "They have beaten us openly uncondemned, being Romans, and have cast us into prison; and now do they thrust us out privily? nay verily; but let them come themselves and fetch us out." A heavy crime it was to scourge a Roman citizen, and it forms the point of one of Cicero's invectives. The words—" I am a Roman citizen," had usually acted like a charm. But the majesty of the empire had been violated in Paul's person—he had been beaten with the lictors' rods; he had not been convicted or even tried; the flagellation had been in public, which, according to law, was an aggravation of the offence, and besides he had been cast into prison. All this indignity had been done in a city which was a "Roman colony;" such a colony being in fact a reproduction of the mother city, Rome—a military settlement founded by Roman citizens and retired soldiers—and not a place built and governed by a body of emigrants.

Why the apostle did not, as afterwards, avail himself of his privilege, we know not. Some suppose that his words were unheard amidst the clamour; and others that he yielded to the outrage for higher ends—showing what he could suffer for Christ's name, and guarding the infant church from extinction through the lesson which he taught the magistrates. Himself says—"Thrice was I beaten with rods"—this being one of the occasions; nay, he was "in stripes above measure;" for he adds—"Of the Jews five times received I forty stripes save one." He would not raise a civil action or make an accusation to the proconsul—though both processes were legally open to him; but he wished that some reparation be made him—that the magistrates should attend in person and liberate him and Silas. These officials "feared," were well aware what a penalty they had incurred; for they had violated the Porcian and the Valerian laws. There were instances, and some of them recent, of the swift and heavy vengeance which Rome took on such as broke those statutes. She was proud of her citizenship, and would not on any pretext tolerate the smallest infraction of its rights. The duumvirs, therefore, "came and besought them, and brought them out, and desired them to depart out of the city." But they would not sneak away like culprits, afraid to be recognized. No, they rejoiced "that they were counted worthy to suffer shame for His name." Boldly and in the face of all "they went out of the prison, and entered into the house of Lydia: and when they had seen the brethren, they comforted them, and departed." Such were the apostle's experiences when he first trode the soil of Europe; and such the first conflict of Christianity with Hellenic heathenism and the savage caprice of Roman authority.

IX.—PAUL AT THESSALONICA.

ACTS xvii. 1–9. 1ST & 2ND EPISTLES TO THE THESSALONIANS.

THE apostle had been beckoned into Macedonia by a vision, and that vision still haunted him. Every temple he beheld, and every form of idolatry he witnessed, brought back the picture. Help was needed everywhere in the province, and he had brought it. The cruel treatment at Philippi did not detain him from the farther prosecution of his labours. His spirit sank not, though he had been subjected to the scourge. That indignity was a severe trial to him—to few more than to him. The knout brings no disgrace to a Russian serf, and wheals are usually found on the backs of American slaves. But the lash must have been felt as an unspeakable ignominy by one of Paul's refined and elevated temperament; and he afterwards characterized the treatment as "shameful." But he bore it as did the Lord before him. He did not sink into sullenness, and feel self-degraded at such outrage done to him as a man, and such a violation of right inflicted on him as a Roman citizen. It did not stand out in solitary gloom and bitterness as—

> "One fatal remembrance, one sorrow that throws
> Its bleak shade alike o'er his joy and his woes;
> To which life nothing darker or brighter can bring,
> For which joy hath no balm, and affliction no sting."

He left Philippi because it afforded no prospect of immediate usefulness. But he prosecuted his great work, and travelled south and west along the Egnatian road thirty-three miles to Amphipolis on the Strymonic gulf, but did not stay there; advanced thirty miles farther to Apollonia, but rested not there either; journeyed onwards other thirty-seven miles, and arrived at Thessalonica. This city, at the head of the Thermaic gulf, had then and has still a large population, and the Jews in it were so numerous as to have a synagogue, which probably was also a place of worship for the Jews of the surrounding district, for the correct reading is—"Where was the synagogue of the Jews." Thessalonica contained a far greater population of Jews and heathen than Philippi—was, in fact, the capital city; but Paul had first visited Philippi, which is called "the chief city of that part of Macedonia." The epithet "chief" or first may admit either of a political or geographical meaning —either a primary city, or the first on his road. If it was the first city of Macedonia that lay on his journey, then he naturally commenced to give it the help which the man of Macedonia had prayed for; if it was a chief city in that part, there was every inducement to fix upon it as the centre of farther operations; and if it enjoyed special advantages as a city and colony, then, its importance in itself, and in relation to other towns and districts, made it a fitting place both for present work and subsequent enterprise. You may either say Paul went to Philippi as the first city on his path, for he had been summoned into Macedonia, and he could never think of passing the first city which he came to; or he formally selected Philippi because of its rank, and because of its privileges as a Roman colony. If the apostle had taken this tour of his own accord, or as the result of plans previously matured; if he had traced out the itinerary of an evangelistic campaign before he set out, then the latter hypothesis would appear the more plausible: but if, as was the case, his purpose was hastily formed, and the general idea of traversing the province, without any distinct regard to the order or arrangements of the visits, was suggested by the prayer of the representative man, then the first would appear to be the more natural and simple hypothesis.

Though the apostle was invited into Europe by a man of Macedonia personating its heathen tribes, yet he never forgot his own nation, but entered at once into the Thessalonian synagogue. Though labouring under a special commission for the Gentiles, he did not deviate from his usual practice, but spoke on three consecutive sabbaths to his countrymen. He and they had common ground—the scriptures. Both acknowledged the divine authority of the Old Testament, and all who read it cherished anticipations of a Messiah. And this was the one point which the apostle discussed. His study was to show how Messiah had been portrayed, and how the portraiture was, feature for feature, the likeness of Jesus of Nazareth. It is plain that an erroneous or one-sided interpretation of these old oracles would either becloud or warp the mind, so that it could not recognize their fulfilment. The Messianic oracles must be understood clearly, fully, and in harmony. No error is safe, and error on certain points is fraught with imminent danger. If a man misunderstand a prophecy, he of necessity misapplies it. The question, whom does it fit—depends on the solution of a previous query, what does it teach? If I take up the notion that teaching was the special and only function of the Messiah—the prophet like unto Moses—that His great work was to enlighten the world by bringing unknown truths into it, and casting a new radiance on principles already established, then the cross and its agony only perplex me, and I am self-bribed to take them simply as seals and attestations of integrity and courage. Or, if a Jew perceived in Him only a promised conqueror and king, with David's sword on His thigh, and David's throne as His seat of exaltation, then the life of the peaceful Jesus would, in his opinion, so far from presenting a fulfilment of prophecy, exhibit such a striking contrast to it that His claims would be at once ignored, and Himself stigmatized as a pretender. It was of high utility, therefore, that the apostle should expound the scriptures, and show what kind of Messiah had been predicted. A sketch from fancy would not suffice. The point at issue was, what is the idea of the Messiah as developed in the Old Testament, and has it been realized. The Jewish mind needed this. Show from the law and the prophets what He was to be, and then tell what Jesus was; depict what He was to do, and then detail the life of this Son of David; and thus it will be seen how the one fitted into the other, how the living person corresponded to the ideal delineation.

Now, there was one point evidently misconceived by the Jewish people, and that one of transcendent moment. The suffering and death of Jesus forfeited, as they thought, all claim on His part to be the Messiah. The cross was a "stumbling-block" to them. They could not imagine the possibility of that man being the Messiah, who had been publicly executed. So foreign was such a thing to all their fancies and hopes, that they could not entertain it, and so sure were they of being right, that they would not examine it. The bare statement was to them its own refutation. The inspired preacher at Thessalonica, knowing what he had to encounter, took the proper course, and showed that the promised Messiah was depicted as a suffering Messiah, that the prophets had distinctly foretold his mortal agony, and that, if their pre-intimations are to be regarded, only He who has died and risen again has any right to be regarded as Israel's hope and God's anointed one.

The apostle, therefore, *reasoned* out of the scriptures—discoursed out of them as his theme; *opening*—explaining or making clear; and *alleging*—advancing and propounding the truth which the preceding or accompanying exposition revealed—" that it behoved the Messiah to suffer and rise from the dead." On the ground of the Old Testament, the apostle showed and proved his position. He took the prophecies and analysed them, and in commenting on them gained his purpose. His argument lay in his exposition. It was no abstract proposition which he discussed, either as to the legal necessity or the atoning value of Christ's sufferings. It was a proof from scripture that He whom Jehovah promised, and the nation had so long and so eagerly expected, was to be one distinguished for his sufferings—sufferings ending in death, and that, therefore, no one could claim to be Messiah who was not notorious for the persecutions and agonies through which he had passed. The apostle entered into no philosophical argument as to the necessity of an expiation, and into no historical proof that Jesus had really died on Calvary; but his object was to prove that Moses and the prophets, in portraying a Messiah, dwelt largely on his sufferings, while they forgot not his kingdom. One that had not suffered, who had met with no hostility, whom the nations had caressed as in his triumphant car he rode from victory to victory, could not be the Messiah, for he did not embody in himself these old inspired predictions. The Christ promised was not only to teach many things, but specially to endure many things; was to die while He conquered. A grave lay between Him and His throne, and His kingdom was to be won by His blood. The work of expiation which was committed to Him involved indescribable agony. The Hebrew mind was filled with giddy imaginations of civil glory and a visible monarchy, and the apostle, therefore, taught that these had no foundation in the Hebrew scriptures, but that the leading characteristic of the Messiah was to be suffering—death.

And he could point to many oracles in support of his opinion as to the necessity and character of Messiah's sufferings. The first gospel in Eden had dimly alluded to it. The typical dispensation had foreshadowed it in the blood of its victims. The paschal lamb typified the Lamb "which taketh away the sin of the world," even "Christ our passover, sacrificed for us." Isaiah had described it with graphic minuteness. "He was wounded for our transgressions, and bruised for our iniquities; the chastisement of our peace was upon him, and with His stripes we are healed." "The Lord laid on Him the iniquity of us all." "He is brought as a lamb to the slaughter," "cut off out of the land of the living." "It pleased the Lord to bruise Him;" His soul made "an offering for sin." "He shall bear their iniquities." "He hath poured out His soul unto death." "He bare the sin of many." The psalmist had pictured Him as the great oblation in man's nature—"A body hast thou prepared me." Daniel had spoken of Messiah the Prince, not as clothed in royal robes, or wielding a sceptre, but as one who "shall be cut off." And the delineations of His conquest and kingdom presuppose his resurrection—He "rose again the third day, according to the scriptures." In dying He conquered, and then had given Him "a portion with the great;" dividing "the spoil with the strong." After the conspiracy against Him which the psalmist depicts in the second psalm, and which ended in His death, He is installed as "king over God's holy hill of Zion." His enemies put Him to death, but He rose and ascended, and, concerning those enemies, "the Lord said unto my Lord, Sit thou at my right hand, until I make thine enemies thy footstool."

Having shown that the Old Testament delineated not simply a suffering Messiah, but one to be noted and known for His suffering — one that as Messiah, or as anointed Redeemer, should agonize and die; the apostle then showed "that this Jesus whom I preach unto you is Christ;" or rather, according to the position of the words, "this Jesus whom I preach to you is that very Christ" who must suffer and rise again. The life and career of Jesus corresponded closely with these predictions—not simply of His birth, but also of His death. The circumstances of that death had been foretold. It was not to be the national mode of execution—not lapidation, but suspension on a tree, to which He was nailed when they "pierced His hands and feet." It was to be preceded by treachery, and an illegal seizure and condemnation. It was a scene in which the heathen were to "rage," implying that Judea should be a conquered country, and under foreign rule. Preparatory to His death He was to be stript of His clothes—"they part my garments among them, and cast lots upon my vesture;" and so it was, as the evangelist tells us. He was to die, and yet "not a bone of Him shall be broken;" to be "numbered with transgressors," and yet to lie in a rich man's tomb. Nay, not only should He suffer at the hands of men, but God should "put him to grief;" and so His bitter wail on the cross was—"My God, my God, why hast thou forsaken me?" It was to be a crucifixion—a violent, voluntary, vicarious death; and it was so. Every feature of prediction was fulfilled. If, then, the sufferings of Jesus, in their source and amount, in their nature and design, in themselves and in their adjuncts, are so closely and universally in harmony with old prediction; if you can find the law and the prophets realized in the agonies of His cross, and the humiliation of His sepulchre; if you perceive that the record of His last days is merely prophecy read as history—that Matthew but relates as past what David had sung of as to come; and that the only difference between Luke and Isaiah is simply that between prose and poetry—between the original and the portrait; surely you will come to Paul's conclusion, that "this Jesus whom I preach unto you is the Christ."

The narrative brings out another feature of the apostle's preaching. The result at Thessalonica was as in other places. The gospel was received by many—*a great multitude*—and not a few of them proselytesses of high social rank—persons who, from their position, were neither fettered by Jewish prejudices, nor clouded with heathen darkness. And not only so, but many heathens were won over—"turned," as the apostle afterwards told them, "to God from idols, to serve the living and true God." The majority of the church seems in fact to have been composed of Gentiles. The Jews, on the other hand, could not conceal their chagrin; and the apostle characterizes them in Thessalonica thus—"Who both killed the Lord Jesus and their own prophets, and have persecuted us; and they please not God, and are contrary to all men; forbidding us to speak to the Gentiles, that they might be saved, to fill up their sins alway: for the wrath is come upon them to the uttermost." They resorted to a very mean expedient; for they took unto them that excitable and profligate rabble that in such towns lounge about the market-place—a class of houseless persons having a defined and well-known character in these days, ready for any mischief, called "dregs and mire" by one ancient author, and "lying and perjured" by another—the canaille, in short, like the lazzaroni of Naples, to which they have been compared. With these allies they easily created a tumult; "assaulted the house of Jason," with whom the apostle lived, and who perhaps was a kinsman (Rom. xvi. 21); but did not find Paul and Silas, whom they wished to bring out *to the people*—the assembly—the word employed meaning the people in a corporate sense. However, they dragged Jason and some other believers before the magistrates, and declared them to be traitors and revolutionists. The "rulers of the city" have here the appellation of politarchs—the term being different from that employed to name similar officials in Philippi; Thessalonica being a free city, and not a Roman colony. The accusers describe the Christians as effecting changes in other places, and as being now in the city prosecuting the same work. The charge is strongly rendered in our version—"turned the world upside down." And, indeed, what better thing could have happened the world than to be so thoroughly upturned? But the point of the charge is that the new sect were rebels, opposing Cæsar's decrees, guilty of treason, "saying that there is another king, one Jesus;" that is, they broke the Julian laws, disowning the authority of the Roman emperor, and proclaiming a rival sovereign.

It is plain that Paul had preached Jesus as king, and that the doctrine was either misunderstood, or that the Jews, knowing what their own hopes were of a conqueror and Lord, gave out in their malice that the Christian creed embracing this tenet taught sedition. The mob cared nothing about a religious question—cared as little for the Jews or their national faith, and would never have been bribed to raise any disturbance about any Jewish dogma. They, therefore, gave their charge a political aspect and edge, which the "lewd fellows of the baser sort," and the people, with the proconsul and his assessors, could at once apprehend. Jesus was prosecuted Himself under the same charge as king of the Jews, and the tablet on the cross bore the accusation—"Jesus of Nazareth, king of the Jews." The apostle's doctrine was misconstrued. He taught that Jesus who suffered was king, but upon no throne of earth; that His kingdom has infinitude for its extent, and eternity for its duration; that the elements of nature do His bidding, as do the loftiest intelligences that bow their heads before Him; that He controls and governs all, and that those who are ransomed by His blood are bound to yield Him the homage of their hearts and the service of their lives. Christ's royal honour has prominence in the apostle's letters to this people, and must have had it also in his discourses. To Him all power is given in heaven and in earth. To Him every knee shall bow, and every tongue confess. On His head are "many crowns." He is "Lord of all," "crowned with glory and honour;" nay, in the apocalyptic vision, while on His white horse He pursues His flying foes, and the breeze tosses back His warlike mantle, the name, written "on His vesture and on His thigh," is seen to be "King of kings and Lord of lords." The gifts of His salvation are royal benefactions, and His sceptre protects and extends His church. That church, on earth and in heaven, is His kingdom; His people suffering for it are "counted worthy of" it, for they are "called to His kingdom and glory."

As we learn from the first epistle of Peter, the same

charge of disloyalty was brought against Christians in other places. Their enemies, in the "ignorance of foolish men," did not understand the genius of that kingdom which "is not of this world," nor believe that spiritual homage is quite compatible with civil obedience. Thus did Tertullian speak in his day, when the reproach of being enemies of the state and the emperor was cast on him and the church—" We pray for the emperor's welfare to the eternal, true, and living God, whom even the emperors themselves would rather have propitious to them than all the rest. They know who has given them dominion; they know, as men, who has given them life. They feel that He is God alone, in whose power alone they stand, to whom they are second, after whom they are first, before all gods. And why not, since they are above all men? They reflect how far the powers of their empire extend, and thus they understand God; they acknowledge that they prevail through Him, against whom they cannot prevail. To Him we Christians look up with outspread, because innocent, hands; with bare heads, because we are not ashamed; finally, without a prompter, because we pray from the heart. We pray always for all emperors that they may have a long life, a secure government, a safe home, valiant armies, a faithful senate, a righteous people, a world at peace, and all that man or emperor can wish for. These things I cannot ask of any other being than of Him from whom I know I shall obtain them, since it is He who alone supplies them, and it is I to whom the obtaining of them is due—I, His servant, who reverence Him alone, who surrender my life for His law, who offer Him a rich and larger victim which He himself has commanded, the prayer proceeding from a chaste body, an innocent soul, from the Holy Spirit. I will call the emperor lord, but only when I am not compelled to call him lord instead of God. Otherwise I am free before him; for I have only one Lord, the almighty and eternal God—the same who is his Lord also."

From the tenor of the epistles to the church in Thessalonica, it is evident that there was also another doctrine which Paul preached, and that was the return of Christ in glory to judge the world—" Remember ye not that when I was yet with you I told you these things." On their conversion they were taught " to wait for His Son from heaven, whom He raised from the dead, even Jesus, which delivereth us from the wrath to come." On delivering to them a weighty message, he adjures them " by the coming of our Lord Jesus Christ." The second advent was the period of hope to which the preacher ever pointed, and which he described as ever near—the period when the dead shall be raised, the living changed, and the happiness of believers perfected — for they shall become " unblameable in holiness before God, even our Father, at the coming of our Lord Jesus Christ with all His saints." He came, and He comes again in majesty, to conclude the history of a world, to obtain His final triumph over death, to raise His people from the tomb in immortal youth and beauty, and carry them in their entire humanity to His own prepared kingdom—to cloudless and endless felicity " for ever with the Lord."

These doctrines preached by Paul at Thessalonica were

all closely connected. The Messiah predicted is to be a suffering Messiah, and such He was. But His suffering terminated in His decease, for He arose again and He ascended to the throne, because He "became obedient unto death." He reigns because He died. And from His throne He comes to gather unto Himself His numerous subjects, whose bodies are sleeping in earth or under ocean, and introduce them into complete and final blessedness. So that they who enjoy the gift and come into His kingdom, trace their honours to His cross, and sing before His throne—"Worthy is the Lamb that was slain."

It may be remarked, too, that the apostle, in these letters written a few months afterwards from Corinth, refers to the style in which he preached at Thessalonica—"Our exhortation was not of deceit, nor of uncleanness, nor in guile: but as we were allowed of God to be put in trust with the gospel, even so we speak; not as pleasing men, but God, which trieth our hearts. For neither at any time used we flattering words, as ye know, nor a cloak of covetousness; God is witness: nor of men sought we glory, neither of you, nor yet of others, when we might have been burdensome, as the apostles of Christ. But we were gentle among you, even as a nurse cherisheth her children: so, being affectionately desirous of you, we were willing to have imparted unto you, not the gospel of God only, but also our own souls, because ye were dear unto us. . . . . As ye know how we exhorted and comforted, and charged every one of you (as a father doth his children), that ye would walk worthy of God, who hath called you unto His kingdom and glory." The purity, simplicity, fidelity and power, and the earnest, loving, unselfish nature of his preaching, are declared by him as being visible to all around him. Nay, he wrought with his own hands—"labouring night and day, because we would not be chargeable unto any of you." He did the same at Corinth, and we shall again refer to it under that head. According to the chronology held by some, a grievous famine at this period oppressed that portion of the world, and it must have taken extraordinary exertion for the inspired tent-maker to earn a livelihood. But during his brief stay at Thessalonica, his friends at Philippi had not forgotten him, for he thanks them and says—"Ye sent once and again unto my necessities." When we read so many warnings against idleness, and so many incitements to industry in both the epistles to this church, we see another reason why the apostle preferred to win his own bread by manual toil. Again and again does he appeal to their knowledge of his character as—"ye know what manner of men we were"—" ye remember, brethren, our labour and travail "—" ye are our witnesses, and God also, how holily, and justly, and unblameably we behaved ourselves among you that believe "—"as ye know how we exhorted and comforted and charged every one of you"—" ye know what commandment we gave you by the Lord Jesus "—" we behaved not disorderly among you."

It is pleasing, in fine, to know that the apostle's lessons were productive of permanent fruits. The magistrates were alarmed at what they heard, were afraid lest the character of their city should be compromised; but they admitted Jason to bail, took from him some security to keep the peace, or perhaps not to accommodate the apostle any longer. A large fine may have been exacted afterwards of him and others, amounting to the spoiling of their goods; for they had suffered like the churches in Judæa, and this was one of the wrongs inflicted on them. In the meantime, lest danger should be incurred, and scenes worse than those at Philippi be re-enacted, "the brethren immediately sent away Paul and Silas by night unto Berea." But he longed to see them again, for they were an exemplary people—"ensamples to all that believe in Macedonia and Achaia"—a loving and generous society "toward all the brethren which are in all Macedonia"—resigned and happy in the midst of suffering: "So that we ourselves glory in you in the churches of God, for your patience and faith in all your persecutions and tribulations that ye endure." Need we wonder that the heart of the preacher warmed toward them, that he sent Timothy from Athens to comfort them, and that he writes them in this jubilant strain—"For what is our hope, or joy, or crown of rejoicing? Are not even ye in the presence of our Lord Jesus Christ at His coming? For ye are our glory and joy." "For our entrance in unto you was not in vain"—"The gospel came not unto you in word only, but also in power and in the Holy Ghost, and in much assurance." Nay, they were a centre of powerful and extensive missionary influence—"From you sounded out the word of the Lord, not only in Macedonia and Achaia, but also in every place your faith to Godward is spread abroad." Thessalonica was, from its situation as a seaport, a city of great commerce, and was brought into connection with all parts of the province and other eastern countries. This intercourse for the affairs of this life was sanctified as an evangelical channel; in many cases "her merchandise and her hire were holiness to the Lord;" and she must have found as the wise man describes it, that "the merchandise of it is better than the merchandise of silver, and the gain, therefore, than pure gold." May not we profit by such an example? Has Britain attained her position, merely for the purposes of colonial superiority and maritime enterprise. "Many isles are the merchandise of her hands," and shall she not delight to send them something better than hardwares and calicoes? "All the ships of the sea, with their mariners, are in her to occupy her merchandise;" and shall they not, whether Lascars or Kroomen, Coolies or Chinamen, when they come into British harbours, meet with evangelical kindness and truth? "O thou that art situate at the entry of the sea, which art a merchant of the people for many isles," when shalt thou appreciate thy solemn responsibilities, and rejoice to hallow thy ships by bringing His sons from far, exporting to the ends of the earth the treasure which faileth not, and conveying thither the men, the weapons of whose warfare are not carnal, but mighty through God?

Such toil and suffering with such a spiritual harvest, such faith and heroism on the part alike of preacher and people, are surely an inspiring lesson. Xerxes, on his invasion of Greece, had halted at Thessalonica, but left behind him no memento save that of rapine and wrong. It was the place of Cicero's banishment, but the illustrious exile could only sob and wail and curse—a pitiable poltroon. Paul, after being scourged at Philippi, comes to the same spot, neither abject nor vindictive, but earnest and forgiving; and he does a divine work, the memorials of which have lasted many ages, and shall never pass away. What the poet says of bards may be applied to preachers like Paul—

> "But the glories so transcendent
>   That around their memories cluster,
> And, on all their steps attendant,
> Make their darkened lives resplendent
>   With such gleams of inward lustre!
>
> "All the melodies mysterious,
>   Through the dreary darkness chaunted;
> Thoughts in attitudes imperious,
> Voices soft, and deep, and serious,
>   Words that whispered, songs that haunted!
>
> "All the soul in rapt suspension,
>   All the quivering, palpitating
> Chords of life in utmost tension,
> With the fervour of invention,
>   With the rapture of creating!
>
> "Heralds still, whose hearts unblighted
>   Honour and believe the presage,
> Hold aloft their torches lighted,
> Gleaming through the realms benighted,
>   As they onward bear the message!"

X.—PAUL AT ATHENS.

Acts xvii. 15—34; 1 Thess. iii. 1.

It was by night that Paul and Silas were sent away from Thessalonica. There had been tumult and violence, and a cry of treason and disloyalty had been raised. At such a time it would have been easy to throw the city into a commotion, and in the midst of it to assassinate the objects of popular dislike. Besides, Jason had given bail, probably to send away the so-called disturbers of the peace, and it was therefore deemed advisable that Paul and Silas should leave quietly and unobserved by the infuriated rabble and their malignant instigators. The missionaries travelled to Berea, fifty-seven miles south-west, and commencing their evangelical labours, found the Jews in that city more docile and less under the influence of prejudice than those in Thessalonica. They "received the word with all readiness;" and were *more noble*—in candour and frankness; more ingenuous, for, instead of scorning the truth and reviling its preachers, they did what really was their duty—" they searched the scriptures daily whether those things were so "—whether the statements made by Paul corresponded with the Hebrew oracles. The inference then is, that he preached in the Berean synagogue the same truths, and in much the same form, as he had done in the previous cities which he had visited. The result was, as indeed always happens when there is openness of mind and study of the Bible, that "many believed," *honourable women which were Greeks*—proselytes of high rank—and "of men not a few."

But Jewish rancour never slept. It had failed in its object so far, but no thanks to it—the apostle still lived. Yet it pursued him with the staunchness of a blood-hound, and go where he pleased, it soon tracked his steps and came up with him. For we are told—"But when the Jews of Thessalonica had knowledge that the word of God was preached of Paul at Berea, they came thither also and stirred up the people." Paul must therefore take leave of the noble Bereans, and still pursue his southward journey; this time without his colleagues. There was work before him, and Jewish spite gave him no rest till he overtook it. Though he had been invited across the Ægean by a man of Macedonia, he must now depart from that province. They "immediately sent away Paul to go as it were to the sea;" Silas and Timothy being left behind. The words—"as it were to the sea," do not mean as they seem to do in English, that his journey sea-ward was a mere feint to elude his enemies, though some have held this notion, but merely that he travelled designedly toward the sea. Probably he might not intend to embark at once—at least for Athens—but might wish to revisit Philippi and Thessalonica. It is not formally stated, but the inference is, that Paul went by sea to Athens. The journey by land would have been one of two hundred and fifty-one miles, and there is no record of it or of any place visited on the way; whereas the voyage, if he took shipping at the mouth of the Haliacmon, might be accomplished in three days. The apostle, after sailing past shores, islands, mountains, headlands, and scenes of imperishable fame—Olympus, Marathon, Salamis, and Sunium—landed at Phalerum, or rather at the Piræus, and wending his way between the long walls built by Themistocles, but now partly in ruins, entered the city—"mother of arts and eloquence"—the intellectual metropolis of the world.

The splendour of Greece had waned, and it had passed under Roman sway. But what had survived the ravages of time and conquerors attested its ancient grandeur. In that region of south-eastern Europe, genius had dwelt incarnate. It had built the loftiest epics, recited the happiest histories, argued in the stateliest dialogues, wept in the saddest tragedies, laughed in the wittiest comedies, harangued in the mightiest orations, discoursed in the subtlest metaphysics, erected the noblest temples, carved the truest statues, painted the divinest pictures, wrestled in the greatest games, spoken the finest language, sung the gayest songs, and fought the bravest battles—that the world ever saw. The studies of the apostle, not at Jerusalem certainly, and least of all at the feet of Gamaliel, but in his native Tarsus, renowned for its cultivation of Grecian literature, must have made him acquainted with these glories of Athens. He had enjoyed the grace and euphony of Xenophon, and been charmed with the simple dignity of Herodotus. He had thrilled under Æschylus, and glowed with Demosthenes, whose intense logic and barbed interrogations he sometimes reproduces. He could be no stranger to the imagery and music of Homer, the depth and beauty of Plato, the arms, oratory, and magnificence of Pericles, or the terse compacted style of Thucydides which he occasionally resembles; and he must have often pictured to himself the groves of the Ilissus, the proportions of the Parthenon, and the keen discussions of the Porch, the Academy, the Lyceum, and the Garden.

The city which he entered was "built nobly, pure the air, and light the soil." The limestone rock on which Athens stands, supplied the ordinary material for its buildings, and also from many of its quarries the marble for its nobler structures. The plain is bounded by ranges of hills—on the north-west by Mount Parnes, on the south-east by Mount Hymettus, and on the north-east by Mount Pentelicus, out of which rises the higher pinnacles of Lycabettus, looking upon the city as Arthur's seat upon Edinburgh. About a mile south-west from it, and in the city, there rose the Acropolis, not unlike Stirling castle in the upper valley of the Forth. West of it was a smaller rock, the Areopagus or scene of judgment—the council meeting in the open air on its south-eastern summit, and sitting on benches hewn out in the rock, which form three sides of a quadrangle. To the south-west, and about a quarter of a mile from it, there was another and lower eminence, the Pnyx, the place of the great popular assemblies—also held in the open air under the deep blue of a Grecian sky—with its *bema* or stone block on which the orator stood and addressed the crowd, which gathered in a semicircular area of twelve thousand square yards before him, and where Solon, Demosthenes, and Pericles often spoke to the assembled "men of Athens."

The apostle is now in this city, not ignorant of its

ancient renown, of its history and literature. And he was alone, having sent word by those who conducted him to Athens, to Timothy and Silas to rejoin him "with all speed." Timothy soon came, but was soon sent off again to Thessalonica, as we learn from 1 Thess. iii. 1, 2. In fact, it would seem as if Paul had originally intended to make Athens only a rendezvous, and not a scene of labour, till he found from Timothy that Macedonia was still shut against him. As he waited, he wandered through its streets with inquisitive and sorrowing gaze, it was so unlike Jerusalem, the city of God. His spirit was *stirred within him*—roused and excited to profound grief and indignation, as he surveyed its glories, not with the eye of an artist, but that of a Christian. The statues and temples were not looked on by him as the creations of genius, but the means and results of debasing superstitions. Intellect, taste, and beauty were alike profaned, for the one God was dethroned. Wherever the solitary stranger gazed, he saw the manifestations of polytheism—nature deified, humanity depicted as superhuman, and virtues, nay, even vices, exalted into divinities. It was an unwonted sight which greeted him. The city was *wholly given to idolatry* —idol-full; crammed, as one might say, with idols—one idolatrous mass. Its public buildings were consecrated as temples, and its streets and forums thickly peopled with statues of the gods. Never had he seen the second commandment so wantonly and systematically violated; never had he beheld so much art and wealth lavished on a wretched idolatry. There had never met his gaze such artistic beauty of appearance with such spiritual deformity of purpose, such symmetry of form and structure with such miserable misconception of the Divine unity and infinity. The epithet "idol-full" given by Luke to Athens, is fully verified by ancient writers both of satire and history. One of the former affirms that it was easier to find a god than a man in it; and one of the latter, that it was one whole altar, one entire sacrifice and offering to the gods. Another tells us how a person could scarce find his way through its streets for the troops of idol-mongers. In the crowds of gods which, turn as you will, your eye gazed upon, were Minerva and Neptune, Jupiter and Ceres, Apollo and Bacchus, Hercules and Theseus, the Muses and the Furies, Venus and the Graces, Diana and the Nymphs of the Dêmos or civic assembly. Altars or temples were erected to Fame, Modesty, Energy, Mercy, Persuasion, Victory, and Oblivion.

But the apostle was no vulgar iconoclast; he did not lift his arm, and in the name of the Lord of Hosts "break down the carved work." He sought to reach the hearts of men, and therefore he first spoke to his countrymen and to the proselytes, and then turned to the Athenian population. These last he met in the *market-place*—forum—which was usually crowded with loungers. This market-place of Athens, surrounded by stately porticoes and colonnades, served not only the purpose of an exchange and news-room, was not only a scene of pleasure as well as business, but philosophers and poets traversed it, and the sharp wit of the people was whetted by a perpetual war of words and exchange of raillery. It was, in short, the heart of Athens, sending forth its vital currents on all sides. Every variety of population was there, and the apostle easily found numbers to listen to his preaching, to batter him with question upon question, to turn his earnestness into ridicule, and toss aside with satiric levity or gay invective the point of his argument and appeals. A man of his experience and practical wisdom could easily secure such admissions and extort such assents from an opponent, as that he should be led, step by step and unconsciously, to an untenable conclusion or one in utter contrast to his original statement, and thus the onlookers would be reminded of the humour and shrewdness of the old Socratic dialogue.

Close upon the agora or forum was a porch or arcade, painted with frescos from the battle of Marathon; there Zeno had taught, and there the Stoics, his followers, still congregated. The audacity of a Hebrew foreigner in daring to ascribe ignorance to the sages of Athens, and in affirming that he was the vehicle of a new and superior philosophy, must have created a sensation which not only surged through the populace, but reached the schools of philosophy. The Epicureans and Stoics, therefore, assailed him, and some of them set him down as a *babbler*—one that fluently retails meaningless scraps, and others as a preacher of new divinities. The last conclusion was nearest the truth, though the expression proved how grievously they misinterpreted the apostle's message. Other some said—" He seemeth to be a setter forth of strange gods." The plural " gods " may be used for the singular, the reference being to Jesus, and to the resurrection as proving his Godhead; but it is a very natural inference from the subjoined explanation, because he preached unto them " Jesus and the resurrection," that the Greek term *anastasis*—resurrection, was taken for a female deity, as if Paul had brought to Athens a new pair of divinities. His preaching opposed the Epicurean theory of creation and the Stoical notion of providence; proclaimed a personal presiding God, who has created all things, whose worship must be spiritual, and on whom man depends for being and well-being; who takes an interest in every creature, and orders all things wisely and well; who has perfect freedom of action, ruling as He wills; whose heart is as tender as His arm is powerful; whose pure and righteous law commands obedience; whose image seeks conformity from man as his highest dignity and perfection, and whose presence and glory in another sphere are the crown of that immortal blessedness which His genuine worshippers are assured of possessing. Such novelties excited both the philosophers and the volatile population, whose passion for news was proverbial. Paul was, therefore, brought out of the noise and bustle of the forum up those sixteen steps cut in the rock to Mars-hill—Areopagus—not to be tried, but to address the assembly on that convenient and hallowed spot. He was not arraigned or put on his defence, but was taken to Mars-hill, only to gratify the inquisitive population, who said, with a tinge of polite irony—"May we," or can we, "know what this new doctrine whereof thou speakest is?" The historian, to explain the cause of this eager procedure, which the apostle met with nowhere else, adds a trait of Athenian character—"For all the Athenians, and strangers which were there, spent their time in nothing else, but either to tell or to hear some *new thing*"—some newer thing than the last news they had gathered. Demosthenes himself cries in his first Philippic

—" Do ye like walking about and asking one another, is there any news? Why, could there be greater news than a man of Macedon conquering the Athenians and directing the policy of Greece?"

On these stone benches had sat the judges so renowned for equity in former times, and there many a solemn appeal and stirring oration had been delivered for and against the culprit. The associations connected with the scene might indeed have overpowered him. There had Socrates, at seventy years of age, been judged and condemned as "a setter forth of strange gods," and he was about to declaim against the prevalent idolatry, standing in the midst of its artistic and architectural glories. Well might his heart be stilled for a moment when he remembered his position where many a brave man had quailed, and when he thought of the fastidious and prejudiced audience before him, and of the solemn and unwelcome truths he was about to announce to them. Yet he stands unmoved, while mighty thoughts are stirring within him. He rises to the occasion, and as his eye takes in the scene, he begins as easily, quietly, and pointedly, as if he had been wont to stand there before—" Ye men of Athens, I perceive that in every point of view ye carry your reverence for the gods farther than most: for, as I was passing along and inspecting the objects of your devotion, I found also an altar on which had been inscribed—" To an Unknown God;" what, therefore, without knowing it, ye worship, that I proclaim to you. The God who made the world and all that is in it, as being Himself Lord of heaven and earth, dwelleth not in hand-made temples, neither is He ministered to with men's hands as if He were in want of anything, seeing Himself is giving to all life, breath, and all things, and did make every nation of men sprung of one blood to dwell on the whole face of the earth, having appointed the times and the limits of their habitation, so as that they should seek God, if by any chance they might feel after and find Him. And, indeed, He is not far from every one of us, for in Him we live, and move, and have our being, as also some of your own poets have said—'For His offspring also are we.' Therefore, being the offspring of God, we ought not to think that the divine nature is like gold, or silver, or stone, the sculpture of man's art and device. The past periods of this ignorance God having indeed overlooked, does now command all men in all places to repent; because He has appointed a day in which He will judge the world in righteousness by that man whom He has ordained, having afforded assurance to all men, in that He has raised Him from the dead."—The address, for the sake of illustration, may be divided into three parts.

Part I.

The apostle thus commences—"Ye men of Athens, I perceive that in all things ye are *too superstitious*"—or, rather, "ye carry your reverence for the gods farther than most." The phrase, "too superstitious," as implying blame, is an unfortunate translation. The apostle appeals simply to the fact, and not to its character. He only uttered a commonplace, for the Athenians were noted among the other Grecian peoples for this propensity. They had preeminence in the scrupulous and unlimited attention paid by them to the national worship. The inspired orator alludes simply to this notorious circumstance, but neither smiles at it in compliment, nor frowns upon it in censure. The implication is, that he came to guide and rectify this tendency of the Athenian mind. It had outcropped in every possible way, and given a multiform expression to itself in sculpture and masonry; but his mission was to turn it into the true course, and lead it to the knowledge of the one, pure, invisible, infinite, eternal, and loving Spirit.

Standing where the apostle did, he saw his words verified all around him. Above him was a temple of Mars from whom the hill took its name; and near him was the subterranean sanctuary of the Eumenides or Furies, but usually called by the first title, from the same feeling which led the old Scottish people to name the fairies the "good folk," though they were a waspish and capricious race. The forum he had left was studded with statues, the altar of the twelve gods being in its centre and the temple of Venus at its eastern end, while on all sides of it were deified heroes of the old mythology. Behind him was the Pnyx sacred to Jove, and before him was the Acropolis, its sides and summit covered with religious monuments, every available ledge laden with its shrine or image, its platforms filled with sculptured groups of gods in various forms and attitudes; on its northern extremity the Erectheum, with its inclosures and its presiding deities; the cave of Pan and Apollo with its sacred fountain not far from its base, and adjoining it the sanctuary of Aglaurus; and the Parthenon crowning the whole, the central glory of the scene; while opposite the magnificent Propylæa, and formed out of the trophies of Marathon, was the gigantic bronze statue of the goddess herself, with spear and shield—the name-mother of the city, and its great protector. In the north-west quarter was the temple of Theseus, and in the opposite direction was that of Jupiter Olympius. A temple of Ceres was close to the Pompeium, in which were kept the robes and vases for the religious processions; and a temple of the divine Mother was near to the great council-house in which also were shrines and altars. There were shrines, too, at the principal gates. The altar of Prometheus was within the groves of the Academy; and the Lyceum, with its tall plane-trees, was dedicated to Apollo. There were also the Pythium and the Delphinium, characteristic names of temples, with those of Euclea, of Castor and Pollux, and of Serapis. Every street, in short, had some object or scene of devotion; every view was bounded and fringed with fanes and idols. Paul had now visited many towns, had been at Antioch, Paphos, and Philippi, but he had seen nothing to compare with Athens in its excessive idolatry.

The apostle then gives the plain reason why he concluded that the Athenians were careful beyond others in this worship—" For as I passed by and beheld your devotions "—rather, "as I was passing along and surveying the objects of your devotion, I found an altar with this inscription—'To the Unknown God'"—more correctly, "to an Unknown God." This is the apostle's proof of his previous statement, and he bases it on his own personal observation. He tells them that what he saw was evidence of their great scrupulosity in matters of worship. Not only did they worship gods whose titles and attributes they knew, but they had built an altar to a foreign god, whose name even they were not acquainted with, and offered homage to an anonymous divinity. They were not contented with their own gods, but they had introduced a nameless stranger, and erected an altar to him. Were they not then, as he had named them, lavish in their worship—so sweepingly attentive in their religion as to recognize in their extravagant devotions the existence of an undiscovered divinity? Ancient writers verify the apostle's statement. Philostratus, in his life of Apollonius, that strange wanderer, says—"It is safe to speak well of all the gods, especially at Athens, where are erected also altars of unknown gods." Pausanias, who visited Athens about a hundred years after the apostle, and has left a full account of the city, speaks of such an altar at Phalerum, one of the ports of the city. How the custom originated, we know not. It is said, that during a plague, when it was not ascertained which of the gods had sent it, an altar was built to the appropriate divinity whoever he was—and they did not identify him for fear of mistake—was built to him who had sent it, and who could alone remove it, though his name was unknown. But, in reality, this impulse was the natural result of polytheism. Amidst the multiplicity of gods, there was great anxiety lest any one should be forgotten, for the neglected deity might be affronted at such an omission, and be provoked to punish it. The worshipper therefore offered homage to all the gods he knew—and to all others, if any existed, though he did not know them. He dreaded the vengeance of some power unrecognized by him; and to secure that every deity was invoked, he might erect an altar to an unknown god. Miserable uncertainty! when the devotee on the one hand feared the revenge of some god, if he did homage to his rival, and, on the other hand, incurred an awful retribution if, in his haste or ignorance, any of the hosts of deities should be unackowledged and slighted by him! Amidst the crowds of known and shrined divinities at Athens, there was one with an altar, but without a name—an unknown god. On the statement of this fact, so patent to his audience, and which probably they accepted as a tribute to their catholic piety, the apostle skilfully and suddenly founds his defence and introduction. In the synagogue he had selected his theme from Moses, but on the Areopagus he takes his text from a heathen altar. To the children of Abraham he proclaimed the Christ, but to the citizens of Athens he "preached Jesus." Nor did he declaim, like an excited Jew, against pagan idolatry, but he penetrated to the feeling which lies beneath it—to that inner necessity under which man must worship; and thus he adds—

"Whom, therefore, ye ignorantly worship, Him declare I unto you;" or "What, therefore, not knowing it, ye worship, that I proclaim unto you." The neuter form makes the declaration more emphatic from its very vagueness. The apostle admits that they worshipped, for a feeling of instinctive devotion underlies polytheism. True, indeed, he argues—"What say I then? that the idol is anything? or that which is offered in sacrifice to idols is anything? But I say, that the things which the Gentiles sacrifice, they sacrifice to devils, and not to God: and I would not that ye should have fellowship with devils." In this passage, addressed to the neighbouring city of Corinth, the apostle dwells on the result or actual character of idolatry. Being such a violation of the divine law, it is a sphere of the devil's operation so contrived that he is adored. It is not Jupiter that is worshipped, since there is no such being or power. Evil spirits lurk behind the idolatrous framework, and make it subservient to their purposes, prey upon man's worshipping instincts, and really receive the homage. Yet there is worship offered on the part of man; his ignorant and fallen spirit knows that there is something above it, something which can and does shape its destiny, with which it is indissolubly connected, and to which it, therefore, erects temples and consecrates altars. It would be rash to affirm that the apostle expressly identifies the "unknown God" with the true God. The unknown God was some being over and beyond their conventional divinities, and there is no proof that the mysterious God of the Jews was intended. But such an altar was a confession that their catalogue did not comprehend all the powers and essences of the universe; that there was or might be some Being beyond the circuit of their recognition, who might be chagrined or angry if Athens should overlook him. This admission the speaker seizes on, and says—There is such a God, unknown, indeed, to you, and Him I proclaim. He thus replies that, in one sense, he is not "a setter forth of strange gods;" but he does not say that the very god who owned the anonymous altar was Jehovah, for the god of that altar must have been really an idol, so far as Athenian imagination pictured him. But he took the idea which the inscription implied, and expanded it. There is a God unknown to you—a being not found in your lists—who has no statue among these numerous groups, and no temple on that eminence; Him so dimly and scantily acknowledged, the one true God, I proclaim. By this very thought he takes Him out of the category of the Greek divinities. He is not one of them, nor yet another of similar nature who claims admission among them. O, no. He is—

"God that made the world, and all things therein, seeing that He is Lord of heaven and earth, dwelleth not in temples made with hands." He is God, the one Creator—of earth, and all in it and on it; its furniture and its population; its botanical productions and its living creatures. The one God made the world—its hills with their crowns of snow, and its valleys with their fields and flowers; its rivers, lakes, and seas; its mines and minerals; its grasses and herbs; its rock and soils; its climates and physical influences; every nation upon it, and all that supports them and gives them occupation or pleasure. Tokens of His existence are on every side—alike in the atom of sand and the strata of majestic mountains; in the lordly eagle and in the insect that sports away its existence during the brief sunset; as well in the instinct which rules the lower creation, as in the reason which dignifies man. The air around, and the breeze which freshens into a hurricane—the tide which lifts the water of the gulf and harbour with such periodical uniformity; the freshness of spring and the life of summer — all are brought into being by the one God on high. Nothing is self-produced. He is the one Maker. Trees may propagate themselves, but their veins and vessels, their secret chemical elaborations, their life and organism, the fruit of the fig and the oil of the Athenian olive, are from Him. The sculptor does not originate his materials, nor the painter his colours; each finding them as made by the great Artist only recombines and applies them. Demosthenes did not invent the language in which he spoke, any more than the nightingale had taught herself the melody which gushes from her throat. The Creator's inspiration gives not only the love of art and the endowments of genius, but He has also supplied what art and genius had wrought upon—the metal out of which the sword of Miltiades had been forged, the parchment on which the laws of Solon had been inscribed, and the ivory and gold out of which the queenly statue of the city-goddess had been constructed. Nor does nature only prove that there is an original vital force, but also that this force, as guided by wisdom and prompted by love, resides in a living personal Intelligence. The world is not eternal, nor is it the result of an eternal series of causes, or the wondrous product of chance. Nay, the more we explore the causes in operation around us, and the farther and higher we carry our analysis of them, the more do we feel them relieved of complexity and converging into unity, and the more clearly do we discern that all causes are themselves but the effects of the First Great Cause, Himself uncaused—the "God that made the world and all things therein."

This conception strikes at the root of polytheism. The Athenians had their gods which they specially claimed, and the nations around them rejoiced in similar property. The gods of the one were not the gods of the other, nor was any alliance recognized among them. Each race had its own tutelar divinity, to whose mythic powers it owed its existence, and sometimes its name. The hill on which Paul stood had its title from one god, and the city had its name from the guardian goddess Minerva—Pallas Athené. But the apostle vindicates the unity of God as sole Creator. He made and filled the earth—"The earth is the Lord's, and the fulness thereof, the world, and they that dwell therein." The Athenians spent their time in continuous inquiries after something new; surely their passion for novelty was now gratified. Creation was a new idea to them. Plato had not dreamed of it; Aristotle had taken it out of the range of possibilities. The relation of matter to mind was not understood among them, nor could they speculate successfully on the origin of the universe. But the apostle's simple statement laid down the truth, that the earth took its being from God's creative power, was not, on the one hand, a fortuitous concourse of atoms, nor, on the other, the result of some necessary law which controlled divinity itself, or acted without the superintendence of a personal governing God. The forms of creation, as shown by modern science, prove it to have been a voluntary act, and not the product of what a French philosopher calls " a necessary force." Nor has the Creator been obliged to repeat Himself. The fossils of the earlier rocks have no analogues among the beds of the tertiaries. Successive acts of creation, and the introduction of a thousand new species, did not exhaust His styles of work. "The Lord God, the Creator of the ends of the earth, fainteth not, neither is weary." He is not, as those Epicureans dreamed, some dim phantom far above the stars in idle and voluptuous indifference; nor is He, as the Stoic argued, the soul of the world, which

> " Lives through all life, extends through all extent,
> Spreads undivided, operates unspent."

God made the earth, and He is above it and apart from it, but yet its active Lord and untiring benefactor; and it is in no sense the complement of His being, or a necessary evolution of His essence. The one Creator is enthroned upon the work of His hands.

Creation is thus ascribed by the apostle to God, and though we cannot comprehend the act or process, we never can doubt it. For, if there has been no creation, then all is eternal, and all is God or an evolution of God. On such a hypothesis there can be no law, no freedom, no personality, and no moral distinctions; for what we term sin would be as really thought or done by God as what we term virtue, since He would be the only thinker and agent in the universe. But, though we cannot understand creation as either the making of something out of nothing, or the eduction of result from latent almighty power, or the image of what is real in the archetypal Mind, we can know it in some of its properties. We can picture a portion of space unfurnished, and then picture it as peopled with worlds. Nor will it avail as an argument against the idea of creation, that it implies change in an unchangeable God; for the purpose to create is eternal, and omnipotence is not changed in essence when it puts forth an effort. The relation of the finite to the infinite is of all things indeed the most perplexing. That the one and that the other exists our consciousness assures us in every act of cognition. To deny the infinite and sink into atheism, or to deny the finite and dream ourselves into pantheism, is a revolt against reason, a vain attempt to burst those limits which are necessarily imposed upon human thought. We enter not on the question as to man's knowledge of the infinite, or as to the form and foundation of his constitutional beliefs. Only it is evident to consciousness that ideas of eternity and infinity surround all our thoughts; for to whatever point of time or of space we reach forth in fancy, we are forced to believe in time and space still stretching beyond. It is true that we can neither grasp infinitude nor span eternity, but we do have a notion of either without a comprehension of them—such a notion as suffices for faith and worship. So feeble is reason out of its sphere, and so true, in fine, is the declaration of the apostle—"Through faith we understand that the worlds were framed by the word of God; so that things which are seen were not made of things which do appear."

And as the sole originator He has the indefeasible right of being sole governor. He is "Lord of heaven and earth," proprietor and ruler of the universe—not earth only, but heaven and earth. The immense spaces that the Greek imagination could roam in, where the sun flamed in splendour, and the moon waxed and waned in serener glory, and the stars shone out like "isles of light," are, when surveyed by the telescopic glass, found to be furnished with innumerable worlds. Nothing like a limit to creation can be discovered; far as man can penetrate he finds star upon star in compacted array. The distant star-dust has been resolved into densely-crowded orbs; and light from the remoter nebulæ must have been two million of years on its journey to us. The Lord of heaven has a kingdom which no imagination can measure in its vastness, nor depict in its variety and grandeur—the firmament thickly strewn with suns and planets. Surely such a one "dwelleth not in temples made with hands." The temples in front of the apostle, around him, and behind him, were the boast of Grecian taste and skill. The gods to whom they were dedicated were supposed, in some vague sense, to fill them. Their respective gods had shrines in them, and claimed them as their residence. They were, indeed, of unsurpassed magnificence. The Theseum was the earliest and most complete; the temple of Wingless Victory was "a thing of beauty;" and there was in front of him the Parthenon—virgin's house, or temple of Minerva—of majestic mass and outline, formed of Pentelican marble, with its forty-six

Doric columns adorned with sculptures and friezes, and its inner walls decorated with choicest paintings. But the Infinite can dwell in no such structure; nor needs He such a domicile. He fills space; infinitude is His temple. "Whither shall I go from thy Spirit? or whither shall I flee from thy presence? If I ascend up into heaven, thou art there: if I make my bed in hell, behold thou art there. If I take the wings of the morning, and dwell in the uttermost parts of the sea; even there shall thy hand lead me, and thy right hand shall hold me." This God whom Paul made known had no rival, no one like Him, no one second to Him; nor could He be supposed to inhabit any edifice built by the hands of man. Such a notion was unworthy of Him; it brought him down to the level of humanity, as if He were one of many tenants, and not the one proprietor. To localize Him would be to degrade Him.

"Neither is He worshipped with men's hands, as though He needed anything;" *worshipped*—served or cared for. The popular heathen idea was that the gods needed to be ministered unto, though the minds of a few thinking men, as Lucretius and Seneca, might rise above such a gross conception. Thus the priest of Apollo remonstrates:—

> "If e'er with wreaths I hung thy sacred fane,
> Or fed the flames with fat of oxen slain,
> God of the silver bow, thy shafts employ,
> Avenge thy servant, and the Greeks destroy."

The god was supposed to be placed under obligation by the service rendered to him, and was expected in equity to repay it. But this notion cannot apply to the Divine

Being, seeing He "giveth to all life, and breath, and all things"—the one universal benefactor. No one has anything which God has not given him; and the highest gift —*life*—conscious being, "life and *breath*"—life and that respiration on which life depends—are from Him; nay, life and *all things*—all that makes life desirable and happy.

He giveth "life," and none but He, the Living One. It is a rill from the Fountain of life. Growth and other qualities belong to plants, such as circulation of sap and respiration by their leaves; but life characterizes man—with its voluntary and involuntary functions, its enjoyments and capabilities, its appetites and instincts, its operations on the world without it, and its conscious possession of its powers within it. Pleasure, glory, and usefulness are bound up with its prolongation. So sweet is it that few choose to part with it, and the cessation of it was regarded by the apostle's hearers as the direst of calamities. He who is our life confers and supports it in His ineffable goodness—for "man liveth not by bread alone."

He giveth "breath," which, as the condition and means of life, is, therefore, singled out by the apostle. Even then the atmosphere was popularly valued as the first of necessary gifts, and, when scientifically examined, its preciousness is not only confirmed, but it becomes a powerful proof of divine unceasing goodness. For the air we breathe is endowed with many qualities, the loss or disturbance of which must be fatal to life. If it lose its gravity, or if its elasticity be changed or become changeable; if it thicken, and darken, and cease to be an invisible medium; if it be deprived of its compressibility, or if any amount of cold could condense it; if the gases composing it were to vary in their proportions; or if it were not universally present, and what is vitiated by respiration purified and restored—animal existence would be extinguished on the face of the earth.

And His bounty is immense, for He giveth "all things." Whatever we have He has given us—the food on our table, and the raiment on our persons, with ability to win them and health to enjoy them. Let there be a scanty harvest, and, when corn cannot be bought with money, there must be famine; let a worm gnaw the cotton plant, and the shadow of death would be cast over Britain—capital useless, gold without circulation, trades unemployed, machinery without motion, empty warehouses, ships without freights, and millions in want of work and bread. Nor let any man boast of being the architect of his own fortune; for the materials out of which he builds it, the skill with which he constructs it, and the propitious season which enables him to rear it without pause or discomfiture—are each of them the gift of the one sovereign benefactor. Discovery, invention, science, art, adventure, commercial shrewdness, literary power, mechanical skill, and political success; the sharp eye that is first to perceive the "tide in the affairs of men;" and the wary enterprise that launches the vessel upon it—are not self-originated. "Every good gift and every perfect gift is from above, and cometh down from the Father of Lights."

Everything possessed by everyone, without exception of gift or person, is of God's bestowal. God is, therefore, independent of man for His happiness; it wells up from an

SPIRITUAL SERVICE. 201

exhaustless fountain in His own bosom. Nor is He in need of such services as are made in human temples—neither the blood of sacrifices to support, nor the odour of incense to refresh Him. For He is the one Giver, always giving and never getting, still bestowing and never repaid—there being a perpetual outflow, but no reflux. If, therefore, all that man has be from God, and all he proposes to supply his divinities with be from the same source, it is plain that He who gives it, and has so freely parted with it, is not in need of it. The wretched anthropomorphism which had crept in among the Jews is thus reproved by the psalmist—" I will not reprove thee for thy sacrifices, or thy burnt-offerings, to have been continually before me. I will take no bullock out of thy house, nor he-goats out of thy folds: for every beast of the forest is mine, and the cattle upon a thousand hills. I know all the fowls of the mountains; and the wild beasts of the field are mine. If I were hungry, I would not tell thee: for the world is mine, and the fulness thereof. Will I eat the flesh of bulls, or drink the blood of goats? Offer unto God thanksgiving; and pay thy vows unto the most High; and call upon me in the day of trouble; I will deliver thee, and thou shalt glorify me." His service must correspond to His nature, and must, therefore, be spiritual service. Those who are so liberally provided for by Him, who live by His bounty and breathe His air, and owe all things to His goodness, will surely rejoice to bless Him; and when they feel that they have no claim on His generosity, and that yet it is so unceasing, will they not invoke their souls and all within them " to bless His holy name?" " Can a man be profitable to God as he that is wise may be profitable to himself?" "If thou be righteous, what givest thou Him, or what receiveth He of thine hand?" He is not worshipped with men's hands, but with men's hearts. The silent hymn of a grateful spirit rolls upward to His ear, though no music should be warbled from the lips. "God is a spirit, and they that worship Him must worship Him in spirit and in truth." When Solomon dedicated the temple, he exclaimed under this impression— "But will God in very deed dwell with men on the earth? Behold, heaven, and the heaven of heavens, cannot contain thee, how much less this house that I have built!" And, in his address before the council, Stephen had said in Paul's hearing—"Howbeit the Most High dwelleth not in temples made with hands; as saith the prophet, Heaven is my throne, and earth is my footstool; what house will ye build me, saith the Lord, or what is the place of my rest? hath not my hand made all these things?"

Part II.

Having shown them the divine independence and self-sufficiency, the apostle proceeds to assert the unity of the human race—as being of one origin, and—no matter how widely they may have been scattered—as being guided and controlled by the one God in their migrations and settlements; their history being but the record of His dealings with them, and His regulation of their movements. He adds —" And hath made of one blood all nations of men for to dwell on all the face of the earth, and hath determined the times before appointed, and the bounds of their habitation." All the nations are of one blood or race. The Athenians boasted that they were autochthones—self-produced, or sprung of the soil of Attica, and looked with contempt on surrounding barbarians. But all had a common origin, and none could vaunt themselves over their neighbours. The Greek with that lofty brow—" the dome of thought" —who lived on the idea of beauty, with whom the arts had found a home, and who had a history so grand from the days of Solon, was a brother of the rude Scythian with the low forehead and stolid visage, who wore a coarse vesture of sheepskin, and was as ignorant in soul as degraded in life. For God "hath *made*—caused—*all nations for to dwell*—settle—on all the face of the earth." Whatever advantage any nation has in the country occupied by it, is due to God. It fills the realm which

God designed for it. Attica had not been chosen by the people on account of its superior qualities, but God chose it for them. It was not Hercules, Cecrops, Pelops, Theseus, or any other ancient mythical leader, that had selected Greece, but God had made the region, and made their forefathers to migrate into it. Bœotia, Sparta, Sicily, and Ionia, with many cities in which they had contended, were sprung of the same stock as themselves. And he who was now bespeaking their attention, whose dark eye and aquiline features showed him to be of a race which they despised, and whose annals they could not appreciate, stood, in point of lineage, on the same level with themselves.

Polytheism is bound up with the notion of distinct and different races. But if all nations be alike in bodily structure, and one blood be in all their veins, and they possess the same range of instinct and appetites, their oneness of origin is demonstrated. That man, no matter what his colour, or stature, or home, is but one species with many varieties, is a truth proved by ethnology, and confirmed by the results of comparative philology. Among the lower creation, the skull of the mastiff differs more from that of the Italian greyhound, than the skull of the European from the central African or the Hottentot, and dogs and horses carried to the hills in India lose their hair and become woolly, like the shawl-goats of the country. Complexion and features are soon altered by climate and physical condition. The third generation of educated and well-fed negroes loses the prognathous type, while filth and famine are known to reduce white victims to a dull and meaningless cast of countenance.

He that made the world and all things therein, is, therefore, God of all the nations. It is a fiction for them to have separate gods, as if each tribe had sprung from a different deity, and owed him homage as lord and guardian. The nations are all brethren, created by the one Divine Being— "Have we not all one Father; hath not one God created us?" It was imagined, too, that the various gods had separate and independent territories, beyond which their jurisdiction did not go, and which they were often obliged to defend against invasion. In the Homeric songs they espouse rival interests, and cabal and quarrel in petty jealousy and revenge. Juno will have her way for her favourites, Venus will not desert hers, Apollo sends a plague upon the Greeks because his priest is insulted, while Jupiter is at his wit's end amid the strifes and antipathies of Olympus. Nay, Minerva (Athené) had contended for the possession of Athens with Neptune, he appealing to a well which had sprung up at the stroke of his trident, and she to an olive which the king had seen her plant on the summit of the Acropolis. The deities of Greece were powerless in Italy, and had neither name nor residence in Persia. Every race had its mythology, and would fight for its idols as readily as for its acres, so that a war between two nations was usually a war between their gods, as well as between their soldiers. But the apostle tells them that the nations, no matter how distant in settlement, unlike in colour, civilization, or worship, descend from a common ancestry, and have a common origin in God. All the power and sovereignty which they assigned to numerous local divinities was, therefore, to be concentrated in one great Being—the Maker of the world, and the Lord of heaven and earth.

And this one Being also "hath determined the times before appointed, and the bounds of their habitations." This doctrine was also taught by Moses—"When the most High divided to the nations their inheritance, when he separated the sons of Adam, he set the bounds of the people according to the number of the children of Israel." The periods of their existence have been defined, and its limits mapped out by God. By the *periods* he means not simply their national duration, but also the crises or turning-points in their national experience. And they had many of them in their own history. Not to speak of such epochs as the return of the Heracleids, the religious mission of Epimenides, the deeds of the Alcmæonids, the despotism of Pisistratus, or the usurpation of the thirty tyrants, there had been the battle of Marathon, when Asiatic invasion was repelled by a gallant handful, and, ten years after, the victorious naval action at Salamis—both of them hairs-breadth escapes for Athens, and both securing against loss of liberty and degradation into a Persian satrapy. These momentous junctures were the fore-appointment of an unrecognized Protector, who settles the limits of nations; for there is a boundary which they can not pass, no matter what their ambition, and what the success of their arms. Their own defeats, and the ostracism of so many of their leaders, had shown this. Miltiades the patriot of Marathon, and Themistocles the hero of Salamis, had been sent into exile for misadventures by which the ambitious projects of Greece were limited, and similar had been the fate of Cimon and Alcibiades. Beyond certain termini Athens could not, with all her skill and valour, carry her arms; an unseen arm defined her bounds, and kept her within them. Minerva could not protect: Xerxes had burned her dwelling, and her spear and shield had neither repelled Philip from the north, nor beaten back the Roman warriors from the west. She stood immovable on that rock, defenceless against the invader. The sudden death of Alexander broke into four principalities the huge empire which he contemplated. But the divine providence is all-embracing, and all history proclaims it. The battle of Zama relieved Italy and civilization from all fears of Carthage. The Saracen power was thrown out of central Europe at a very critical period, and the tide of Turkish fanaticism was finally checked under the walls of Vienna. He blew with His winds and dispersed the Spanish armada. Borodino, Leipzig, Trafalgar, and Waterloo set bounds to France in recent times, and Blenheim and Ramillies in days gone by. Bunker's-hill put an end to British supremacy in the older American colonies. The fall of Sebastopol has retarded the southern march of Russia for a season. The congress of Vienna appointed bounds to the nations on selfish and political principles, but how long shall they last, and how soon may the map of Europe need to be remodelled? "God is the judge; He putteth down one and setteth up another." "He ruleth according to His will in the army of heaven and among the inhabitants of the earth; and none can stay His hand, or say unto him, What doest Thou?"

And the moral purpose of God in the allocation and

government of the different nations was a special one—"That they should seek the Lord, if haply they might feel after him, and find Him, though he be not far from every one of us." To *seek* Him, is to acknowledge and worship Him, to *feel after* is to grope, as if in darkness, in the dim light of the gentile world, as he admits, but the last clause shows that the search after Him might not have been in vain. He was still within reach of discovery. There were revelations, not, indeed, in clearness and expressness like those given to the Jews, but still sufficient to have kept the nations from atheism, polytheism, and idolatry. The human race have been formed into nations, not to set up exclusive national divinities, but that they should know and adore the *Lord*—or God, as perhaps is the better text. The finding of God should have been their chief concern; the acknowledgment and worship of Him the business of their lives. It might require anxiety and study—there might be doubts to be overcome and difficulties to be removed—but what intimations they had they should have followed, and what surmises rose within them they should have diligently pursued. They might occasionally blunder, but they should not have abandoned the inquiry. He that gropes may stumble, but he is not to desist; he may weary himself, but still he should cast about for the object of his search. For God was near to everyone, and therefore his duty was not so hard as the investigation of some theorem, hopeless from its darkness and the distance of its conclusion from the first step of its demonstration. God was near them; their eyes saw the stately steps of His majesty, and their ears heard the melody of His choirs.

God's great object, as he has thus shown, in organizing nations, in giving them duration, and in raising a mountain here and opening a channel there as their boundaries, is that Himself may be discovered and served. Nations forget this, and think of national greatness—armies, literature, commerce, colonies, and government. Mahometan tribes have at least the " form of godliness," as they begin their public documents with the word "Bismillah"—In the name of God. There is nothing, however, which a nation may legitimately covet that is incompatible with the homage due to God. For, what is science but the discovery of those laws which He has in His wisdom established? What is art but the embodiment of those ideas of beauty, symmetry, and power, which He has implanted in the soul? What is legislation but the human expression of His equity and benignity, which should reign supreme through all ranks and in all the occupations of society? What is commerce but the necessary interchange of the results of that labour which He enables men to perform? What is agriculture but the application of chemical skill to the agencies of the soil?—the skill that He imparts to the agencies which He has arranged and perpetuated; "for His God doth instruct the husbandman to discretion, and doth teach him." And what are manufactures but man's cunning manipulations of those products which He so bountifully provides from His sun and rain, and his versatile adaptation of them to his physical wants? God may be felt and adored in all, and ought to be felt and adored in all.

And why do nations cease to be, and why are their bounds

invaded and broken down? Simply because they do not own or follow out this divine purpose. They deify themselves, and forget Him who is above them—live but for themselves, and "feel after" aggrandisement, and not after Him. The Canaanites were ripe for expulsion on the invasion of Joshua, and so were the Jews themselves before the Roman Titus. The liberties of Greece had been struck down on the fatal field of Chæronea, and many a nation has been dispossessed of its soil. No people have an irrevocable charter to it; they possess it only so long as they are worthy of it, and act in harmony with Him who planted them in it. And they are displaced that the new occupant may be put upon its trial, too. In this light may be viewed those conquests which are establishing modern colonies—the conqueror in turn is judged, and will, if God decrees it, be in turn exiled. The Anglo-Saxon has driven back the Celt to the verge of the Atlantic, but the Sclave may be commissioned to exercise the same force upon the Anglo-Saxon if he do not service as God's tenant of His lands. And thus God shall be for Britain, so long as Britain is for God.

"He is not far from every one of us," says the orator; "for in Him we live, and move, and have our being." There seems to be neither climax nor anticlimax in the expression. But our existence is viewed on all sides—life and motion are *in Him*—as their sphere; in Him we live, and move, and *are*—continue to be. This statement gives no countenance to that mysticism which holds that every thought and act is not ours, but God's; thus destroying moral freedom and responsibility. But His existence includes ours. As we are and walk in the atmosphere, so really are we in God, and in Him we live and move. Every pulsation of our hearts depends on His sovereign beneficence. The nerves have no sensibility, the muscles no motion, the eye no vision, the blood no circulation, the tongue no voice, and the brain no energy but from Him and in Him. Let a single organ be deranged, and death may follow; let some cerebral atoms be disturbed, and reason is destroyed. If "in Him we live, and move, and have our being," then surely He is not far from us. We touch Him on all sides of us, and at every moment. Men need not feel far or long after Him; for He envelopes them with continuous pressure. Nay, they sustain a close relationship to Him—such a relationship as should impress them with His nearness and glory—

For the apostle adds—"As certain also of your own poets have said, For we are also his offspring." The word "for" is a portion of the quotation, which belongs to more poets than one, showing that the doctrine was not unknown to the Grecian mind; and to this fact he gives prominence —"certain poets of your own." The sentiment occurs in two of them, especially in Aratus of Cilicia and in Cleanthes the Stoic. The first, a countryman of Paul's, in his "Phenomena"—an astronomical poem, extolled by Ovid and translated into Latin by Cicero—says—

> "From Jove begin we, whom we should never leave
> Uncelebrated. Of Jove the public walks are full,
> And all the councils of men; the sea is full of him,
> And the shore. All that we always enjoy is from Jove;
> For we are also his offspring;"

this last clause being the apostle's quotation, and forming

half a hexameter. The commencement of the famous hymn of Cleanthes to Jupiter may be thus rendered—

> "Great Jove, most glorious of the immortal gods,
> Worshipped by many names, always almighty,
> Author of nature, governing by law the universe—
> Hail; for mortals all may lift their voice to thee,
> For we thine offspring are."

Both these poems acknowledge the apostle's doctrine—that man springs from no idol, but from a superior power often felt by the bards, if not excogitated by the philosophers —perceived by the soul, if not always admitted by the intellect. There had been, as was proved by the dedication of an altar to an unknown god, a belief with thoughtful men that there was some Essence or Power higher than all collected in the Pantheon—a conviction which originated such a sentiment as that quoted by the apostle. The Hebrew stranger was not ignorant of their literature, and could apply it to his purpose. Indeed, he was speaking their current tongue, though it was not, in many respects, that of their famous fathers.

The lesson is—that men are God's *offspring*—not His creation simply, but His offspring. The argument turns on this idea—the Fatherhood of God. Men are His offspring —His children possessing the paternal likeness. Sheep and oxen, the nightingale that warbled among the olives by the Ilissus, and the bees that ranged among the flowers on Mount Hymettus, were God's creatures, but not His offspring. This is in fact the doctrine of the genealogy in Luke, that Adam was "the son of God;" the doctrine of the earliest record, that "God created man in His own image—in the image of God created He him." Many features of that image have not been deleted. Holiness has been obliterated, and happiness has gone with it. But man yet preserves his capability of regaining this departed purity and felicity. And he still possesses his manhood though he is under sentence of death; still enjoys his erect mien, nor have reason and immortality been penally wrested from him. What belongs to his constitution he retains; what belongs to his character has been lost. Still has he those mental powers which fit him for speculation—for the attainment and application of knowledge. Conscious of his being, he can feel impressions from without, and perceive their cause; can think, and recall what he has seen, heard, or known, and can perform acts of mental abstraction and generalization. He can classify and decide, and can imagine and follow out long trains of thought and imagery under the influence of association. Nay, he can not only take cognizance of relations and differences, but ascend to ultimate and universal truths; and he is crowned with the gift of language through which his ideas and convictions are correctly expressed and conveyed. His heart can be stirred to emotion—to love or hatred, to joy or grief, to anger or gratitude, to fear what is to come or to hope for it, according to its character. And he is endowed with conscience—a witness and judge of his actions—God's vicegerent within him—while he is sensible of his moral freedom, that he is no series of sensational phenomena, no victim of impressions which he cannot control, or of mechanical laws which bind him in links of stern necessity.

These are features of God's image borne by His offspring —intelligence, liberty, personality, and conscience. Man, therefore, stands in a nearer and more tender relation to God than any other creature on earth—being to some extent still a shechinah—the Divinity resident within him. His life is sacred, because he bears the image of God. Mind in some sense belongs to the lower creation; but reason is not theirs, nor conscience, nor that higher spiritual nature by which man approaches and resembles God, and God by His Spirit works upon man. Look at that horse, he is strong, and " paweth in the valley," but he cannot rise in idea beyond his rider and his groom. "The ox knoweth his owner," and forms no higher conception; "and the ass his master's crib," with no apprehension of a world beyond.

> "The lamb thy riot dooms to bleed to-day,
> Had he thy reason, would he skip and play?
> Pleased to the last he crops the flowery food,
> And licks the hand just raised to shed his blood."

Is it not godlike on the part of man to be lord of the lower creation, a divine representative to them? Is it not godlike for "the spirit of man" to know "the things of a man," even as "the Spirit of God knoweth the things of God?" Is it not godlike to be able to say as God says —"I know all the fowls of the mountains?" Is it not godlike to be able to do as God does, to "tell the number of the stars and call them all by their names?" to adapt nature for every purpose, even for the instantaneous transmission of thought? Is it not godlike for him, by his faculty of invention, to imitate God's power of creation? Is it not godlike for him to have all things subservient to him, for he is an end to himself, at the same time as the means of glorifying his Creator? Certain of their own poets had said—" For we are also His offspring;" and one of their own philosophers had said—"On earth there is nothing great but man, in man there is nothing great but mind." So true it is, that even in fallen humanity, the divine image is still to be found—a protest against idolatry.

And man, as God's offspring, feels an instinctive impulse to recognize his Divine Father; has the means of knowing Him, of understanding this filial relationship, and profiting by it. The child calls for help when in danger, and presents its thanks when relief has been vouchsafed. It seeks to know the Divine will, as did the Greeks at Delphi; it is conscious of having offended, and devotes a victim. It hopes for some home nearer the Father when it leaves the world—some Elysian field, such as many could picture whom the apostle addressed. Idolatry is a confession of man's need that he must know his Father; the heart cannot be at rest without some deity to look up to and adore, to trust in and to obey. Polytheism may be irrational, but atheism is unnatural. To say that there are many gods is folly, but to say that there is no God is treason against man's own constitution, " for we are also His offspring "—not products simply, but children, formed, fed, and clothed; mentally and morally endowed by Him whose image we bear, though its brightness has been darkened by sin. What a blessed doctrine, then, that we are the divine offspring — children of one father. How high our dignity! how rich our patrimony! Wherever we are, in whatever portion of His universe, we are still in His house—our home. We can never outstep our heritage. The Father has fitted nature not merely to supply our wants, but also to minister to our delight—the glitter of the star and of the dew-drop, the colour and scent of the flower, freshness and beauty for the eye, and song and melody for the ear. Our Father's house is not barely furnished, but richly ornamented. Rocks are piled into hoary mountains and picturesque heights; the woods are budding forth into life in spring, laden with foliage in summer, or swinging their great boughs to the tempest of winter; the sky folds its curtains and trims its lamps; the waters dance in torrents and leap in cascades, as well as fill the seas; there is gold as well as iron, gems as well as granites, the blush and fragrance of the blossom, as well as the sweetness and abundance of the fruit. The human frame, too, has symmetry as well as strength—possesses far more than is merely essential to life and work; the eye, lip, and brow are rich in expression and power. There is not only the power of thought essential to business and religion, but there is the garniture of imagination, poetry as well as science, music in addition to speech, ode and oracle as well as fact and doctrine in scripture, the lyre of the bard no less than the pen of the apostle. Above sensation there rises the power of discovery—invention blends with experience. In man and around him there is not mere provision for necessities; there are profuse luxuries. "His offspring" walk in the lustre of His love. It rejoices them to know that the power which governs is no dark phantom veiled in mystery; no majestic and all-controlling force—a mighty and shadowless sceptre; no mere omniscience—an eye that never slumbers; no dim Spirit, having its only consciousness in the consciousness of man—but a Father with a father's heart to love us, and to the yearnings of which we may ever appeal—a father's ear to listen to us, and a father's hand to bless with kind and continued benefactions. And, as we have wandered, shall not each of us say—"I will arise and go unto my Father?" Will not He accept the returning child, giving us the adoption of sons, revealing Himself graciously through Christ the Elder Brother who leads us to cry in true filial devotion—"Our Father which art in heaven?"

In the next verse the apostle states his inference—"Forasmuch then as we are the offspring of God, we ought not to think that the Godhead is like unto gold, or silver, or stone, graven by art and man's device." At that moment the speaker stood in view of such idols and sculptures. Art had reached its perfection; device had exhausted itself in forms of sublimity and beauty. The market-place was thronged with the statues of the gods. The Acropolis before him had three statues of the great goddess, one of them the original image, which, like that of Diana at Ephesus, was believed to have fallen from Jupiter; another of them, in the shrine of the Parthenon, made of ivory and gold, the masterpiece of Phidias; and the third, the colossal image of the same divinity, towering in front of him, armed, and on guard—the top of whose spear might be seen by the mariner crossing the Saronic gulf. He was in the midst of a crowd of metal and marble deities, the like of which for symmetry and stateliness, for loveliness and majesty, no other nation had ever produced. But he does not denounce them and endanger himself; he appeals to his hearers, and presents an argument which their acute spirit could scarcely fail to appreciate. The neuter term rendered "Godhead," signifies the divine nature or essence; *graven by art and man's device*—means, "sculpture of the art and ingenuity of man."

The argument, then, is—being the offspring of God, we ought not to think that the Divine nature can ever be imaged in metal or stone, no matter what skill and art may be employed in the sculpture. Our filial relation to God should teach us this. It is a spiritual relation, and should convince us of the spirituality of the Godhead. We cannot image ourselves, far less God. What is spiritual in us, what makes us the offspring of God, can neither be pencilled on canvas, or be carved by the chisel. The portrait, or the statue which flows from the furnace are not we, they are only an effigy of us, or rather only of our external appearance. Vital action, mental power, and spiritual susceptibility, cannot be so depicted. True a statue may be made, and it may resemble a man in form, attitude, and drapery. The likeness may be so vivid as to startle you; and as you gaze you almost expect it to move and speak. But it is chill and changeless—a lump of immobility—not even representing fully the shell or corporeal tabernacle of man. For much in it is beyond the reach of such vulgar delineation—the nerves conveying sensations and transmitting volitions; the lungs at work in their chemical laboratory; the heart in its dilatations, contractions, and propulsion of the vital fluid; the blood in its rapid arterial and venous courses, depositing tissues and clearing itself from impurities; the swelling and straining of the muscles and tendons; the motions and secretions of the joints; the secret functions of the skin; the optical wonders of the eye; the acoustic chambers of the ear; and the mighty and mysterious action of the brain—that complex process, in short, which we call life. Man's art and device cannot reproduce his living self in gold, silver, or stone.

Still more as those organs are his, but not he, therefore what he really is—his reason, soul, conscience, genius, and immortality—defy all representation. No power can shape them, Zeuxis could not paint them; Praxiteles could not figure them; gold, silver, and stone cannot body them forth. The apostle's thought then is—If as the offspring of one God, we cannot produce any likeness of ourselves, containing this relationship to Him, how can we imagine that we can produce any likeness of Him, containing His relationship to us. Spirituality is lost by being shadowed out to sense. How shall we depict His infinitude or omnipotence, His omniscience, His goodness and truth, or any of those qualities which have the reflection of themselves within us, and our possession of which proves us His offspring? If you cannot picture out the godlike in man, why attempt to picture out God Himself? If the image defy you to grasp and embody it, why dare to make trial upon the original? Idolatry is therefore false as well as foolish; his own likeness, far less the likeness of his Father, man cannot fabricate. Give the artist precious gold and silver, so ductile to his hand, and so brilliant in the polish which they take from it; or give him the pure and veinless marble of Pentelicus, out of which he can produce a shape so exquisite in limb and feature, and what is the result? The so-called likeness is only that of the outer form of a bold and graceful man, or a beautiful and lovely woman. The statues of their gods were quite the same as those of their heroes, sages, and orators, with the exception of some symbol—painted thunder or a crown of glory. The uninitiated eye could not tell the one from the other—the man from the god. Man's own dignity is a living argument against idolatry and polytheism. How absurd in him, therefore, so to limit and degrade his object of worship.

According to this report of his address, the apostle did not pursue farther his exposure of idolatry. He left his hearers to their own reflections—to follow out the lessons which their own poets had suggested. By knowing what they were themselves, they would come to know what God was. One, indeed, dares not gaze upwards on the sun as he pours out his burning radiance, but he may contemplate his image in the lake or river at his feet. Men may not pierce to the uncreated splendour, but they may see God in themselves—the likeness of the Father in His child. While we cannot believe with some modern philosophers that the physical creation is unable to prove to us the existence of God; while we differ from that notion of cause which those thinkers maintain, and believe it to be a reality, and not merely a logical form of thought—still we hold that man's mental and moral constitution presents the highest and fullest argument for the existence, personality, and character of the Supreme. Man knows God because he knows himself, or perceives the image of the All-Father within him. The revelations which God has made in scripture, he is enabled to understand in the same way, or with the same intuitional assistance. The terms employed to represent the character and attributes of God, I can understand only as they are descriptive of properties or processes in myself. If I am told that God possesses knowledge, I gather the meaning of the statement by a reference to my own mind and its information. Or, if I am told that God loves or hates, then, knowing what these emotions are within myself, I instinctively ascribe them to Him in infinite purity and degree.

Part III.

Changing his theme, the apostle advances—"And the times of this ignorance God *winked* at "—literally " overlooked." That is to say, He did not declare his special disapprobation of them, and sent no heralds with articulate denunciations of them. His oracles were given only to one nation. Man was left to the exercise of his own reason, and the results of his idolatry should have checked him. The argument had just concluded with this idea—that man's own nature should have taught him the spirituality of the divine nature. There was therefore no apology for "this ignorance." But still it was ignorance—lamentable ignorance, and the temples and statues of the Acropolis were a sad memorial and witness of it. The eye of Greece was sealed in spiritual gloom. It did not look within it to discover its own dignity, or above it to obtain a glimpse of the divine glories. There had been guesses at the truth, and crude and vicious idolatry with correspondent tales of mythology had sometimes been reprobated as a national scandal. But the mass of the people were never reached by such speculations; to them the idol was the god, and no mere symbol or representative of an unseen person or power. In fact the absence of faith produced idolatry. Man could not endure as "seeing Him who is invisible," and longed to have a palpable god, one that he could handle and carry about with him—one on his hearth as well as in his temple.

Actuated by this very principle, the Jews asked a king; losing faith in a divine, invisible Sovereign, the Lord of Hosts, their Guardian, they clamoured for a visible leader with helmet and sword to lead them forth to battle. And polytheism was the natural result of idolatry. The various powers of nature in operation around them could only be pictured by symbols, and each symbol soon rose to be an independent divinity. The omnipresence of the one God was lost sight of, or divided as a domain of numerous gods. His thousand modes of appearance and operation were deified. The tokens of His presence were hailed as indications of separate gods; the movements of His arm were personified, and temples were built on the prints of His feet. What higher knowledge and faith are possessed by us!

> "There's not a strain to memory dear,
>   Nor flower in sacred grove;
>   There's not a sweet note warbled there,
>   But minds us of thy love.
> O Lord, our Lord, and spoiler of our foes,
> There is no light but Thee, with Thee all beauty glows."

But the period of divine forbearance had expired. Such ignorance God had overlooked, " but now commandeth all men everywhere to repent"—chargeth this on everyone everywhere—to repent. "Now" is opposed to the past "times." He had overlooked such ignorance then, but his command is urgent now—no person is exempted, and no place is omitted. The men of Athens were under the injunction; with all their boasted wisdom, the proud Stoic, the light-hearted Epicurean, and the volatile populace were solemnly charged by the great God to repent. The command was new indeed, for it had been recently given, and it was to repent—to desist from those follies, to feel their guilt, and look to God for deliverance. A complete change of mind was implied; they were to unlearn their past creed and abandon their previous life, for Christianity proclaimed no truce, and admitted no compromise. And the grand and solemn reason is affixed, that a period of judgment is coming and inquest would be made, for He who had issued the command would examine into the treatment it had met with. Unless they repented, they could not meet God in the judgment with hope of acceptance.

And that judgment-day was fixed—"Because He hath appointed a day in the which He will judge the world in righteousness." The judge is the great God, "Lord of heaven and earth." He simply changes His throne of majesty into a tribunal. He has the right to issue the command to repent, and He has the right to inquire if it be complied with. He is not, as those Epicureans thought, indifferent to or unobservant of the actions of men, for He legislates now, and He will judge hereafter. Nor is he, as those Stoics dreamed, so much identified with His universe as a portion of Himself that he cannot sever Himself from it, and sit in judgment upon it as responsible to Him. Nay, the period of the judgment is irrevocably set down —a period known only to the Judge Himself. It is not left to the course of events, but every day leads to and prepares for the "last day," when the human species shall have completed its cycle. It will not be antedated, and it cannot be postponed. And the world is to be judged—all its population—whatever their character or country. The judges of the Areopagus shall stand before a higher tribunal. No resistance will avail. No room is there for escape, for all must appear; the order of the judge cannot be set aside, and there is no moment for repentance, for time has been completed. Solemn thought for a human spirit to be arraigned before its Creator, whose eye sees at once its entire history—motive as well as action, wishes that may never have been expressed, desires that would have shuddered at their own gratification, and misdeeds which had long since faded into oblivion. Judgment implies omniscience, a perfect comprehension of the whole character of every man. If "in God we live and move, and have our being," He knows us, and each of us may say—" O Lord, Thou hast searched me, and known me. Thou knowest my down-sitting and mine uprising; Thou understandest my thought afar off. Thou compassest my path, and my lying down, and art acquainted with all my ways. For there is not a word in my tongue, but lo, O Lord, thou knowest it altogether. Thou hast beset me behind and before, and laid thine hand upon me."

Nor can the world object to be judged. Every man has been created by God for Himself, and all his mental and moral endowments have been conferred upon him with this view. Instinct may not bring along with it such a result, but the gift of reason and freedom implies responsibility. We have been made by God to live to God, and this is the standard of judgment; or, putting it into a more direct evangelical form, God has provided salvation for us, and may He not ask whether we have accepted it, or whether we have scorned His gift and destroyed ourselves? For all that God has made him, for all that God has done for him, for his belief as well as for his life, is man accountable to God.

While God, who creates, upholds, and governs us, has the right, and, from His omniscience, has the qualification to judge us, we are assured at the same time of His perfect rectitude. He will judge the world *in righteousness*—not only in the exercise of perfect equity, but His equity necessitates such a judgment. Justice belongs to His nature, and characterizes all his proceedings. Without it as the unchanging substratum, mercy might degenerate into weakness, and power stretch itself into tyranny. "Just and true are Thy ways, Thou King of saints;" "Thou only art holy." His laws are the expression of His rectitude, and His providence exemplifies it. In it Adam was expelled from Paradise, and the old world drowned—Israel sent into captivity, and ultimately dispersed. In it, and by its process of self-vindication, the drunkard undermines his health and shortens his life; nay, in the midst of many disturbing influences, vice is, in a true sense, its own punishment, and virtue its own reward. "Verily there is a reward for the righteous, verily He is a God that judgeth in the earth." "With righteousness shall He judge the world, and the people with equity."

For He cannot err, or be charged with unconscious injustice or partiality. A human judge may blunder, may fail to identify the criminal, or leave out of view some aggravating or some extenuating element in the evidence. His mind may be prejudiced insensibly by the face of the culprit, or swayed by the apparent candour of some hostile and unscrupulous witness. Even on that hill where the judges of the Areopagus had sat under night, that they might simply hear proof on either side and be unmoved by appearances, sentences at variance with equity had been pronounced, in spite of their rigid impartiality and severe and patient investigation; for they could not always get at the facts, or did not in every case give each fact its just weight in their deliberations. But the divine judge can never be imposed on. "All things are naked and open unto the eyes of Him with whom we have to do;" all motives and thoughts, all the complex elements that mould and make up character, are utterly known to Him. The scales of His justice are so delicate, that they vibrate under what would be utterly inappreciable before an earthly tribunal. As a man really is, so shall he appear before God, but man takes cognizance only of what appears, not what is.

For even the universe presents infallible witness. The following is the awful statement of one well qualified so to speak—"Whilst the atmosphere we breathe is the ever-living witness of the sentiments we have uttered, the waters and the more solid materials of the globe bear equally enduring testimony of the acts we have committed. If the Almighty stamped on the brow of the first murderer the indelible and visible mark of his guilt, He has also established laws by which every succeeding criminal is not less irrevocably chained to the testimony of his crime; for every atom of his mortal frame, through whatever changes its several particles may migrate, will still retain, adhering to it through every combination, some movement derived from that very muscular effort by which the crime itself was perpetrated. The soul of the negro whose fettered body, surviving the living charnel-house of his infected prison, was thrown into the sea to lighten the ship, that his Christian master might escape the limited justice at length assigned by civilized man to crimes whose profits had long gilded their atrocity, will need, at the last great day of human account, no living witness of his earthly agony. When man and all his race shall have disappeared from the face of our planet, ask every particle of air still floating over the unpeopled earth, and it will record the cruel mandate of the tyrant. Interrogate every wave which breaks unimpeded on ten thousand desolate shores, and it will give evidence of the last gurgle of the waters which closed over the head of his dying victim, confront the murderer with every corporeal atom of his immolated slave, and in its still quivering movements he will read the prophet's denunciation of the prophet-king—*Thou art the man.*" But even this strange and indelible record, legible only to the eye of omniscience, is imperfect; for there are many thoughts and purposes, hidden volitions and cravings, which belong solely to mind, and make no external impress. Yet these are not unknown, nor are they forgotten. They form the character, and that character meets with infallible judgment; or, according to the impressive figure, " the judgment is set, and the books are opened." Everything takes place in God, for " in Him we live and move, and have our being," and in God is it therefore laid up beyond possibility of error or oblivion. Nor can God pronounce any verdict not holy in the highest sense, and equitable to the fullest extent. "Every word of God is pure; He is a shield unto them that put their trust in Him." No sentence of His can be improved —"Add not thou unto His words, lest He reprove thee, and thou be found a liar."

Nor, perhaps, is it rash to say that our past history is so laid up also in ourselves, that God's touch can at any time evoke it into sudden consciousness. "Memory," said one of their own poets, "is the queen of things." Its storehouse is vast and secret, and what appears to be forgotten may in a moment start up under some impulse or association. The mind apparently never ceases to act, even in sleep, for a person suddenly roused wakes always out of a dream, and probably nothing ever really passes into absolute oblivion. Abnormal states of mind in somnambulism and in cerebral disease, prove the amazing power and compass of involuntary recollection—in repeating long arguments or pieces of poetry, in depicting scenes long ago visited, and in speaking languages unused since childhood—feats found to be utterly impossible in a sound and healthy condition. Innumerable instances of this nature show that, in all likelihood, no sensation received by the mind, no judgment formed, desire entertained, decision come to, acquisition made, or emotion felt by it, ever fades into nothing, as if it never had been; but that all is treasured up in it, and needs but a word from Him who made it to bring it into light, and to reproduce in a moment to a man all he ever was, or thought, or did, so that in a moment of intense and surprising consciousness he shall live over again the whole of his existence! May not he that stands before the tribunal be thus enabled to read himself in the light which God's eye flashes in upon him?

Thus every one at His awful tribunal will admit the justness of that decision pronounced upon him—not decision in the ordinary forensic sense, implying either previous ignorance or doubt before trial, but decision as the simple declaration of a living omniscience. Every one will feel that "God is justified when He speaks, and clear when He judges." For were any one even of those condemned to have doubts, or to feel that God had acted hardly towards him, such a sense of injury would nerve him to the endurance of all the agony which might be sent upon him. "He will judge the world in righteousness," and show it to be so. Believers are not justified by works, though they may be judged by them. Their character is declared to be, not the foundation of their acceptance, but the token or fruit of their union to Christ, and their love to Him; it is their service to Him by service to His, and their preparation for the kingdom prepared for them. Divine grace has so changed and blessed them, that they prove their meetness for heaven by their possession of its spirit—a spirit of love to Jesus and all who bear His image. The test is a sure one, and the rectitude of the judge cannot be impugned—"Inasmuch as ye have done it unto one of the least of these my brethren, ye have done it unto me."

But there is another and a special revelation. What the apostle had said might be admitted, for it is what the religion of nature could not deny. But he adds the startling peculiarity—"He will judge the world by that man whom He hath ordained"—*by that man*—in Him—as His representative and image. By a man? What would his audience now think? He had a few seconds ago been censuring their idolatry—telling them that statues can never be a likeness of Deity, and that He does not reside in hand-made shrines—and how then will He by a man do this solemn and divine work of judging the world? The apostle was not allowed to explain, or he could have easily solved the mystery as to the character and relations of the man whom He hath *ordained*—set apart to this high office. For that man is more than man. A man He is, and we rejoice to know it, but his manhood is a second and assumed nature. He is God—the Son of God—equal with God. That omniscience and equity which are requisite in a judge, meet in Him. "The Father judgeth no man, but hath committed all judgment unto the Son, and hath given Him authority to execute judgment also, because He is the Son of man." In His mediatorial position He is the Father's servant, and the judgment is the last great function of the mediatorial reign. Therefore the man Jesus is judge—He who loved us and died for us—and His question is, have you relied on my love, and accepted my atonement? Farther, man has been placed in a new position by Christ's incarnation. He has been allied to Divinity, that he might be brought back to the divine favour and image. Our nature had died under the penalty of the old covenant, but a new representative man has been given us, that a new spiritual life might be originated and developed within us. The Word was made flesh, that flesh might become divine. By Christ's becoming one of us another epoch commences, and a new path is opened up through our union with Him. God became man to win man back to Himself, and He who is the second Adam—"that man," man's Saviour and Brother—is to be judge.

And O what consolation in the thought that He is to be judge! How appalling the prospect of standing "before this holy Lord God"—of being enveloped and permeated with His brightness—of being conscious that every part of our naked nature is so filled with His presence and inspection! But He who is on that judgment-seat is Christ—the man Christ Jesus, with His heart of sympathy and tongue of comfort. And though He come in glory, surrounded by a dense and bright retinue—the armies of heaven following after Him; and though He seat Himself on the great white throne, amidst the wreck of elements and convulsions of nature, and other tokens of homage to His presence and majesty, yet He is our kinsman clothed in our nature—that very nature in which He lay on the Virgin's bosom, and died on the accursed tree.

And the proof is not lacking—"Whereof He hath given assurance unto all men in that He hath raised Him from the dead;" *given assurance*—literally afforded faith or the means of belief. How the apostle would have developed the proof we know not, for at this period he was rudely interrupted. Into the array of proof we do not enter, and we may find subsequent occasion to refer to it. But we may say, that the resurrection of Jesus proved His mission to be divine, and showed Him to be the head of humanity, and, therefore, entitled to be its judge. His resurrection is also the proof that all men are to be raised; not a token that they may be raised, but a pledge that they shall be raised. As by His resurrection He becomes judge, so they are raised in order to be judged. And thus assurance of judgment is given unto all men.

The apostle could easily have given them indubitable evidence that Christ had been raised from the dead; as, for example, that His tomb was guarded, and that the sentinels only befooled themselves and those who suborned them, by their contradictory announcement—" His disciples came and stole Him away while we slept." Roman soldiers asleep on special duty, and forward to confess it—asleep on a post which they were warned might be assailed—all of them asleep at the same instant, and when under orders of unusual strictness—asleep, and yet able to tell what happened, what was done, and who did it, too, when their eyes were shut in unanimous slumber—all of them asleep, and yet not one of them awakened by the noise and concussion of the earthquake which preceded the resurrection! Nor had these disciples any motive to do the act imputed to them. They had no idea that their Master should rise again, and all their hopes were buried along with Him. They could, therefore, never dream of such an attempt as stealing His body, it being of no use to them, as they had no romance to base upon its absence; and if they had, the eleven poltroons who " forsook Him and fled " at the sight of the soldiers in the garden, would never have ventured to attack a Roman guard of sixteen men under the bright moonlight of the eastern heavens. Farther, He who had risen appeared to His former friends who could identify Him, and on the spot, too, where He had been put to death. It was not as if one supposed to have risen in Glasgow should be said to have appeared first in Inverness, where he was a comparative stranger. It was not as if it were alleged that one had risen, but that the story was only first heard of half a century after the imagined event. At the time when, and in the place where He had died and been buried, did the Lord appear, when full investigation could be made into all the circumstances, and into the testimony of crowds of living witnesses. But those who should have originated and conducted the inquiry shrank from it under the impression that the result would not be to their satisfaction, and resorted to the miserable refuge of authority, "straitly threatening" the witnesses to say no more on the matter; while they who were "witnesses of these things" had no end to gain, and no worldly advantage to secure; on the contrary, proscription and death resulted from the avowal of their belief in this momentous tenet. And the apostle might have referred, in conclusion, to his own conversion, when the Lord appeared to him and gave him that commission under which he was at that moment speaking on the Areopagus.

But the simple mention of the "resurrection" led to a burst of laughter on the part of some, and destroyed all anxiety to hear any farther on the part of the whole. They did not deem it worth their while to listen any longer; and they felt so and said so, just when the argument had reached a crisis, and a chain of evidence was about to be woven—just when Christ was about to be specifically preached to them, they contemptuously shut the preacher's mouth, and told him that really they had heard enough, that their curiosity was satisfied, and that it would be a mere waste of time for him to proceed. The apostle must have felt this treatment very keenly; never had he had such an opportunity, and never had he failed so egregiously. He had made no general impression. The anxiety to hear him had been keen, but he could not even command attention to the close of his address. No wonder that after this severe disappointment he entered Corinth, the next Greek city he visited, as he says, " in weakness, and in fear, and in much trembling." Not that the preacher could blame himself, as if he had selected a wrong topic, or had not handled it with sufficient skill and power; but apprehensions of his success in southern Greece seem to have filled him with despondency. He was in a new scene, and the synagogue seems to have afforded no basis of operations. He had often battled with Jewish obstinacy, and to some purpose; had been in contact with Cyprian licentiousness, and had succeeded to a marvel; had mingled with the dissolute populations of Antioch, and gained hundreds of converts; had so impressed the rude men of Lycaonia that they took him for a god; had been the victim of Roman ferocity in Philippi, yet had formed a church; had preached in Thessalonica, and reaped compensatory fruit — but in Athens, the eye of Greece, where he first confronted " the wisdom of this world," he could not even succeed in stirring opposition or stimulating inquiry. He would rather have been persecuted than put off so gently in this way —would rather have been scourged as a peace-disturber than dismissed as a crazy enthusiast. What he had said had told so little upon his volatile audience that they affronted him by breaking up and leaving him in the midst of his harangue. Need we wonder that the apostle hasted to be off, or that we read—" So Paul departed from among them?" Though he was afterwards in Greece, nay, at Corinth, he never again visited Athens. But his work was not wholly fruitless: "Howbeit certain men clave unto him; among the which was Dionysius *the Areopagite*"— one of the judges of the Areopagus, and, therefore, of the best blood in the city—"and a woman named Damaris, and others with them." This woman must have been of some note that she is thus named. Possibly she belonged to the notorious class of Hetairai—mistresses—the class to which Aspasia, Lais, Phryne, and Lastheneia belonged— courtezans, indeed, and usually slaves or foreigners, though some of them, by superior education, boldness, and wit, rose to influence in the state, and held in their houses reunions of its chief statesmen, philosophers, and orators.

The Greek worship, with its magnificent architecture and sculpture, was a powerless institution. It had failed to lead men to true theology. The speculations of Thales, Pythagoras, and Zeno on the origin and phenomena of the universe, could not bring their disciples to this truth— "God made the world, and all things therein; He is Lord of heaven and earth." And though Socrates reclaimed many to the study of themselves, this self-knowledge made little or no impression on the masses. For their religion had a disastrous influence over their lives; the actions of their gods being a stimulus to depravity. Men became, like their objects of worship, sensual and debased, and gloried in pleading the example of the gods—examples we should blush to describe. As the mind did not arrive at truth, the conscience could not find repose. A veil lay upon the other world, and they scoffed at a resurrection. As the apostle was about to expatiate upon its certainty, they rose in their levity and bade him desist—they could not tolerate the mention of it. When "the man, the best of all his time, the most wise and just," stood on Mars-hill and received sentence of death as "a setter forth of strange gods," he is reported to have said—"To die is one of two things: for either the dead may be annihilated, and have no sensation of anything whatever; or, as it is said, there is a certain change and passage of the soul from one place to another. And if it is a privation of all sensation, as it were a sleep in which the sleeper has no dream, death would be a wonderful gain. For I think that if any one, having selected a night in which he slept so soundly as not to have had a dream, and having compared this night with all the other nights and days of his life, should be required on consideration to say how many days and nights he had passed better and more pleasantly than this night throughout his life, I think that not only a private person, but even the great king himself, would find them easy to number in comparison with other days and nights. If, therefore, death is a thing of this kind, I say it is a gain; for thus all futurity appears to be nothing more than one night. But if, on the other hand, death is a removal from hence to another place, and what is said be true, that all the dead are there, what greater blessing can there be than this, my judges? For if, on arriving at Hades, released from these who pretend to be judges, one shall find those who are true judges, and who are said to judge there, Minos and Rhadamanthus, Æacus and Triptolemus, and such others of the demigods as were just during their own life, would this be a sad removal? At what price would you not estimate a conference with Orpheus and Musæus, Hesiod and Homer? I indeed should be willing to die often if this be true." Thus doubt and fluctuation seem to have disturbed the mind of the sage, though he is depicted as arguing elsewhere the immortality of the soul as boldly and truly as unassisted reason ever could. But his philosophy had fallen so dead, that the Athenians, with all their love of news, declined to listen to a new appeal on the subject from a bold and eloquent stranger. What was speculation with Socrates is certainty with us. Our assurance is, that the spirit at death is conveyed to the bright spirit-world—the throne of God in its centre, and the Lamb the object of enraptured homage; that the true and the good are there; Abel and the martyrs; Enoch and the antediluvian witnesses; Abraham and the patriarchs; Aaron and the spiritual priesthood; David and the holy kingdom; Elijah and the prophets; the apostles and the early church; the saints of all ages and countries—all who have believed on Christ, done His work, and borne His image. What a glorious assembly to mingle with and enjoy, as we hold

THE FOLLY OF GRECIAN WISDOM. 239

fellowship and offer worship with them—partakers all of us of the "common salvation."

But "the world by wisdom knew not God." Nay, in those degenerate days there was such indifference produced by this so-called wisdom, that "philosophers" did not deign to listen to what was highest philosophy. Pride of intellect has ever been the hardest barrier against the truth: "Seest thou a man wise in his own conceit? there is more hope of a fool than of him." "Simplicity and godly sincerity" were wanting at Athens, and the truth was rejected. Yes, even Athens, of which Lucretius sings—

> "Athens, of peerless name, to savage man
> First taught the blessings of the cultured field,
> His life remodelled, and with laws secured.
> She, too, the soul's sweet solaces first oped
> When erst the sage she reared, whose boundless breast
> Swelled with all science, and whose lips promulged"—

this Athens was indifferent to the noblest of blessings, which had brought down the "hidden manna" from heaven, with laws which are the expression of infinite love, and joys which spring from the fellowship of the soul with its Creator, as it becomes more intensely conscious of bearing His image and possessing His love. Yes; Athens, blinded by its wisdom and its worldliness, saw no truth nor beauty in the divine philosophy conveyed to it by a Jewish traveller in whose glance—

> "There lurked that nameless spell
> Which speaks, itself unspeakable."

May we not, in fine, fetch a lesson to ourselves? Are there no idols among us in this age of hero-worship? We allude not to the strange fact, that some months in our years are named from Roman idols, and that all the days of our week are named from Saxon idols. But is there no pride of reason nursed by intellectual ascendancy? In what does homage to force or genius, irrespective of the end to which they have been applied, and in oblivion of the One Giver, differ from idolatry or nature-worship—from that process which made a god of tutelar power, and a goddess of patriotic wisdom? Are there not those that bow the knee to Mammon in the exchange, who would not bow it to Jupiter in a temple? Are there not many who in boasted illumination cast aside the teaching of scripture, or who, in the enjoyment of wealth and power, feel not their need of it? This age is a strange one. There are open defenders of atheism, impugners of sabbatic obligation, and public revilers of Christianity, as if it were effete and worthless—denying God's existence and unhallowing God's day. One has written a book to show that religion is so feeble that it has had no influence on civilization; and another in a neighbouring nation, who is so proud as to believe and call himself a combination of Aristotle and Paul, proclaims that new gods should be introduced and adored—heroes and saints—Moses and Homer, Confucius and Shakspeare, Hercules and Frederick the Great. It is one hypothesis that man is but an elevated monkey, and that he and the universe around him are but developments out of the atoms of an ancient fire-mist; and it is another, quite in keeping, that the heavens, which of old declared the glory of God, now declare only the glory of Newton and Laplace. That God had become man, was once a faith to be gloried in, but with many the proposition has been reversed, and their creed is, that man has become God. Some maintain the grossest materialism—that there is no spirit in man; some, admitting that they are the "offspring of God," refuse to call Him Father, and unfilially style Him Nature; and others deny the responsibility of man for his belief even to that God who presents him with evidence, and has conferred upon him powers by which he can sift it and come to a right conclusion. Are not "wise men after the flesh" dealing with the gospel as the Epicureans and Stoics dealt with Paul? A resurrection to the one and the other sect was impossible in theory, and undesirable in hope; for with them the soul itself was supposed to sink into unconsciousness at death, either by being dissolved or being absorbed into the great sum of existence. So it is that philosophic minds still refuse the revelation of Christ, or strip it of all that is distinctive and remedial, before they profess to receive it. For some it is too simple, and for others too mysterious; one class objects that it takes too little notice of man's present interests; and another, that its morality is too transcendental. Inspiration is pared down, and the authority of scripture is lowered by this party; and by that party the truths of scripture are thought to be good enough for the age which produced them, but deficient in breadth and adaptation for the enlightened nineteenth century. By such seekers after wisdom, the gospel is dismissed as quietly and effectually as was its great apostle from Mars-hill.

O that all this wildness and passion were stilled by the remembrance that He " hath appointed a day in which He will judge the world in righteousness by that man whom He hath ordained—whereof He hath given assurance unto all men in that He hath raised Him from the dead." Is Christ risen—ay or no? The controversy turns on this—Is it fact or fable? If His resurrection be a demonstrable reality, then surely His voice must be listened to, and His warnings pondered. His gospel has a claim which no other form of truth presents—it is God's immediate and authentic revelation. It can be superseded by no dialectics, and rung out by no poetical peal. The light of science is unable to eclipse it, the treasures of art equal not its "pearl of great price." Legislation dares not displace it, for it gives law to the conscience, and without it civilization is but a whited sepulchre. Freedom rests upon it as a solid basis, because its disciples are not to be the "servants of men;" and national progress, true prosperity—greatest happiness to all—are measured by its development. For it gives nobility to the meanest, and the best of the graces to the highest—presents every one with an aim worthy of his nature—sanctifies every pursuit as a calling on which he may "abide with God"—sends a cheering influence through all the relations of life—relieves the poor and needy—visits the "fatherless and widows in their affliction"—sets its brightest jewel in the crown, and guards the purity of the ermine—breathes a just and generous spirit into legislation—opens up a widening circle of spiritual brotherhood, and blends earth with heaven: realizing the Saviour's natal anthem—"Glory to God in the highest, and on earth peace, goodwill toward men." Such a religion can have no rival, and admits of no substitute.

XI.—PAUL AT CORINTH.

ACTS xviii. 1—18.   1ST & 2ND EPISTLES TO THE CORINTHIANS.

ON leaving Athens, Paul set out for Corinth—the capital of Achaia, and the "city of the two seas." It lay about forty-five miles west from Athens, on an isthmus with a seaport on each side—Lechæum, about a mile distant, on its western, and Cenchrea, about eight miles distant, on its eastern shore. It was a thriving entrepot for the commerce between northern and southern Greece, and it had been in other days a strong military post, the key of the Peloponnesus. The famous isthmus was about three miles and a-half in breadth at its narrowest point; and boats being sometimes conveyed across it from the Ionian to the Ægean sea, it resembled in this respect those necks of land in Scotland called Tarbet—from two words, meaning, "to draw the boat." Thus in 1203 the Norwegians sailed up Loch Long, dragged their boats over the isthmus of Tarbet, under two miles in breadth, and launching them upon Loch Lomond, slew and plundered the natives, who had taken refuge on its islands, and had never dreamed of such a stratagem. But the importance of Corinth as a military station had almost ceased when it passed under the Roman yoke. Its citadel, Acrocorinthus, two thousand feet high, rising as abruptly as the rock of Dumbarton, and not unlike it, still remains a prominent feature in the landscape—

> "Yet she stands,
> A fortress formed to freedom's hands;
> The whirlwind's wrath, the earthquake's shock,
> Have left untouched her hoary rock,
> The keystone of a land which still,
> Though fallen, looks proudly on that hill;
> The landmark to the double tide
> That purpling rolls on either side,
> As if their waters chafed to meet,
> Yet pause and crouch beneath her feet."

Corinth was at this time the residence of the Roman proconsul, and Gallio, the brother of Seneca, held the office. In its best days it had been depraved in the extreme. Its obscene impurities had passed into a proverb, and from its very name a word was coined to denote wanton indulgence. The Isthmian games in its vicinity brought crowds of dissolute strangers to it, and a thousand priestesses or courtezans had been attached to the temple of Venus. The basest passions were consecrated in this city which has given to architecture its most florid order; and the tub in which Diogenes kennelled in the principal promenade, was a surly protest against surrounding pomp and luxury. Many changes had passed over it, but its immoral character was unaltered; it still delighted in show and pleasure. The consul Mummius had burned it, but Julius Cæsar rebuilt it, and peopled it as a Roman colony. The spoils of the city—the work of the potter and silversmith—were prized at Rome, as far surpassing anything that Italy could produce. If Athens was wholly given to idolatry, Corinth was wholly given to lust and revel, and one of the famous of its abandoned women had a splendid tomb in the outskirts. Nor had it been in reality less idolatrous than Athens. Neptune was the presiding deity of the maritime city; it had its sacred fountain, where Bellerophon had captured the winged steed Pegasus; temples and gods were abundant; chariots of Phaethon and the Sun, with statues of Apollo and Venus.

In this gay and dissipated city Paul took up his residence with Aquila and Priscilla, Jews who had recently been banished from Rome; and being " of the same craft, he wrought with them, for by their occupation they were tent-makers." It was the custom of the Jews to teach their children a trade, even though they should be destined to a professional life. Tents were in great demand in those days, for no one could travel without them, as indeed is still the case in eastern countries. The traveller must carry all accomodation along with him, as none can be had or found on the road. Paul's native province of Cilicia had a species of goats with long hair, out of which tent-cloth called *cilicium* was woven, and it was easy and natural for him to learn this occupation in his youth. This hair, or the cloth made of it, must have been a common article of commerce, so that Paul could exercise at Corinth the craft which he had been taught when a boy in Tarsus; and he wrought with his own hands, not only because he had claim as yet on no one—for we cannot say that his host and hostess were believers at this period—but because both here and at Thessalonica there were those who might impugn his motives, and reckon him as seeking and valuing a secular interest in his labours and his converts.

He knew his right and could maintain it, but he waived it from higher considerations. In the case of Corinth he is unusually resolute, a proof that there was some reason of unusual urgency: "Have I committed an offence in abasing myself, that ye might be exalted, because I have preached to you the gospel of God freely? I robbed other churches, taking wages of them, to do you service. And when I was present with you, and wanted, I was chargeable to no man: for that which was lacking to me the brethren which came from Macedonia supplied; and in all things I have kept myself from being burdensome unto you, and so will I keep myself. As the truth of Christ is in me, no man shall stop me of this boasting in the region of Achaia. Wherefore? because I love you not? God knoweth. But what I do, that I will do, that I may cut off occasion from them that desire occasion; that wherein they glory, they may be found even as we."

It is almost impossible for us to realize the apostle as a tradesman—dressed in an humble garb and handling the implements of his calling, undistinguished in appearance from the operatives round about him, either at their work or at their meals. According to his own maxim, he must have wrought with diligence; not with reluctance, as if he were self-degraded, not idling on pretence of preaching, but "from the heart" doing the one thing which was his duty. How amazing to think of that mighty mind which discussed the divine decrees and argued out a free justification, busying itself with weaving, shaping, or stitching those pieces of coarse haircloth. He who preached the "unsearchable riches of Christ," holds out his hand to receive the wages which he has earned by his industry. He who felt that, in his highest functions, it was "a small thing to be judged of man's judgment," must submit to have his work inspected and approved before he is paid for it. Christ's servant, to arrest and commission whom He had left His glory, to whom He had assigned such work and given such promises and qualifications, is not heralded on his way, is not greeted with applause, nor welcomed by the noble and received into lordly mansions, but is obliged to board with Jewish exiles, and eat his bread "in the sweat of his face." We can with difficulty picture the fingers that wrote the epistle to the Galatians plying a shuttle or handling scissors and needles, and that for daily bread. What thoughts were passing through that heart when he was at his toil—a heart at one with Christ, and embracing the welfare of the world! Its greatest benefactor, next to its Saviour, might be found in a workshop; found there from no reverse, but from deliberate purpose—the orator at Athens a mechanic at Corinth! And when the task of the day was over, he would be found speaking to some group, or meeting some anxious inquirers, or labouring to remove the doubts and prejudices of some unbelievers. And then on the Sabbath day what a change, as he rose in power and zeal to address the synagogue or the church, as an apostle of the Lord Jesus—what an outflood of soul as he reasoned or entreated, or spoke of the life of Christ within him, or the constraining love that lay upon him! Is this the tent-maker?

The preacher did in Corinth what he had done in every town which he had previously visited—he "reasoned in the synagogue, and persuaded the Jews and the *Greeks*"—Greeks, proselytes to the Jewish faith; laboured to convince them that Jesus was the Messiah—the only Saviour on whom they should at once and without hesitation believe. Every available proof from the Old Testament would be brought to bear upon them, as in Antioch, Iconium, Thessalonica, and Berea.

He had been alone in Athens, and alone he had come to Corinth, and for some time he had been evangelizing there before Silas and Timothy joined him. When they arrived, they found him painfully occupied *in the word*, that being the truer reading, and not " in the spirit," as our versionists took it. They found him absorbed *in the word*—in preaching it—more than usually anxious about his labour and the result of it. The " word" which engrossed him was testifying to the Jews that *Jesus was Christ*—discussing and witnessing as to Christ Jesus. The train of proof must have been the same as on former occasions, showing how the oracles of the Old Testament were all so minutely and wonderfully realized in the life and career of the Son of Mary. It would seem as if, up to the arrival of Silas and Timothy, the teaching of the apostle had been more general, but that after their joining him, it had become more pressing and pointed in its great and solitary lesson—that Jesus is the Christ. He had foreseen the result, and had postponed it as long as he could; but when he was joined by his colleagues, and was thus enabled to look to and overtake the gentile field, he at once became so earnest that matters were brought to a crisis. The Athenians would not believe their own poets, and the

Jews would not believe their own prophets. The unbelieving Jews "opposed themselves and blasphemed" as in other places, and the preacher used a symbolic warning and farewell—"shook his raiment, and said to them, Your blood be on your own heads"—this awful expression being taken from Ezekiel. He had done his utmost, had left no means unapplied, had been "instant in season and out of season," and had brought to bear upon them every form of argument which prophecy contained. Therefore he could do no more; the responsibility rested with themselves, and he could only weep over their infatuation and ruin. "I am clear," he adds—no guilt attaches to me, in God's strength I have done my duty—"from henceforth I will go unto the Gentiles;" that is, to the Gentiles in that city, or, if the comma be erased—With a good conscience, and having been rejected by you, I will go, or feel at perfect liberty to go, to the Gentiles.

Accordingly the apostle left the synagogue, resorted no more to it, but selected as his place of preaching the house of a proselyte—Justus—in the immediate vicinity. Whether the Jew Aquila was converted at this time, and whether Paul ceased also to lodge with him, we know not. But his labours had not been without fruit—"the chief ruler of the synagogue believed on the Lord with all his house;" and "many of the Corinthians hearing"—not that Crispus had become a believer, but hearing the gospel—"believed, and were baptized"—probably by Silas and Timothy; for the apostle himself, as he tells us, baptized only Crispus, and Gaius, and the household of

Stephanas; fearing lest it should be surmised that he liked to make men Paulites as well as Christians.

It seems plain from the context that Paul now apprehended danger — such danger as had assailed him at Antioch, Thessalonica, and Berea. He may have either seen the symptoms of it—heard the low moaning of the ocean before the storm—or he may have ascertained that his old enemies were again upon his track. Having missed him in his fortnight's stay at Athens, they might discover him in Corinth; and the fear of this danger may have quickened his desire to revisit Macedonia, into which he had been specially summoned. At all events, the apostle had some grounds of alarm, some apprehensions of a conspiracy, which induced him to think of leaving the city. There are moments when the bravest spirits quail from reaction. Elijah, after confronting the power of the kingdom, matching himself, unaided and alone, against the national idolatry—a single man against eight hundred priests and prophets of Baal—suddenly lost courage when he heard of Jezebel's resentment, and for fear of one woman "went for his life to Beersheba," and, lying under a broom in the desert, sank into such despondency as to say—"Now, O Lord, take away my life, for I am not better than my fathers." The vision vouchsafed to Paul could not, at all events, be unnecessary: *the Lord*—Jesus, whom he served and whom he preached—appeared to him as at Jerusalem, and said—"Be not afraid, but speak, and hold not thy peace." This charge implies that the apostle had some misgivings, but he was at once reassured by the pledge—

"For I am with thee, and no man shall set on thee to hurt thee; for I have much people in this city;" *much people*—not already converted, but to be certainly won over to the gospel through Paul's preaching. "I am with thee" —a repetition of the original promise to the eleven; and no higher pledge could be offered. "I am with thee"—I, the almighty and all-present Living One—a light to cheer him and a shield to protect him, a power to clear up his path and a blessing to crown his labours. "With thee;" not away when expected; not a periodical guard, absent when needed—but with him always and everywhere. So that under this encouragement, and with these hopes, "he continued a year and six months," and during all that period was teaching the *word of God* among them—not any theories of his own, but the divine record of salvation through the blood of Christ. The history in the Acts does not contain any further account of the theme and style of the apostle's preaching at Corinth; but his two epistles to this church afford us the requisite information. He refers in these letters again and again to his subjects of illustration, and to his feelings and circumstances.

And first, he fully and over again states his unvarying theme to have been the cross of Christ—"For I determined not to know anything among you, save Jesus Christ, and Him crucified." More especially and in detail— "Moreover, brethren, I declare unto you the gospel which I preached unto you, which also ye have received, and wherein ye stand: by which also ye are saved, if ye keep in memory what I preached unto you, unless ye have believed in vain: for I delivered unto you first of all that which I also received, how that Christ died for our sins according to the scriptures; and that He was buried, and that He rose again the third day according to the scriptures; and that He was seen of Cephas, then of the twelve: after that He was seen of above five hundred brethren at once; of whom the greater part remain unto this present, but some are fallen asleep. After that He was seen of James; then of all the apostles. And last of all he was seen of me also, as of one born out of due time. For I am the least of the apostles, that am not meet to be called an apostle, because I persecuted the church of God. But by the grace of God I am what I am: and His grace which was bestowed upon me was not in vain; but I laboured more abundantly than they all: yet not I, but the grace of God which was with me. Therefore, whether it were I or they, so we preached, and so ye believed."

Such was the burden of the apostle's message, which he delivered to them *first of all*—first in time, and first also in importance. His first and foremost theme at Corinth was the death of Christ; for His death truly is the central fact of the gospel. What He taught prepared for it, and His power in glory applies its results. He came down not simply to instruct, but also to atone; not only to reveal the will of His Father, but to offer propitiation for the sin of the world. No matter what revelations He has given us, if guilt remain unexpiated, and the sentence of death unrepealed. He took upon Him the nature of man, that He might possess the capability of dying for man. And in man's place, and under his legal liabilities, He did die —obeyed the law and endured its penalty. What more glorious message than this could the apostle proclaim? —God's infinite pity for us; His unspeakable gift of His Son; the Lord Jesus, in unfathomable grace, taking upon Him our nature, and suffering and dying in order to deliver us from the curse of that law which we had broken, Himself yielding to it a voluntary and perfect obedience and enduring its sentence of death.

The apostle preached that Jesus Christ died *for our sins* —on account of them, to make expiation for them. And why should He die if His death had not been indispensable? for, to use His own figure—" Except a corn of wheat fall into the ground and die, it abideth alone; but if it die, it bringeth forth much fruit." There is no harvest without previous death—the seed dies, and by its decomposition nourishes the life of the future plant. We stop not to argue the necessity of Christ's death out of any abstract speculation on the nature of God, the evil of sin, or the principles of the divine administration. Yet, may it not be said that a distinction must ever be maintained between sin and righteousness—that the majesty of law must be vindicated—that a separation must be made between the perfect and the transgressors—that statute must not be weakened by repeated acts of mercy to its violators—and that the unchanging holiness of God must for ever reign paramount in all His ways and works? Normal procedure must have involved the sinner in ruin; but the abnormal process of an innocent one self-offered in room of the guilty, satisfies the claims of justice, exhibits the rectitude of the Judge, and manifests His compassion for the fallen, on whom, but for His infinite love, the original penalty must have been inflicted.

And Christ died for our sins *according to the scriptures*— the Bible contains clear information on the subject. It tells us that though man has incurred the penalty, there is mercy for him—that mercy, however, being always connected with the death of a victim in his room. "Without the shedding of blood there was no remission," under the old economy. Pardon is declared to be based on sacrifice— "The priest shall make atonement for his sin, and it shall be forgiven him." The sacrificial type, while it exhibited the penalty in the vicarious infliction of it, not only showed how deliverance was to be attained, but also predicted the atoning death of Calvary. The phraseology of the Old Testament is employed to describe Christ's death in the New Testament. It was a sacrifice; violent death—a "body broken;" voluntary death—"He gave Himself;" vicarious death—"the just for the unjust;" a death endured as an expiation—"blood shed for remission of sins unto many." Had not such an agony been necessary, why should it have been endured? Of other plans possible to infinite wisdom, this was preferred as being the best to illustrate the divine character, maintain the authority of the divine law, show the true evil of sin, secure the allegiance and harmony of the universe, and provide salvation for mankind.

It is a cheering truth that Jesus endured the penalty— justice being diverted from its natural course, and falling upon the surety; so that the original transgressor escapes.

MISREPRESENTATIONS OF THE ATONEMENT. 255

And why should this procedure stir up such hostility? why should so many men be so anxious to caricature it, and disavow their belief in it? Thus one, and he a transatlantic unitarian, describes it as if the Creator, "in order to pardon His own children, erected a gallows in the midst of the universe, and publicly executed upon it, in the room of the offenders, an infinite being, the partaker of His own supreme Divinity." Another pictures it as if Saul, missing his stroke at David, "had, in disappointed fury, dashed his javelin at his own son Jonathan." A third affirms that the atonement likens God to some heathen divinity who must be appeased—"a thought which refutes itself by the very indignation it calls up in the human bosom." "A relic of heathen conception," says one; "an elaborate process of self-confutation," cries another. That the just should suffer, even though willingly, for the unjust, is not justice, one opponent asserts; and his fellow responds that a man's debt may be freely forgiven, and why not God's? All these objections appear to us frivolous and baseless. The language of scripture gives them no countenance. It declares that God is infinite love and purity; that He vindicates His righteousness while He extends His mercy, and upholds His law while He forgives its unworthy violators. We say not that He is vengeful, and strikes wildly in His anger; but that, in the vindication of His government, He consults the happiness of His universe. For if His law be wantonly broken, and the criminals are treated quite as the unfallen and loyal, then it might be surmised that moral distinctions were obliterated. The vicarious and willing suffering of Jesus is not inconsistent with highest equity, though human analogy fails to illustrate it; and if language have meaning, the phraseology of the New Testament declares that Christ died as a substitute. Are we not "healed by His stripes," "bought with a price"—His "precious blood;" "redeemed from the curse of the law, Christ being made a curse for us?" The plan arose in love, and in love was perfected, when the Father "spared not His own Son, but delivered Him up for us all." The distinctive feature in the atonement is not the unjust sentence which led to it, nor its ignominy or external agony; the nakedness and nails of the cross, nor the personal virtue of the sufferer, though it shone in bright serenity; nor the great penal example which it afforded—but the representative character or position of Him who died—the Son of God who "gave Himself for us an offering and a sacrifice to God." O, this is the precious truth which lifts the burden from the conscience, and leads us to adore and serve the Lamb.

> "Talk they of morals? O, thou bleeding Love,
> The grand morality is love of Thee."

In connection with the death of Christ, the ordinance which commemorates it was enjoined upon the Corinthian church: "For I have received of the Lord that which also I delivered unto you, that the Lord Jesus, the same night in which He was betrayed, took bread: and when He had given thanks, He brake it, and said, Take, eat; this is my body, which is broken for you: this do in remembrance of me. After the same manner also He took the cup, when He had supped, saying, This cup is the New Testament in my blood: this do ye, as oft as ye drink it, in remembrance of me." Paul was not present at the first celebration, but the account which he gave them he received *of the Lord*—by immediate revelation from Him. The institution vividly sets before the mind the love and the death of the Lord Jesus—not His birth or His life, His miracles or His teaching; but His death, and that death as the one source of salvation. It is a communion with Him and with one another over the emblems of His suffering humanity, and a eucharist or scene of devout thanksgiving —an anticipation of the gratitude and song of heaven; but more especially is it a feast, in which, as we " eat of that bread and drink of that cup, we do show the Lord's death till He come." Doctrine is presented in vivid symbol, and participation is imaged as the enjoyment of a banquet. And yet the Corinthians profaned that ordinance or the accompanying love-feast—one being hungry, another being drunken.

Farther, the apostle preached that " Christ was buried." Before the synagogue in the Pisidian Antioch he had also dwelt on this, declaring that "they laid Him in a sepulchre," but yet that " He saw no corruption," as had been predicted of Him by the royal psalmist. He was laid in a borrowed tomb, and in one which had not been previously occupied. Nay, according to the prophet, " He made His grave with the wicked and with the rich in His death ;" or rather, more literally, " there had been appointed to Him His grave with the wicked, but He was with a rich man in His dead state :" that is, three tombs had been prepared for the three men that day to be executed; for any one dying under sentence of law could not be buried in the sepulchre of his fathers. But "a rich man of Arimathea, named Joseph, begged the body of Jesus, and laid it in his own new tomb," "wherein was never man yet laid." Thus prophecy was fulfilled, and the truth of the resurrection confirmed. As we have seen under the last head—" Paul at Athens"—the tomb of Jesus was guarded, and the story of the guard was an inconsistent falsehood. It was a solitary tomb, occupied by its first tenant, and disputes about identity were, therefore, precluded. The burial proved also the reality of the death, and the resuscitation was, therefore, a resurrection. He left the "linen clothes lying, and the napkin that was about His head, not lying with the linen clothes, but wrapt together in a place by itself"—a proof of His calmness and composure as He rose from the realms of the dead. The act of rising was seen by no one; but the tomb was found empty, and ample proof has been vouchsafed. The last honours were paid in haste to His corpse, and the entombment was a melancholy deed to all concerned in it. Because they "trusted that it had been He which should have redeemed Israel," the two disciples on the road to Emmaus were "sad"—all their prospects had been dashed.

But the apostle farther preached that—

"He rose again the third day, according to the scriptures." The proof which the apostle refers to is that of testimony— the testimony of credible witnesses, so placed that they could not be imposed upon, and so honest that they could not stoop to deceive others. He appeared to them in different places, and at different times, the variety of the appearances itself affording evidence of their truth. A man in one position may be deceived, but a number of men in separate circumstances cannot surely be all duped in succession. The apostle selects a few of these appearances, and some of them are not recorded in the gospels. "He was seen of Cephas"—Peter, who had run to the tomb and found it empty, but did not meet the Lord there, as did Mary Magdalene—*seen* of him probably in the forenoon of the day on which He rose. Peter had been singled out for the kind message—"Go, tell my disciples and Peter;" and perhaps he was the first of the apostles to whom singly the Lord showed Himself. "Then of the *twelve*"—the familiar round number being employed to designate the eleven; to the ten, Thomas being absent, He appeared on the first day of His resurrection, and eight days after to the whole eleven, vouchsafing to Thomas the palpable proofs of His identity. The next appearance is not referred to in the gospels, but implied, and it is thus described—"After that He was seen of above five hundred brethren at once; of whom the greater part remain unto this present, but some are fallen asleep." This large assemblage was specially honoured, the only assembly of the size on earth which has enjoyed the singular felicity. Probably in some remote spot, some retreat among the mountains of Galilee, did the spectacle greet the eyes of the five hundred, many of whom had known Him in Nazareth, heard Him in Capernaum, and followed Him by the shores of Tiberias. Was it possible that this whole company were cheated by some hallucination, or made to believe that there was among them He who had been executed in the capital—the true and loving teacher, the illustrious wonder-worker at whose word thousands had been feasted, and every form of disease had vanished? The apostle adds, "After that He was seen of James"—some special manifestation—and "then of all the apostles," prior to His ascension.

Such is a summary of the proof which the apostle adduced in his preaching. All these men bare witness to the resurrection, and they were worthy of credit, as they only testified what they had seen, and they could surely trust their own senses.

Now the resurrection proves the Messiahship, for it not only verified prediction, but proved that Jesus was all in person and commission that He professed to be. If He rose again by His own power, then indeed He was God, and if the Father raised Him, Jehovah could not accredit a deceiver. He was crucified under a charge that He called Himself the Son of God, and He was "declared to be the Son of God with power, by His resurrection from the dead." Put to death as an impostor, He rose again in token that He was "the faithful and true Witness." "If Christ be not risen, then is our preaching vain, and your faith also is vain." It also proved His death to be a perfect atonement. The debt was cancelled when the surety was released. He died to satisfy the law, and rose again as a proof that His death was all which the law demanded, and that the law so satisfied will not demand another victim, or exact another penalty. We point to His empty tomb as evidence of His completed atonement. On the other hand, "if Christ be not raised, your faith is vain, ye are yet in your sins;" there has been no expiation, and there can be no forgiveness. And the apostle, in the sequel of his argument, maintains that Christ's resurrection secures that of His people—" Christ the first-fruits, afterward they that are Christ's at His coming." And they are raised in incorruption, in glory and in power, possessed of spiritual bodies, bearing the image of the last and heavenly Adam, fitted to dwell in a world which "flesh and blood cannot inherit"—the sting having been extracted from death, and the grave spoiled of its victory. "If Christ be not raised, then they also which are fallen asleep in Christ are perished."

Further, when at Corinth, the apostle insisted on the plainest truths—" And I, brethren, could not speak unto you as unto spiritual, but as unto carnal, even as unto babes in Christ. I have fed you with milk, and not with meat; for hitherto ye were not able to bear it, neither yet now are ye able." He did not stretch away into the region of ultimate truths, did not prelect on the " deep things of God," though his great mind had strong likings for the profound, and he loved to tread on the borders of the incomprehensible. But he restrained himself, and set before the Corinthian minds the simplest truths, the clearest facts of redemption. He did not amaze them with compacted argument, or dazzle them with glowing imagery, or transport them with rhetorical displays. Man's sin and Christ's salvation were the twin-truths which he illustrated, without bewildering them with the divine purpose of a past eternity, or the divine developments of an eternity to come. He addressed the Corinthians out of the fulness of his own soul, uttered before them all his convictions, spoke from the heart, in the hope of reaching the heart.

Nay more, the apostle preached at Corinth the plainest truths with the utmost simplicity—"And I, brethren, when I came to you, came not with excellency of speech, or of wisdom, declaring unto you the testimony of God; for I determined not to know anything among you, save Jesus Christ, and Him crucified. And my speech and my preaching was not with enticing words of man's wisdom, but in demonstration of the Spirit and of power; that your faith should not stand in the wisdom of men, but in the power of God." The apostle, then, did not repeat at Corinth the kind of discourse which he had tried at Athens; did not, as he might say of himself in his boyhood—

> "Having lost one shaft,
> I shot another of the self-same flight
> The self-same way, with more advised watch,
> To find the other forth."

No, he preached the cross, and that alone, and having secured such results, having gained so many who were "epistles of Christ," he was anxious that no other form or theme of teaching should be introduced—"According to the grace of God which is given unto me, as a wise master-builder, I have laid the foundation, and another buildeth thereon. But let every man take heed how he buildeth thereupon. For other foundation can no man lay than that is laid, which is Jesus Christ." That foundation is stable and sure, and will support the edifice. The truth concerning Christ does not grow old any more than creation. It is still fresh and mighty, new to every succeeding age which receives it, and is ever to be kept free from contamination or foreign admixtures. Every doctrine must be homogeneous with the great central truth, of the same nature with it, and dependent upon it. He says, *"I determined"*—made a formal resolution, "not to know anything among you, save Jesus Christ;" such a determination seeming to imply that he was under temptation to waver, and to mingle up other allied topics in his addresses, and that he may have felt such a temptation in Athens, when he spoke to its wise men. But he had vowed within himself, that at Corinth the one topic should occupy him, though it should appear "foolishness;" for, by the preaching of that very foolishness, they who believed were saved by God. He also refers to his style more especially, as it may have been brought in contrast with that of the "eloquent" Apollos, and may have been compared with it to the apostle's disadvantage. He spoke without the aids and ornaments of rhetoric. He placed the gospel before them in pure light. A showy eloquence might suit the degenerate taste of the city, but the apostle would not indulge it. He wished to gain men to the truth for the pure love of it, and not for any attractions which might be thrown around it. He would not throw a rainbow over the fountain of life, but wished that thirst and not curious gaze should bring men to it. He would not charm them by his oratory, lest some inferior motive should influence their conviction. He would not put himself in the foreground, and leave his Master in the shadow. He was anxious that men should not praise the preacher to the neglect of his sermon. Himself was nothing, Christ and His cross were everything.

Nor did he array the gospel in the garb of *wisdom*—philosophy. It was, in truth, the highest wisdom—true in its views of man and God, and of the relation between them. Its theology is just, for it reveals a perfect God, and its ethics fit into man's nature. Its God is one to be believed in, loved, and served, faith in such a God being productive of peace and happiness; and its obligations so suit themselves to us, that we feel their equity, and cannot refuse them, assured that obedience will train us to the high end of our being. Given, man's nature as it is—what other creed so speaks home to its spiritual instincts and satisfies them, and what other code of duties so approves itself to his reason, or so brings him under its imperative sway, by simply quickening his consciousness of its authority and truth? But the apostle did not proclaim it in the language of philosophy, did not bury it under rich and redundant illustration, did not employ pretentious terms, or borrow the phrases of the schools. He spoke to them in the tongue of common life—that which they most easily understood: "Which things also we speak, not in the words which man's wisdom teacheth, but which the Holy Ghost teacheth." When a man is in danger, the simplest cry is the most significant to him. But this example set by the apostle has been often lost sight of, and the Bible has been made to speak the nomenclature of human systems: sometimes Aristotelian, sometimes Platonist, and sometimes modern antichristian errors. Thus the combination of two natures in the Redeemer has been profanely taken as a mystic delineation of pantheism—the union of Creator and creature; eternal life has been explained to be, not the immortal happiness of the individual, but only the duration of the species; and the Trinity has been degraded into a metaphysical symbol shadowing out the subjective, the objective, and the relation between them, or the thinker, the thought, and the link that connects them.

To dwell upon the central fact of Christianity—salvation by the cross; to connect all truth with it, and trace all blessings from it; to present it as the living source of hope, and the one stimulus to duty, bringing with it pressure of obligation and ability to comply; to put forth every power in doing this from love to Christ and love to souls; and to do it all the while in earnest simplicity, affectionate fidelity, and constant dependence on Him who " giveth the increase "—that is to preach like Paul.

The apostle when at Corinth was in a state of great dejection—" in weakness, and in fear, and in much trembling." It was a dark and desponding mood, to which a variety of causes might contribute. His signal failure at Athens must have deeply vexed him, and he must have had nervous apprehensions as to his success at Corinth. The scenes were new, and he trembled at his responsibilities. His physical constitution was not robust, and the scourging at Philippi may have seriously impaired it. All men of such susceptibility as Paul are liable to depressions, and when they are exhausted by exertion, and find their great wishes unrealized, the sky darkens over them, and they sink into themselves with grief and alarm. For some weighty reason, implying vexation or difficulty, the apostle at this time put himself under a vow, which lasted till he set sail from Cenchrea. It could scarcely be the formal vow of the Nazarite, but it may have been one of similar self-denial and restraint, his hair being all the while allowed to grow in token of his entire subjection to the will, and devotion to the service of God. Such vows were taken, Josephus says, " by those who were afflicted with disease, or any other distress." The incident shows that Paul during his stay at Corinth was in some critical state —infirm and nervous—and filled with unwonted agitation. His enemies at Corinth said—" His bodily presence is weak," and perhaps he was smarting at the same time from the prickings of the thorn in the flesh, and the buffetings of the messenger of Satan. Still, on a review of his frailties, he could say—" Truly the signs of an apostle were wrought among you in all patience, in signs, in wonders, and mighty deeds." For the preaching of the apostle was sustained and confirmed by supernatural attestation. The Master was with him, as He had been at Iconium, giving " testimony to the word of His grace."

The preaching of the cross produced great results in dissipated Corinth—among the chief of sinners. After enumerating some hideous and revolting classes of sinners, he says to them—" Such were some of you," vilest of the vile, " but ye are washed." Athens in its wisdom had resisted the gospel, but Corinth in its depravity had received it. Their sins became bitter to them, as—

> " The sweetest honey
> Is loathsome in its own deliciousness."

Boasted philosophy closes the soul more effectually against Christ than notorious vice. The heart comes to know its burden, and longs for deliverance; but such philosophy tells it that no deliverance has been provided for it, for its plan is not in accordance with "wisdom." It will not listen in docility, but rejects whatever is not in harmony with its own prepossessions. No physician in Europe above forty years of age believed in Harvey's discovery of the circulation of the blood. They had made up their minds that it could not be true, and nothing could convince them to the contrary. Not a few in the apostle's days, as at all times, preferred opinion to truth, and would not have their cherished notions disturbed or rectified. The scribes refused Christ, but sinners accepted him. Caiaphas doomed Him, while the labouring and heavy-laden found rest in Him. Whence hath He this wisdom, cried some in scorn, but the stilled demoniac sat at His feet. Pilate's wife dreamed of Him, but the Magdalene clung to His knees.

The successes of the apostle, it may be added in conclusion, stirred up his old enemies at Corinth, and "the Jews made insurrection with one accord against Paul, and brought him to the judgment-seat" of Junius Annæus Gallio the proconsul, Achaia having been a few years before handed over to the senate by the Emperor Claudius. They charged Paul with breaking the law—with teaching men "to worship God contrary to the law"—the charge being designedly a vague one, brought before an inexperienced governor. Gallio would not listen to the accusation, and, as the apostle was on the point of replying, he said—"If it were a matter of *wrong* or *wicked lewdness*"—were it really an offence against the state or against morality, "O ye Jews, reason would that I should bear with you; but if it be a question of *words*,"—mere verbal controversy, and "*names*"—such as Jesus or Messiah, " and of *your law* "—your national law, in contrast with the Roman law, "look ye to it, for I will be no judge of such matters." Such disputes did not come within his jurisdiction. Regulate your religious matters in your own way; so long as the peace is kept, I choose not to interfere. "And he drave them from the *judgment-seat*"—the tribunal so sacred to a Roman governor—dismissed them and their case with summary contempt. The heathen hangers-on at once laid hold of the chief complainer, and beat him in the presence of Gallio, either because the Jews had annoyed him and he had so curtly sent them off, or they seized the opportunity because the feud between Jew and Gentile was constant and bitter. The judge had frowned and they struck, glad to have such encouragement. "And Gallio cared for none of those things"—perhaps thought the beating of Sosthenes a just punishment for his forwardness—observed a perfect neutrality between contending religious parties, and, from his well-known gentleness of nature, practised the law of toleration. The reference of this last clause is not to moral or religious indifference, but to his official behaviour as Roman judge on this occasion.

The promise of the Master had been—"No man shall set on thee to hurt thee," and the promise was kept; men had set on him, but they had not been able to hurt him. Remaining in Corinth a considerable time he was unmolested, and then "took his leave of the brethren, and sailed thence unto Syria;" that is, from Cenchrea he crossed, in the first instance, over to Ephesus, Syria being his remoter destination. Though he remained but a brief period at Ephesus, yet he commenced his usual occupation—" entered into the synagogue, and reasoned with the Jews." On being pressed to remain, "he consented not, but bade them farewell, saying, I must by all means keep this feast that cometh in Jerusalem, but I will return again to you, if God will." The feast was probably Pentecost, and by the law, as Josephus describes it, he was bound to appear within thirty days after the shaving of his head in token of the expiry of his vow, and obtain absolution through a certain ritual in the temple. To accomplish this he hastened from Ephesus, " landed at Cesarea," went up to Jerusalem, and "saluted the church." Thus ended the second great missionary journey of the apostle.

XII.—PAUL AT EPHESUS.

Acts xix. 1—41. 1 Cor. xv. 31, 32; xvi. 8, 9. 2 Cor. i. 8, 9, 10.
Epistle to the Ephesians.

On leaving Jerusalem for his third missionary circuit, the apostle "went down to Antioch," and "spent some time there." This city had many attractions for him; there he had laboured with signal success, and in the midst of the brethren his heart was cheered. Leaving it, "he went over all the country of Galatia and Phrygia in order, strengthening all the disciples." At length, "having passed through the *upper coasts*"—inland districts to the east—he came to Ephesus, or returned to it according to promise. Built chiefly on two heights near the mouth of the Cayster, Ephesus had a capacious harbour, where ships of all countries discharged their cargoes, and it had access also to the far interior by the defiles of mount Tmolus and up the valley of the Hermus. Not only had it an extensive trade, but it was also the highway from Rome into Asia. Its situation gave it importance, for it might become a great centre of evangelizing influence. Its ships traded with Greece, Egypt, and the Levant, and the Ionian cities poured their eager and inquisitive population into it at the annual festival in honour of Diana.

On his arrival at Ephesus, where he was to stay for so long a period, Paul found *certain disciples*—Christian converts; and these twelve men were in much the same situation as Apollos is described to have been towards the conclusion of the preceding chapter. They were imperfectly informed, but they were sincere; and they were conscientious in walking up to the measure of their light. The apostle at once accosted them. "He said unto them, Have ye received the Holy Ghost since ye believed? And they said unto him, We have not so much as heard whether there be any Holy Ghost." It is plain that their defective Christianity had struck the apostle with wonder, and suggested these interrogations. The previous conversation is not, indeed, recorded, the results only are given us. The precise point of the question is lost in our translation, for it really is, "Did ye receive the Holy Ghost when ye believed?" The inquiry is not whether at any point of time since their conversion they had received the Holy Ghost, but whether, when on a profession of faith they had been baptized, they had been endowed with the "heavenly gift," especially in its palpable form and manifestation. And their reply is—" But (so far from this) we did not even hear if there is a Holy Ghost." At their baptism they did not hear His name mentioned, far less did they enjoy any effusion. Christian baptism, as the initiatory rite, makes mention of the Holy Ghost, but their baptism was silent about Him. The meaning is not that they were ignorant of the existence of the Holy Spirit promised in the Old Testament, for they were Jews; but that they heard not His name at the critical period referred to. Their answer is, therefore, a strong denial to the question. The apostle at once asked them again, "Unto what then were ye baptized? And they said, Unto John's baptism." This reply explained the peculiarity. Their baptism, omitting all reference to the Spirit, could not be Christian baptism. "Into what baptism, therefore, were ye baptized," is the question, and the reply is, "Into John's baptism"—the baptism administered by him to his countrymen, with its own formula and profession. They were not, however, disciples of John, but of Christ; for John preached Christ, and baptized only those who professed faith in Him as the promised Messiah. But John's baptism was an imperfect ordinance now that Jesus had suffered and died, and gone to glory.

The apostle at this point explained the nature and purpose of John's baptism—"Then said Paul, John verily baptized with the baptism of repentance, saying unto the people that they should believe on Him which should come after him, that is, on Christ Jesus." John's baptism was that of repentance, its watchword being *repentance*—a change of mind and heart, as the preparation for Christ's advent. The apostle used the same terms concerning John in the synagogue at Pisidia, and under that head we have explained them. As he was baptizing, John invariably instructed the people, and his uniform charge was, that they should believe not on himself, but on Christ. And he characterized the Messiah as the One coming after him; for, being His herald, John's descriptive language is, "He that cometh after me;" "there cometh one mightier than I after me;" "He it is who, coming after me, is preferred before me;" "I am not the Christ, but I am sent before Him." Probably "He that cometh after me," was the appellation of Christ formally employed by John when he dispensed baptism. He demanded faith in the Coming One, and the applicant avowed his faith in the Coming One. He did not, indeed, call Him Jesus in his discourses, but the apostle adds in explanation, that Jesus was the individual referred to. The Baptist preached the Christ, and Jesus was the Christ. These men had believed ideally in a coming Messiah when they were baptized; but as they were now to believe really in Him who had come, even Jesus, the old ordinance was not sufficient for them. They were not to be content either with John's doctrine or John's baptism, for both were anticipative. Higher privileges were now presented to them, and they at once embraced them—"When they heard this, they were baptized in the name of the Lord Jesus." It is needless to refer to the notion sometimes advocated, that this verse is a portion of Paul's address in reference to John's hearers, for it simply describes what took place at Ephesus as the result of the apostle's explanation. John's baptism was not Christian baptism. It was administered under commission from the Father, who "had sent him to baptize," and not under commission from the Son. It referred to a coming Saviour, and not to one who had died and was glorified; the Holy Spirit was not named in its formula, for it was the distinctive prerogative of Jesus to confer Him, and many, not all indeed, to whom John had administered the rite, submitted to it again when they were introduced into the church, as on the day of Pentecost. The apostle laid his hands on the men after they had been baptized, "and the Holy Ghost came on them, and they spake with tongues and prophesied."

The gift of tongues was then a common spectacle. It had been conferred at Pentecost, and had spread and perpetuated itself in the church. The plain meaning seems to be, that those who enjoyed it could speak in living languages which they had never learned. This sudden capacity was miraculous, for all of us know what toil is required to master a foreign language, so as to use it with the correctness and fluency of one's native dialect. The linguistic endowment was not only striking, but also useful, for those who had it might employ it as missionaries in other lands, and, though it was abused, the abuse could injure no one. A man might speak many tongues, and indulge in an ostentatious display of them, as seems to have been the case in the Corinthian church; but no one was hurt by his polyglott exhibition — a very different result from what might be imagined had there been bestowed upon the early converts the faculty of inflicting judgments, or of raising the dead.

The prophesying was a species of excited declamation, under the impulse of the Holy Spirit. The persons who enjoyed it were inspired improvisatori, pouring out song and doctrine in animated and exalted phrase. They were not prophets in any official sense, for prophets ranked next to apostles; but they could speak, as the apostle describes it, to "edification, and exhortation, and comfort." Prophesying, whether as an occasional or stated exercise, was useful chiefly "for them that believe." It excited and instructed them, as it rose so freshly out of the spiritual consciousness, and described the high aspects and bearings of Christian truth and ethics. The Spirit so lighted up their spirits, that they saw with a new vision, and He so impelled them, that they could not but speak what they thus beheld.

As his wont had been, the apostle began his evangelical labours in the synagogue. For three months did he labour in it, and in the same strain—"spake boldly, disputing and persuading the things concerning the kingdom of God;" *disputing*—using every form of argument; *persuading*—labouring to convince; *the kingdom of God*—viz., the new dispensation, often predicted under such a title. But the result was as elsewhere—"divers were hardened and *believed not*—disbelieved—gave a positive refusal to the gospel; and not only so, but "spake evil of that way before the multitude"—maligned Christianity so bitterly and boisterously that the apostle's efforts were wholly frustrated. He and the believers, therefore, seceded from the synagogue, and met in the school of one Tyrannus, who might be either a rabbi or a Greek rhetorician. There he was "disputing daily," vindicating the gospel against its assailants, combating their fallacies, and demonstrating the truth of what they opposed and misrepresented. The apostle continued this course "for two years; so that all they which dwelt in Asia heard the word of the Lord Jesus, both Jews and Greeks." The fame of the apostle spread through the province, all round the coasts and far away into the interior—the region of the "seven churches." As he describes it himself, " a great door and effectual is opened." Masses of the heathen population were reached, whether by short journeys of the apostle, or by their thronging into the Ionian capital, or pitching their tents round about it. The reference in the clause last quoted may have been to the period of the Pan-Ionic games, when a vast concourse of strangers crowded into the city, and for a month—the month of May—held holiday in honour of Diana. The apostle would not want an audience amidst such idle masses of the people bent on gratifying curiosity.

If it be asked what the apostle preached during his prolonged sojourn at Ephesus, the answer is easily given, and on his own authority. There was, first, a special polemical contest with the Jews, proving the Messiahship; and that so keen, that they seem to have hated him yet more virulently than did their brethren at Berea or Corinth. And there was, secondly, the exposition and enforcement of the great and distinctive truths of the gospel. But from the context, from the valedictory address at Miletus, and from the epistle to the church of Ephesus we may glean some more special information.

And first and generally, the apostle proclaimed the gospel as a true, divine, and saving revelation. Writing from Rome he says to the Ephesians—"After that ye heard the word of truth, the gospel of your salvation." It was brought by him to them under this character. It was not a new opinion, or a recent speculation, or a system elaborated with infinite ingenuity and effort; but it was the word of truth—an oracle without fiction or ambiguity. As this the apostle proclaimed it; not as its originator, but simply as its herald. He told it, because he had been commissioned to tell it; told it not in fragments, or in shapes of growing clearness and symmetry, but at once in all its fulness and perfection. It is truth; therefore accept it, and live by it. Refuse it; ah! if you refuse it, it is at the peril of your souls; for it is not only truth, but gospel—the *gospel* of your salvation—good news, of which salvation is the theme. Men cannot know what the salvation is till they feel what the danger is. And that danger is beyond description—the guilt and misery of sin—guilt that man cannot expiate, and misery out of which he can by no effort or sorcery charm himself. The sentence of death is upon him—it is in him—" dead in trespasses and sins." And what power but God's can awake him? what pity but God's can touch him? It is perdition if there be no relief—sin being at once its own penalty, and bringing down upon it also the anger of the judge. It is of the essence of sin to entail agony—there being " no peace to the wicked," by an inviolable law of the universe; and not only so, but a positive punishment has also been decreed against it. There is no escape, and those words and images of God contain an awful truth— " Though they dig into hell, thence shall mine hand take them; though they climb up to heaven, thence will I bring them down: and though they hide themselves in the top of Carmel, I will search and take them out thence; and though they be hid from my sight in the bottom of the sea, thence will I command the serpent and he shall bite them: and though they go into captivity before their enemies, thence will I command the sword, and it shall slay them: and I will set mine eyes upon them for evil, and not for good." Must it not, then, be good news to hear of deliverance? not of what it should be, but of what it is; not of the idea of it, but the fact of it; not of it as contemplated, but as provided; not of it as provided only, but also as offered, and offered so freely and universally that any one may accept and possess it. The Ephesians heard Paul preach and they believed, and on their belief were "sealed with that Holy Spirit of promise."

Secondly and personally, Paul preached Christ as the one theme in this word of truth, and the one agent in this salvation. The Ephesians are said on hearing it to have believed on Him—" in whom ye also trusted"—" in whom also ye were sealed"—faith on Him, union to Him. The vagabond Jews, exorcists, used as their spell these words—"We adjure thee by Jesus, whom Paul preacheth." They characterized his preaching by this, and they characterized it truly. He preached Jesus—no one but Jesus—Jesus on all occasions and everywhere—the same in the school of Tyrannus as it had been in the synagogue—the same at his second visit as at his first—the same for two whole years as it had been during the earlier "three months." What nobler theme could he expound than the person of Christ and the work of Christ? the Son of God who veiled His glory and lay in the cradle, "made of a woman"—who " increased in wisdom and stature"—who wrought at His father's occupation, submitting to the curse—who enjoyed " the Spirit without measure," and baffled the assaults of Satan—who spoke such words of love, and did such deeds of kindness—who never sinned in thought or act, and left a pure and attractive example—who opened His heart to the vile and unworthy, receiving sinners and eating with them—who could touch the leper without fear of being infected, and walk in a guilty world without risk of being contaminated—who never showed respect of persons in His intercourse with men, while no form of misery appealed to Him in vain—who suffered Himself to be betrayed, apprehended, tried, scourged, buffeted, blindfolded, spit upon, insulted in every possible way—and who was at length nailed to the cross without reluctance, and in perfect self-devotion to the will of God and the salvation of mankind. This Jesus the apostle held out as the one Saviour, yet living and loving, pleading and sending down His Spirit, giving light to the blind and peace to the disturbed, riches to the poor and health to the diseased, sympathy to the afflicted and comfort to the bereaved—a Saviour, in short, able, and none can doubt His ability—a Saviour willing, and none can impugn His willingness; for the love that brought Him to the cross still glows in His bosom before the throne. Nor could he refrain from preaching Him as Master, presenting a perfect example, and giving ability to copy it—changing believers " into the same image from glory to glory" by His own Spirit given to them. And, as at Athens, he must have pointed to Him as judge, to sit upon His own tribunal and award an infallible and eternal destiny—to welcome His own people to Himself and the glory prepared for them, and doom the unrighteous to " everlasting fire, prepared for the devil and his angels."

In one portion of his letter to the Ephesian church, the apostle says that Christ " came and preached peace to you which were afar off, and to them that were nigh"—preached it through His apostle—preached peace between Jew and Gentile, and reconciliation between both and God;

for "through Him we both have access by one Spirit unto the Father." This Jesus, our Saviour and our peace, Paul preached. Never himself did he preach, or any other than Jesus—the one Saviour and sole foundation of acceptance before God. And what is a discourse without Him? what saving life or power can belong to it? As he writes to them—"Now, therefore, ye are no more strangers and foreigners, but fellow-citizens with the saints, and of the household of God; and are built upon the foundation of the apostles and prophets, Jesus Christ Himself being the chief corner-stone." Christ is the chief corner-stone, and the apostle preached always under this conviction—"that the man, 'Jesus,' who was 'Christ,' the divinely-appointed and qualified and accepted Saviour, unites and sustains the church. Saving knowledge is the apprehension of that truth about Him which Himself has announced—saving faith is dependence on the atoning work which He has done—hope rests in His intercession—the sanctifying Spirit is His gift—the unity of the church has its spiritual centralization in Him—its government is from Him as its King—and its safety is in Him, its exalted Protector. Whether, therefore, we regard creed or practice, worship or discipline, faith or government, union or extension, is He not in His truth, His blood, His power, His legislation, and His presence to His church 'Himself the chief corner-stone?'"

Thirdly and doctrinally, the apostle preached, as himself describes it, "repentance towards God, and faith towards our Lord Jesus Christ." Repentance towards God is that state of heart which every sinner ought to cherish before God, whose law he has broken, and whose sentence he has merited. Surely it is meet for him to feel his sin in all its guilt and aggravation, and especially in this element of it—that it has been committed against God; not to feel it only, but to mourn over it, and confess it frankly and without reserve or apology; and not only to confess it, but to hate it; and as he asks the forgiveness of it, to resolve to forsake it, and now in God's name and in God's strength to follow after holiness. Evangelical contrition is very different from selfish despair; for its language is—" Against thee, thee only, have I sinned, and done this evil in thy sight." And it is equally different from " the sorrow of the world, which worketh death;" for it is the first pulsation of life. It is not the mere remorse which Judas felt when he " went and hanged himself;" for, as there is the hope of forgiveness, the mercy of God is apprehended in the cross of Christ. Sin is seen to be exceeding sinful only in the sin-offering of the Lamb, and the eye of faith alone can realize the vision—" They shall look on Him whom they have pierced and mourn." *Faith toward our Lord Jesus Christ*—faith resting on Him as its one object. For Christ is not Saviour to any one in reality till He be believed in. The heart must rely on Him, assured of His claims. The link of connection between the soul and Christ is faith—the belief of the truth about Him, and earnest and simple reliance upon Him. Faith is thus the cardinal or distinctive grace, and the want of it is fatal; for the message of God is in that case treated as a lie, and Himself as a liar. The apostle preached Christ as an object of faith, and declared that up till the first moment of faith, no saving change is produced on the heart. His order was—Believe Him, and then you may know Him; believe Him, and then you shall love Him; believe Him, and then you cannot but serve Him, and be one with Him: "The life which I now live in the flesh I live by the faith of the Son of God, who loved me and gave Himself for me."

Repentance and faith were his twin doctrines; repentance towards God, as He it is who loved us, though we so heinously sinned against Him; and faith towards our Lord Jesus Christ, as He it is who, bearing the penalty, is "the propitiation through faith in His blood." For repentance and faith are united closely—repentance conditioned by faith, and faith urged and necessitated by repentance. Salvation is forced by God upon no one, and no one can accept salvation till he feel his need of it. The first consciousness of need is the first element of repentance. Conviction of sin begets desire of forgiveness, and such a desire is responded to by God. He who is most deeply sensible of what he is, who knows most truly what sin deserves and what sin is, and who has been alarmed by those heartquakes which it produces, and sighs and groans under his burden—he kneels the most lowly, longs the most vehemently for the grace of God, and cries most earnestly for pardon and peace. The spirit so subdued and softened is prepared for the possession of faith—faith resting on Him who died for sin, who invites and accepts the weeping penitent, and gives "beauty for ashes, the oil of joy for mourning, and the garment of praise for the spirit of heaviness." The process is described in Ps. xxxii., where the royal bard sings his own experience, beginning with the blessedness of that forgiveness, to which he had at length attained; but there had been anguish and groans day and night, when sin lay on his conscience a burning torture, and his nature was not relieved till he made acknowledgment to God. The tale of guilt breathed into the ears of a fellow-man eases the bosom, and lightens its load. So when the soul owns its condition to God, and weeps and mourns for its trespasses against Him, it betters itself in the very act; for it is the first token of confidence in Him. Prior to this hearty and humble confession, the soul is like one in fever, with burning skin, throbbing brow, parched tongue, and utter prostration—his "moisture turned into the drought of summer;" but when he opens his heart to God in earnest trust, it is as when the fever abates, and the aching subsides, and the morbid tension of the frame is reduced, and gentle slumber gives evidence of returning health.

And fourthly, the apostle taught ethically the necessity of holiness, and its connection with heaven as the preparation for it. He says to the Ephesians in reference to his own preaching—"But ye have not so learned Christ; if so be that ye have heard him, and have been taught by him, as the truth is in Jesus: that ye put off, concerning the former conversation, the old man, which is corrupt according to the deceitful lusts; and be renewed in the spirit of your mind; and that ye put on the new man, which after God is created in righteousness and true holiness." And again—"For this ye know, that no whoremonger, nor unclean person, nor covetous man, who is an idolater, hath any inheritance in the kingdom of Christ and of God." In both passages the apostle evidently alludes to his previous and personal instructions—"Ye have not so learned Christ"—"This ye know." When among them he had insisted on purity of heart and life, on entire renovation, the putting off of the old man, renewal in the spirit of the mind, and the assumption of the new man. This purity is called learning Christ and obedience to the truth "as the truth is in Jesus." And he says— "Ye know" it; ye know what holiness and unworldliness are incumbent upon you as expectants of glory.

For Christ is Master as well as Saviour, the object of imitation as well as the object of faith. The design of His death is to bring man back to his primeval state— "righteousness and true holiness." Pardon prepares for holiness—they who are justified are of necessity also sanctified—delivered from the power of sin as well as from its burden—are "turned away from their iniquities." The love of sin must die within them—of every form of sin, no matter what temptation there is to it, or how prevalent is its sway, how lightly the world thinks of it, or how leniently it speaks of it. The sins which the apostle censures in the Ephesian church are yet far from uncommon among us. Intemperance, for example; how many jocular and palliative names are given to it; and impurity—what neutral, nay, graceful terms have been coined to cover its baseness! But Christ's authority interposes, and we dare not tamper with sin; the purity of heaven is before us, and we must be made meet for it. To take sin out of us, to perfect us, to bring us back to what God made us—this is the work of spiritual restoration which Christ effects within us, and which, by resisting temptation, and casting off past habits, and imploring and cherishing grace, we are ever to be forwarding within us. They who seek happiness elsewhere than in Christ, and strive, in the indulgence of appetite or the accumulation of this world's goods, to create a heaven for themselves, have no part in God's heaven, and cannot have any "inheritance in the kingdom of Christ and of God;" for they have no relish for it, neither the hope of it, nor yet any meetness for it. And how, then, can they dwell in it?

Such is a brief sketch of that doctrine which the apostle preached in the city of Diana—no novelty, but the same truth which he had proclaimed in every place he had visited. He knew that this was the only saving truth, to be ever preserved in its simplicity and power; for to add is to impair, and to alter is to corrupt, and to improve is to adulterate it. Restless minds have not been satisfied with the gospel preached by Paul, but would ingeniously modify it. What is called "the new or negative theology," resembling Paul's in little but in name, has been satirized by an American essayist in the form of a parody on the "Pilgrim's Progress," averring that, by the expertness of modern engineering, the old and difficult footpath has been converted into a railway; that the Slough of Despond, into which "twenty thousand cart-loads of wholesome instructions had been thrown without effect," has been filled up with numberless tomes of French philosophy and German rationalism; that the burthen which lay so heavy and galling on the traveller's shoulders till he saw the cross, is snugly deposited in the luggage van; that the roll, which of old was sometimes cumbersome, has been pared down to a neat and elegant ticket; that the Hill of Difficulty has been tunnelled, and with the rock and rubbish excavated from the heart of it, the Valley of Humiliation has been filled up; that the defile of the Shadow of Death is lighted with innumerable jets of brilliant gas which itself exudes from the soil; and that the last chilly river which Christian waded with no few anxieties is now regularly crossed by a capacious steam ferry-boat. The satire is too true. Are not men taught that faith in Jesus is a vanity—that a vague confidence in all-giving Goodness is enough—that sage resolution supersedes change of heart—that the old struggle between flesh and spirit may be neutralized—that the oppression of sin is a self-created dream and burden—that spiritual progress is only daily experience—and that death is but the debt of nature, which no one can grudge to pay?

Alas! for the delusion. Still must each one feel his guilt and look to his Saviour's cross; still must each one enjoy the vital change by which he is born into "newness of life;" still must each one battle with unsubdued appetites and passions, that he may be more than a conqueror; still must each one by himself meet death, and only through Him that died obtain a triumph. It is not every one that hopes for heaven who will enter it; for it is no accidental destiny, neither is it a necessary termination of our career. It is by no law of nature, as the fruit succeeds the blossom, or the insect bursts from the chrysalis, that we come into possession of it.

Christ has died to open up the path, and is Himself "the way, the truth, and the life." Our moral nature is appealed to, that it may credit the testimony of God. Faith, as it secures forgiveness, reunites us to the source of life; the Divine Spirit imparts life to the soul and fosters it there; the kingdom is promised only "to them that love Him"— and faith worketh by love: "Thou wilt guide me by thy counsel, and afterward receive me to glory." O that all of us in humility accepted the Lord, and gave our souls to him—learned at His feet, and leaned upon His bosom— implored, possessed, and never grieved His Spirit—subdued every lust, and flung off every weight—grew into His likeness, and revelled in fellowship with Him—felt His presence to be our chiefest joy and strength—and were prepared "to depart and be with Christ, which is far better." Salvation and heaven are ours only by faith like the centurion's, tears like those of Mary, earnestness like that of the Syro-Phenician mother, and prayer like that of the thief on the cross. Christ, and He alone, is Saviour: "Neither is there salvation in any other: for there is none other name under heaven given among men whereby we must be saved."

Thus did the apostle preach and labour. Opposition, as usual, was stirred up against him, and on one occasion so fierce and brutal was it, that he compares it to fighting with beasts after the manner of men at Ephesus. "There are," he says, writing from Ephesus to Corinth, "there are many adversaries." He shed "many tears," for his countrymen were his principal adversaries. He ceased not "to warn every one day and night with tears." He had no rest, for he taught "publicly, and from house to house." There seem also to have fallen on the apostle other dangers, which have not been recorded: "For we would not, brethren, have you ignorant of our trouble which came to us in Asia, that we were pressed out of measure, above strength, insomuch that we despaired even of life; but we had the sentence of death in ourselves, that we should not trust in ourselves, but in God which raiseth the dead; who delivered us from so great a death, and doth deliver; in whom we trust that He will yet deliver us." We know not to what the allusion is. It can scarcely be to the tumult about Diana, but to some other peril, either sickness, or perhaps assassination all but accomplished through what he calls "the lying in wait of the Jews." For weeks he was a doomed man, and was so aware of it that he despaired of life. The wonder is not that conspiracies were formed against him, but the wonder is that he escaped them all. The shadow of an assassin again and again crossed his path, daggers were pointed at him by invisible hands, oaths were sworn against him, but he bore a charmed life—his hour was not yet come: he "must also see Rome." And with all this earnest and incessant toil, there was no vulgar declamation, for the apostle and his colleagues were solemnly absolved from the charge of being "robbers of churches or blasphemers of the goddess." The missionary proclaimed the truth, and allowed the truth to work its way, and it had "free course;" "all they which dwelt in Asia heard the word of the Lord Jesus, both Jews and Greeks." Nay, Demetrius declares— "Moreover, ye see and hear, that not alone at Ephesus, but almost throughout all Asia, this Paul hath persuaded and turned away much people, saying that they be no gods which are made with hands."

During his stay at Ephesus, the preaching of the apostle was aided by *special* miracles—unusual miracles—"So that from his body were brought unto the sick handkerchiefs or aprons, and the diseases departed from them, and the evil spirits went out of them." As we have elsewhere said—Surprising results sprang from the slightest contact with the wonder-worker; diseases fled at the approach of those light articles of dress which he had touched as the symbols or conductors of divine power; and the "evil spirits," formally acknowledging his supremacy, quailed before him, and were ejected from the possessed. These miracles, as has been well remarked, were of a kind calculated to suppress and bring into contempt the magical pretensions for which Ephesus was so famous. None of the Ephesian arts were employed. No charm was needed, no mystic scroll or engraven hieroglyph; there was no repetition of uncouth syllables, no elaborate initiation into any occult and intricate science by means of expensive books, but shawls and aprons were the easy and expeditious vehicles of healing agency. The superstitious "characters" which the Megalobyzi and Melissæ—the priests and priestesses of Diana—had so carefully patronized and made popular amulets throughout the Eastern world, were shown by the contrast to be the most useless and stupid empiricism. That indeed they were so in themselves, is evident from their structure. An old Greek lexicographer, himself a native of Alexandria, in the fourth century, gives a specimen of the gibberish—Aski, Kataski, Lix, Tetrax, Damnameneus, Aision; adding that according to tradition the first word meant darkness, the second light, the third the earth, the fourth a year, the fifth the sun, and the last truth. The construction of such recipes had risen to the rank of a popular science.

Some Jewish exorcists—a class which was common among the "dispersion"—attempted an imitation of one of the miracles, and used the name of Jesus as a charm. But the demoniac regarded such arrogant quackery as an insult, and took an immediate vengeance on the impostors —"Jesus I know, and Paul I am acquainted with, but who are ye? And the man in whom the evil spirit was, leaped on them, and overcame them, and prevailed against them, so that they fled out of that house naked and wounded. And this was known to all the Jews and Greeks also dwelling at Ephesus, and fear fell on them all, and the name of the Lord Jesus was magnified." This sudden and signal defeat of the seven sons of Sceva produced a deep and general sensation among the Jews and Greeks, and "the name of the Lord Jesus was magnified." Nay more, the followers of magic felt themselves so utterly exposed and outdone, that they "confessed and showed their deeds." They were forced to bow to a higher power, and acknowledge that their "curious" arts were mere pretence and delusion. Books containing the description of the secret power and application of such a talisman must have been eagerly sought and highly prized. Those who possessed them now felt their entire worthlessness; and, convinced of the inutility and sin of studying them, or even keeping them, gathered them and burnt them "before all men"—an open act of homage to the new and mighty power which Christianity had established among them. The smoke and flame of those rolls were a sacrificial desecration to Diana—worse and more alarming than the previous burning of her temple by the madman Herostratus. The numerous and costly books were then reckoned up in price, and their aggregate value was found to be above two thousand pounds sterling. The sacred historian, after recording so decided a triumph, adds with hearty emphasis—"So mightily grew the word of God and prevailed."

But "no small stir" was made by the progress of Christianity, and its victorious hostility to magic and idolatry. The temple of Diana or the Oriental Artemis had long been regarded as one of the wonders of the world, and "all Asia" worshipped the goddess. The city claimed a title which, meaning originally "temple-sweeper," was regarded at length as the highest honour, and often engraved on the current coinage. The town-clerk artfully introduced the mention of this honour into the commencement of his speech; for though the whole province claimed an interest in the temple, and it was often named the temple of Asia, yet Ephesus enjoyed the special function of being the guardian or sacristan of the gaudy edifice. And the Ephesians were quite fanatical in their admiration and wardenship of the magnificent colonnades. Their quarries of Mount Prion had supplied the marble; the art and wealth of Ephesian citizens, and the jewellery of Ephesian ladies, had been plentifully contributed for its adornment; its hundred and twenty-seven graceful columns, some of them richly carved and coloured, were each the gift of a king; its doors, ceiling, and staircase were formed respectively of cypress, cedar, and vinewood; it had an altar by Praxiteles, and a picture by Apelles; and in its coffers reposed no little of the opulence of Western Asia. A many-breasted idol of wood, rude as an African fetich, was worshipped in its shrine, in some portion of which a meteoric stone may have been inserted, the token of its being "the image that fell down from Jupiter." Similar superstitions belong to various countries, such as the Palladium of Troy, the Ceres of Sicily, the Minerva Polias of Athens, and the Diana of Tauris. Somewhat of the same nature were the shield of Mars at Rome, the black stone in the Caabah at Mecca, that in the temple of the Sun at Baalbec, and the Lia Fail, or stone of destiny, on which the Scottish kings were for many centuries crowned at Scone. Popularly supposed in those ancient times to be a portion of Jacob's pillar, it was thought to be so connected with the destiny of the kingdom, that wherever it happened to be, there should reign the Scottish race, and though it was removed by Edward to Westminster Abbey, where it now forms the support of the coronation chair of the British sovereign, the old prophecy was fondly believed to be verified when James VI. ascended the English throne on the death of Elizabeth.

Still further, a flourishing trade was carried on in the manufacture of silver *shrines*—medallions, or models of a portion of Diana's temple. These are often referred to by ancient writers; and as few strangers seem to have left Ephesus without such a memorial of their visit, this artistic business "brought no small gain to the craftsmen." But the spread of Christianity was fast destroying such gross and material superstition and idolatry; for one of its first lessons was, as Demetrius rightly declared—"They be no gods which are made with hands." The shrewd craftsman summoned together his brethren of the same occupation, laid the matter before them, represented the certain ruin of their manufacture, and the speedy extinction of the worship of Diana of Ephesus— "So that not only this our craft is in danger to be set at nought, but also that the temple of the great goddess Diana should be despised, and her magnificence should be destroyed, whom all Asia and the world worshippeth." The trade was seized with a panic, and raised the uproarious shout—" Great is Diana of the Ephesians!" "The whole city was filled with confusion." A mob was gathered, and seemed on the eve of effecting what Demetrius contemplated, the expulsion or assassination of the apostle and his coadjutors by lawless violence, so that no one could be singled out or punished for the outrage. The emeute was so sudden, that "the most part knew not wherefore they had come together." As usual on such occasions in the Greek cities, the rush was to the theatre, to receive information of the cause and character of the outbreak. Two of Paul's companions were seized by the crowd, and the apostle, who had escaped, would himself have very willingly faced the angry and clamorous rabble if his friends, seconded by some of the Asiarchs, or presidents of the games, had not prevented him. A Jew named Alexander, probably the "coppersmith," and, as a Jew, well known to be an opponent of idolatry, strove to address the meeting, probably to vindicate his own race from being the cause of the disturbance, and to cast all the blame upon the Christians. But his appearance was the signal for renewed clamour, and for two hours the theatre resounded with the fanatical yell—" Great is Diana of the Ephesians." The "town-clerk" or recorder, a magistrate of high standing and multifarious and responsible functions in these cities, had the dexterity to pacify and dismiss the rioters, first, by a judicious admixture of flattery, and then by sound legal advice, telling them that the law was open, that the great Ephesian assize was going on, and that all charges might be formally determined before the sitting tribunal. Such a scene could not fail to excite more inquiry into the principles of the new religion, and bring more converts within its pale. After the tumult, the apostle, having called unto him the disciples and embraced them, immediately left the city.

XIII.—PAUL AT TROAS.

Acts xx. 5—12.

BEFORE he left Ephesus, the apostle had formed the resolution of visiting Macedonia and Achaia on his way toward Jerusalem. In the meantime he had sent as his pioneers into Greece, Timothy and Erastus the chamberlain. But after the tumult in the city of Diana, he left at once for Macedonia—"And when he had gone over those parts, and had given them much exhortation, he came into Greece." It would appear that the apostle stayed some time at Troas, where "a door was opened unto him of the Lord." But having "no rest" in his spirit because he found not Titus, and unable longer to endure the suspense, he sailed by himself for Macedonia. Somewhere in this province Titus met him, and though he says, "Our flesh had no rest, but we were troubled on every side—without were fightings, within were fears," yet he admits that the good report which Titus brought from Corinth filled him with comfort and joy. It is probable that at this period he extended his journey to the west, and travelled as far as Illyricum, preaching the gospel, as he tells the Roman church in an epistle written soon after. In Greece, that is, southern Greece as distinguished from Macedonia, he "abode three months." "As he was about to sail into Syria," the Jews, unchanged in their animosity, laid wait for him, so that he altered his determination, and purposed to return through Macedonia. Seven friends accompanied him, representing the Asiatic and European churches, and probably intrusted with the offerings made for the poor saints at Jerusalem; and "these going before tarried for us at Troas." Leaving Philippi, the apostle, after a few days' sailing amidst adverse winds and currents, arrived at Troas, and there "abode seven days," the last of them being a Sabbath.

The "first day of the week" appears to have been the usual period of assembly, and no doubt was selected and consecrated by apostolical authority. It was held in honour of the Saviour's resurrection—that event which proved His mission divine, His mediation effectual, and His combat with death and hell victorious. Being the day of the Lord's resurrection, it was noted as His day—"the Lord's day," when His people meet for His worship and His truth is expounded, His name chaunted, His Spirit poured down, His presence enjoyed, and His death showed forth. The place of meeting in Troas would be an humble one, with no architectural decorations, the private dwelling of some large-hearted disciple, in whose upper chamber the sacred feast was observed. It would appear that at first in Jerusalem, when the disciples kept free table, or "had all things common," every meal was a sacramental feast, or that it was connected with every meal, as it had been with the paschal banquet. It was therefore not as with us, the mere emblem of a feast—only the symbol of a symbolical feast. Out of this old practice may have sprung its early division into a love feast and a sacrament. The church at Troas may have possessed no regular organization, but the disciples could meet in hearty fellowship, and eat and drink in memory of the crucified One. Twice had Paul been in that city before; the first time when he was hurried across to Europe, and again on his second visit to Macedonia, when he seems to have lingered some time waiting for Titus. During this third visit he stayed a week, and preached on the Lord's day.

The disciples must have rejoiced at their privilege, and eagerly embraced it. What could keep any of them back from enjoying Paul? Alas! that so many in modern times regard so little the first day of the week, or weary on it only for the coming of the second, reckoning Sunday a mere interruption between Saturday and Monday, or otherwise profaning it in the pursuit of lawless pleasure or pastime. And even of those who "come together," how many stay away for very trivial reasons, a passing cloud throwing a chiller shadow upon their souls than it does upon the earth, and betokening a fall in their religious affections deeper than the depression of the barometer. If one may thus absent himself, why may not all; the minister, too, as well as any of the people? Who keeps at home for such a paltry reason from a scene of secular enjoyment, or the place of ordinary business? Are there not many sicknesses so cunning in their coming and going, so endowed with forethought as never to invade a week-day, but to appear with the dawn of Sabbath and disappear on its evening? Is it not a law of our nature that difficulties grow with indulgence, and if weather regulate church-going, other barriers will soon make themselves be felt—irregularity followed by long pauses, and ending in utter spiritual remissness and death. Does not such fluctuation in duty deprive one of the divine promise, and may it not rob him of the very word which was adapted to his benefit? And if heaven is an eternal Sabbath for which this recurring Sabbath prepares, how can any one hope to enjoy it who cries out as to "the weariness" of the periodical rest on earth—who finds not exceeding luxury in social worship, or who regards not the day which God has blessed and sanctified as the happiest, holiest day of all the seven?

> "Light of light! enlighten me,
>   Now anew the day is dawning;
> Sun of grace! the shadows flee,
>   Brighten Thou my Sabbath morning.
> With Thy joyous sunshine blest,
> Happy is my day of rest!
>
> "Kindle thou the sacrifice
>   That upon my lips is lying;
> Clear the shadows from my eyes
>   That, from every error flying,
> No strange fire within me glow,
> That Thine altar doth not know.
>
> "Let me with my heart, to-day,
>   Holy, holy, holy, singing,
> Rapt awhile from earth away,
>   All my soul to Thee up-springing,
> Have a foretaste inly given
> How they worship Thee in heaven.
>
> "Hence all care, all vanity,
>   For the day to God is holy;
> Come, Thou glorious Majesty,
>   Deign to fill this temple lowly:
> Nought to-day my soul shall move,
> Simply resting in Thy love!"

"And upon the first day of the week, when the disciples came together to break bread, Paul preached unto them, ready to depart on the morrow, and continued his speech until midnight." Paul preached unto *them*—the Trojan church. Preaching was his function. It was the high office to which he had been set apart by Him whom He preached. The inspired men under the Old Testament did not preach. They proclaimed the will of God in a variety of forms. Moses enacted statutes, prescribed duty, and predicted national results, as patriot and legislator; Joshua, after his sword was sheathed, swore the nation to fidelity; Samuel judged and taught with divine authority; David sang as saint and king, and gave utterance to emotions common to the church in every age; Elijah challenged and battled for God in days of idolatrous degeneracy; Solomon embodied his experience in pithy and pointed sentences—each as a "nail fastened in a sure place"—and even in that book where he calls himself "the preacher," he declaims chiefly on the vanity of human pursuits and enjoyments. The prophets as a body portrayed present obligation and future crises. The burdens pronounced by Isaiah ring over Babylon, sweep through the wilderness, and are borne up the Nile. Jeremiah, Ezekiel, and Daniel interest themselves with national affairs and theocratic history and relations. Obadiah seals the fate of Edom, and Haggai and Malachi censure the selfishness of their age. These old seers foretold Messiah, but did not exhibit Him; they pictured Him, but did not preach Him. Their style is often dark in its gorgeous drapery. Figure and hyperbole, sudden changes and dramatic visions distinguish them. Now it is the warlike note of a trumpet, and now it is the wail of a dirge; now it is a peal of thunder, and now a night of woe and havoc; and now a flood of that "unearthly lustre which ne'er was seen on sky or shore." But the apostle preached—taught the simplest truths in direct and plainest shape, threw around them no embellishment, but placed them under clear sunlight, so that each might perceive and comprehend them. He spoke not of the fortunes of nations, but of churches; detailed not the annals of kingdoms, but strove to make each man's history an image of Christ's, dating from a new birth and opening into life eternal. His work was with souls—their condition and duty; and he portrayed the one and enforced the other so lucidly and fully, that each saw himself in the portrait, and recognized his obligation in the appeal

The Greek critic Longinus says, "that Saul of Tarsus, as an orator, was the first who excelled in undemonstrated statements," which probably may be taken by us as meaning that he spoke and wrote with such a consciousness of truth, that he did not reason out his assertions as if they might be doubted, or state premises and draw formal syllogistic conclusions. His was no artificial rhetoric, elaborated according to rule and method—"We also believe, and therefore speak." He threw out his glowing thoughts rudely sometimes, but never feebly; in broken sentences and disorderly constructions, but ever with a force that proved his sincerity, and tended to beget a sympathy with his fervour. He who delivers an oracle must speak very differently from a practised sophist. He who had seen the Lord in glory could not tell of Him in tardy or doubtful terms, could not waste his time in wading among neutral questions, and could not speak as if he were propounding some philosophic novelty which needed a high effort of logic and oratory to recommend it.

Paul preached unto them—it had been his wont. It was his usual mode of address. Wherever he found himself he preached. If he travelled, it was to preach; at the stages where he rested he preached, and when he came to the end of the journey he preached. No matter who composed his audience—the Jew or the Gentile, the rustic or the intelligent, the philosophical people of Athens or the debauched residents of Corinth—he preached. He never feared frown nor scourge, the sneer of the sophist nor the senseless laugh of the profligate. Meet with him where you will, you hear him preach. You do not discover him surveying ruins or measuring temples, admiring works of art, or mingling with the populace for the sake of amusement, that he might smile at their follies or learn their customs. You do not find him at Troas exploring the scenes of the great legend, the " tale of Troy divine," before which Achilles fought, Agamemnon ruled, Ulysses counselled, and Ajax heaved his strength—" the bulwark of the Greeks "—by the banks of the Simois and Scamander. No; every man he beheld filled him with sorrow and hope, for that precious soul was soon to pass into the presence of the Judge. He saw him as Christ saw him; not as a Greek or a Jew, a rich man or a poor man—but a human being, guilty and helpless, to whom salvation might be offered, and by whom it should be accepted; saw his soul in its value and destiny—undone if unbelieving—and urged him to accept Christ and His cross. And therefore he preached, "warning every man, and teaching every man in all wisdom."

Paul preached unto them; what else could he do? Necessity was laid upon him—"Yea, woe is unto me," says he, "if I preach not the gospel." What other substitute for preaching can be devised? Ceremonial will not do; souls may perish in ignorance amidst genuflections and music. Satire will not suffice. What effect had Juvenal and Martial on their age, or on the world? It is far from being a perfect work to cast contempt on society for its frivolous and unmanly attachments; to expose the hollowness of civilization, and call its pursuits a sham. To exhaust the vocabulary of scorn and vituperation, or to denounce with bitterest eloquence the want of faith and sympathy, exposing what is evil, without pointing what is good and wooing men to do it; to throw gleams of ethereal beauty over the darkest picture of man and his misery, with the genius of a poet and the grim mood of a prophet, and yet to open up no refuge for him, and ply him with no arguments to rush into it—is only to mock him—to give him a stone for bread when he is hungry. This is not the preaching of the apostle. His was a nobler work. If he cursed, he likewise blessed; if he thundered, he also wept; if he scathed and killed, he at the same time brought life and health. It is no gospel to tell men what they are, without showing them what they might be; to prove them dupes and wretches without pressing upon them truth and blessing. One can conceive the glee of a fiend as he alternately frightened and soothed men—indulging in the work as a prime gratification—for it did no good, but only inflicted misery. But far different was Paul. He taught salvation—preached Christ; showed the path of glory; never spoke of guilt without speaking of the blood of expiation; never expounded our condition without inviting us to deliverance; or declared our destiny without assuring us that life and immortality have been brought to light. If preaching was the presentation of the good news, what else could the apostle do than preach?

Paul preached unto them; what better could he do? Had he any other news which could be called good news, or any other speculation fraught with spiritual power and joy? Was there any salvation but by the cross—any other road to heaven but that by Calvary? He had no alternative gospel, and he allowed no choice. He might have done many things—might have prelected on Jewish history or Grecian philosophy; delivered his views of man's mental and moral nature; described what he had passed through—the peoples he had seen, and the scenes he had visited; how he had been lacerated by the scourge, and tossed upon the billow; delineated what was striking in his experience of men and manners—sometimes the materials of a comedy, and oftener those of a tragedy; or he might have given readings from the bards of Judea, or the orators and dramatists of Greece. But with such employment never could he have saved a soul, or gathered a church. Preaching far excels philosophy and oratory, and yet it is genuine philosophy and living oratory. No romance equals in wonder the story of the cross; no shapes of wonder have the divine style of Christianity; and no mode of speaking can surpass, in pathos and penetration, that of a man to his sinful fellows, on the themes of God and eternity, Christ and heaven. A sermon is not a harangue constructed so as to be praised for its depth, its fancy, or its elaborate paragraphs; nor is it a piece of rhetoric to be executed before an admiring audience. The preacher is not like Demosthenes declaiming on Macedonian invasion, Cicero on Catiline's conspiracy, Chatham on continental hostilities, Burke on the French revolution, Pitt on democratic aggression, Fox on the repeal of an obnoxious tax, Canning on the balance of power, Brougham on slavery, or Peel on fiscal regulations. For he has a higher aim than to repel the invader, and deliver his country from change, turmoil, or tyranny—a higher aim than to emancipate the fettered, secure peace among nations, or fill their harbours with ships and their warehouses with costly imports—a higher aim than to raise and enlighten the masses, loosen the shackles of commerce, and lighten the springs of industry, so that none may stand "in the market-place idle" because no man hath hired him, and every one hired be amply compensated for bearing the "burden and heat of the day." These may be the results, but they are not the end. While the preacher may not withhold himself from the advocacy in its place of any just and liberal measure having man's good in view in any respect—his aim stretches beyond all those aims; for they may be enjoyed, and yet the object of the gospel not be realized.

Nor must he wait till those ends be secured. Shall

the physician abnegate his function, and refuse to attend the sick man till he is convalescent? The gospel does not haughtily stand back from the slave, and refuse to embrace him till his chain be broken, but it gives him spiritual hopes and freedom in his captivity. It does not pause at the frontier of a nation groaning under tyranny, but it enters and gives its liberty to the oppressed. It meets man in any condition, and cheers and blesses him. It needs not civilization to precede it. It does not require that man shall have all that earth can give him, ere it turn his hope to heaven. No; as it finds him, it appeals to him and bids him believe it. Still, though it be independent of external influences, its results are all of an ennobling character, and it gives stability to education, liberty, government, and commerce. The advancement of man's spiritual good tends to elevate his temporal condition. It gives him the consciousness of being a child of God and an heir of immortality, and teaches him to act in no sense inconsistently with his dignity and prospects. It leads its disciple to glory, but forgets him not on his journey toward it. His title to heaven enables him to assert his position on earth. Christ has bought him, and why should he be the slave of man? If he can be free, he will "use it rather." He may not at all times succeed, but, though the day of his death be the first day of his emancipation, he has been ransomed by the precious blood of Christ, and he enters into rest. Is not this the glory of the gospel, that it salutes man everywhere and in every condition? It is not ashamed of his fetters, nor repelled by the colour of his skin. It shrinks not from the gloom of the dungeon, or the dreariness of the work-house, and revolts not at the bleeding couches of the hospital. It is neither awed by a coronet, nor shamed away by the bared and cold hoariness of age. It offers itself as freely to him in purple and fine linen in the mansion, as to him who is huddled in rags at the gate. It crosses the frontier and laughs at the sentinel's bayonet; it has its good centurions in the army; it enters the barrack in spite of its dissipation; its sunshine fills the cottage; nay, it "is found in kings' palaces," and it triumphs in the midst of licentiousness and blood—"They that are of Cæsar's household salute you."

Paul preached unto them—what better could the apostle do than preach? preach with all that power which distinguished him, as well as with that knowledge and application of the scripture, that keen insight into human nature, that perfect mastery of motives, that entire self-abnegation, and that earnest and repeated pressing of his theme upon his audience, for life and death were at stake—by which his reported addresses are characterized. He was unpretending, indeed, in appearance, feeble in health, and agitated by the various passions of his soul; his strength was in his frailty; "his speech was contemptible," "rude," as he admits, possibly in accent and gesture, but glorious in its theme, and mighty in the faith and fervour of him who employed it—

> " Weary souls by thee are lifted;
> Struggling souls by thee are strengthened;
> Cloud of fear asunder rifted;
> Truth from falsehood cleansed and sifted;
> Lives like days in summer lengthened."

It may be inferred from the narrative, that, as an apostle,

he presided at the ordinance of the Supper. How memorable such a scene in that church on the night when Paul broke the bread of life in the Master's name, and gave thanks over it after the Master's example! From the lips of that weak and worn-out traveller, what words of truth and power would flow! How he would speak of the death of Christ—he who had himself been "crucified with Christ!" With what impressive power he would revert to the scenes of the last sufferings—the agony in the garden, the capture and trial, the sentence and the scourging, the procession to the cross, and the torture endured upon it, till He "bowed His head and gave up the ghost!" How he would glow as he spoke of that love which the Redeemer displayed in dying for lost souls; of the meekness of His character and the openness of His heart; of the tears He shed, and the wise and affectionate words which He uttered; of the deeds of mercy He did, and the pure and fascinating life which He led! How his heart would melt, and his accents thrill, as he repeated the words—"Take, eat; this is my body." How he would speak, as he felt from the deeps of his own enraptured experience, words of electric power, stirring those whom he addressed into kindred emotion.

The eating of bread and drinking of wine betoken a feast and a family circle. Might not the apostle dilate on that love which Christians should display to one another — each loving the image of Christ — praying for one another's welfare, and striving together for it; drawing the bonds of the gospel closer round them; "kindly affectioned one to another"—"in honour preferring one another?" O what a cheering banquet it must have been, with the principal part of the conversation sustained by Paul, on his last journey to Jerusalem, and under the solemn impression that his career was drawing to a close. The fragrance and softness of heaven would breathe in his words, as he counselled the communicants to remember Jesus, to grow in faith on Him, to pray for more likeness to Him, to serve Him yet more devotedly, and suffer for Him yet more joyously—to bear Him in their hearts, and manifest Him in their lives.

The apostle "continued his speech till midnight"—the interview, as being the last, was naturally prolonged. There were "many lights in the upper chamber"—the moon was but young—and the assembly cared not though they were seen of all men. A young man seated on the bottom of the unclosed window became overpowered with sleep, and fell into the court from the "third loft," in which the upper room was situated. But the consternation at this fearful incident was hushed at once, when Paul, acting like Elisha, "went down and fell on him, and, embracing him, said, Trouble not yourselves, for his life is *in him*"—as restored to him by miracle. After the miracle the conversation was renewed, and carried on till the morning broke upon the heights of Ida: then the sad farewells were exchanged— "so he departed."

XIV.—PAUL AT MILETUS.

Acts xx. 17—38.

On leaving Troas, the companions of the apostle took shipping for Assos, and left him to walk to that town by land. The distance is twenty-four Roman miles, and we do not know why the apostle preferred a solitary pedestrian journey, but we are told, "for so had he appointed, minding himself to go afoot." No doubt he wished to be as long with the Trojan converts as possible, and he saved himself a tedious voyage, as the vessel had to round the promontory of Lectum before it reached Assos. He met his company at Assos, and embarking with them "came to Mitylene," the capital of Lesbos, a voyage of about thirty miles. The next day they were "over against Chios," the modern isle of Scio; the following day they arrived at Samos, remaining for the night at Trogyllium, and on the morrow they came to Miletus, a seaport about thirty miles from Ephesus. The reason why the apostle did not visit the latter city is thus given—"For Paul had determined to sail by"—that is, past—"Ephesus, because he would not spend the time in Asia; for he hasted, if it were possible for him, to be at Jerusalem the day of Pentecost."

The apostle could not go himself to Ephesus, either lest his presence should be the occasion of another tumult, or lest his journey to Jerusalem should be retarded, and his arrival before Pentecost rendered impossible; nor could he summon the entire church to him, as such a large concourse might have excited suspicions, and led to dangerous consequences. But he convened the elders, as the rulers and representatives of the church, and delivered them his counsels. His very words seem to have been preserved, and thus he spoke—" Ye know yourselves, from the first day that I came into Asia, after what manner I have been with you during the whole time, serving the Lord with all humility, and with tears and trials befalling me through the plots of the Jews; how I have kept back none of the things which are profitable to you, so as not to tell and to teach you in public and from house to house, testifying both to Jews and also to Greeks repentance towards God and faith towards our Lord Jesus Christ. And now, behold, I go bound in spirit to Jerusalem, not knowing the things about to encounter me there: save that the Holy Ghost testifies to me from city to city that bonds and afflictions await me (in Jerusalem). But I hold my life of no account, not even so precious to myself as to finish my course with joy, to wit the ministry which I have received from the Lord Jesus, to testify the gospel of the grace of God. And now, behold, I know that you all, among whom I went about preaching the kingdom, shall see my face no more. Wherefore I take you to witness this very day that I am clear from the blood of all; for I have not kept back from declaring to you the whole counsel of God. Take heed to yourselves, therefore, and to all the flock in which the Holy Ghost has made you overseers, to feed the church of God which He has purchased with His own blood. I know that after my departure shall grievous wolves enter in among you, not sparing the flock. And also out of your own selves shall men arise, speaking perverted things, so as to draw away disciples after them. Therefore watch, remembering that, for the space of three years, night and day I ceased not with tears to warn every one of you. And now, brethren, I commend you to God, and to the word of His grace, even to Him who is able to build you up, and give you an inheritance among all them that are sanctified. Silver, or gold, or raiment of no one did I covet. Ye yourselves know, that to my wants, and to those who were with me, these hands ministered. In all ways (by example as well as by doctrine) I showed you that it is bounden on you so to labour as to support the helpless, to remember, too, the words of the Lord Jesus, that Himself said—'It is more blessed to give than to receive.'"

Part I.

INTRODUCTORY APPEAL TO THE PAST—HIS FIDELITY.

The apostle begins by appealing to their own experience of himself. His whole conduct was patent to them—" Ye know from the first day that I came unto Asia after what manner I have been with you *at all seasons* "—the entire time. His object is not to glorify himself, or so to picture his life as to induce their admiration, as if they had not already paid him sufficient homage. But he bids them follow his example, and imitate his patience, his courage, his tenderness, and his unwearied effort to win souls to Christ. His was no life of idleness; he travelled but to labour, and laboured that he might find leisure to travel again and work at the end of his journey.

And he characterizes his career as that of one "serving the Lord." The Lord had special claims on his service; for he had arrested him, and had changed and blessed him. The Lord had bought him, and he could not but serve such a master. The bond of redeeming love laid him under solemn obligations which he uniformly felt. His, too, was special service, that which the Lord both enjoins and exemplifies. The Lord's work in heaven is salvation, and Paul's service on earth was identical with it. The instrument he wrought with was the highest form of truth —the gospel; and the sphere of his operations was the most precious on earth—man's immortal soul. And he served not as a hireling; his heart was wholly in his work; the conversion of sinners was a pure passion within him. He spent himself in this work, and delighted to spend himself in it. He could not live for a holier purpose, nor die in a nobler cause. And though his honour was commensurate with his toil, yet he served "with all humility." He never was elated, as if he had done too much, or even was satisfied, as if he had done enough. "Less than the least of all saints," he styles himself in a letter to this church, the elders of which he was now addressing.

Though his preaching had provoked fierce opposition, his brave heart quailed not, but he wept as he laboured—he served "with many tears." He wept not for himself, but for his foes. His tears were wholly unselfish, like those of his Lord over doomed Jerusalem. "Temptations," he adds, "which befell me by the lying in wait of the Jews:" his trials sprang from his countrymen, whom he loved in spite of their rancour. The incidents are not given in the narrative, but we gather from other allusions that the apostle had met in Ephesus with ferocious opposition. In that city he had, "after the manner of men," fought "with beasts;" "a great and effectual door was opened, but there were many adversaries." This language, so strong and pointed, warrants the idea that the apostle's enemies had both been malignant and numerous, and that he had been among them like a victim braving at fearful odds the lions in the arena—one against many; a single man in front of bloody and unscrupulous antagonists eager to spring upon him, and yearning for his death.

The "lying in wait of the Jews" was more to be feared than the blunt fury of the guild of silversmiths whose craft had been endangered. The worshippers of Diana were open and lawless in their rage, but the Jews crouched and watched the opportunity offered, stooped to any artifice and submitted to any ignominy so as to gain their object. Such conduct well-nigh broke the apostle's heart. It did not agitate him with terror, but it filled him with sorrow. He did not curse—he wept over such blindness and obstinacy.

But the furious opposition of the Jews did not induce the apostle to mutilate the gospel which he preached. He "kept back nothing that was profitable," no truth that could secure their spiritual benefit. If it was to be of advantage to them he gave it prominence, no matter how repugnant it might be to his opponents. He still insisted on the Messiahship of Jesus, and on his atoning death as His prime work. Nor did he publish these tenets in whispers, or give dubious expression to them in darkened chambers. He dilated on them, gave them ample and repeated illustration, or, as he declares—"but have showed you publicly, and from house to house;" in the synagogue, in the school of Tyrannus, and in the more private and occasional assemblies. The apostle then succinctly states the invariable theme of his preaching—"Testifying both to the Jews, and also to the Greeks, repentance towards God, and faith towards our Lord Jesus Christ." Repentance without faith is but remorse, and faith cannot exist without repentance. Faith in Christ gives repentance its distinctive character. For vainly would our hearts be broken unless His body had been broken for us, and vainly would our tears be shed unless for us his blood had been shed. Paul's preaching ranged round these two grand topics which we have considered in the previous chapter. Such is the record of his labour; earnest, faithful, and unremitting evangelical labour, watered with tears and carried on amidst deadly hostility.

Part II.

ANTICIPATIONS OF THE FUTURE—HIS COURAGE.

He then turns to himself, and his own future. He was proceeding to Jerusalem, ignorant of what specially awaited him there, but *bound in the spirit*—either under an impulse from the Holy Spirit, or under a constraining sense of duty, but having no detailed foresight of what lay before him. He was no traveller choosing his own paths for pleasure or mere gratification, nor was it any inferior motive that took him to the metropolis. Still he was aware that, wherever he went, ruthless opposition was excited to him. By no conjecture, by no reading of the future in the past, by no insight into Jewish character verified by Jewish practice, but by special information from the Holy Ghost, vouchsafed *in every city*—in city by city as he visited them—was he made aware that *bonds and afflictions*—imprisonment, and the restraints and tortures attendant upon it—were abiding him in Jerusalem. Such revelations fulfilled the early promise—"I will show him how great things he must suffer for my name's sake." He was not left without warning, but his courage sank not. He did not shrink for fear of bonds. Liberty was dear to him as to every one; dear to him as to every one who walks and wanders from place to place, and especially to him, as he moved about under the commission of an evangelist. Nay, though the bonds *were abiding him—*

ready to be thrown around him, as if they yawned to receive his limbs into them, he did not hesitate—"I am going" says he, on my perilous journey. At Tyre he was cautioned not to proceed, and at Cesarea Agabus warned him, but still he held on his course; nay, in a letter to the church at Rome, written a short period before, and with this journey in prospect, he asks them thus to pray for him—"that I may be delivered from those that do not believe in Judæa."

The apostle lived in suffering, and felt its mellowing influence every day of his life. He knew not what it was to be exempted from it, for his heart was steeped in it, while past memories pressed upon him, and anticipations of trial ever haunted him. His soul, like that of Moses, was bowed down under daily cares and troubles, while innumerable difficulties and dangers always beset him. There were the Gentiles, who hated him as a religious innovator, and a destroyer of the popular gods; the Jews, who cursed him with bitter ferocity as a renegade; and the Judaizers, who no less thwarted and grieved him, for they maintained their law in all its rigorous claims, and fell into the absurdity of putting the "new wine into old bottles." So beset with foes, the apostle was the less and less attached to earth, to which nothing bound him but his love of the churches and his unquenchable ardour to benefit them; and he was more and more desirous "to depart and be with Christ," for it was far better to enjoy Him than even to preach Him. The spirit of his Lord filled him, and he entered into "the fellowship of His sufferings." Nay, he had that deep experience of divine comfort and sympathy which, but for his sufferings, he could not have enjoyed. His soul was so subdued and tender, that Christ's grace and power were not an occasional pleasure to it, but formed its daily luxury—" As the sufferings of Christ abound in us, so our consolation also aboundeth by Christ." Service and suffering have been often and similarly associated—not such wounds as men frequently inflict upon themselves by wit or rivalry, folly or commercial speculation, but such sufferings as, springing out of the service done, render it acceptable, and are the libation poured out upon the sacrifice. Perfection is reached through suffering—as with Christ so with Christ's. He suffered these things, and entered into His glory; was made " perfect through suffering." He " learned obedience by the things which He suffered." Obedience is easier than suffering; to endure is harder than to act, for action draws around it a cluster of motives and pleasures. Patient suffering is purest obedience; pang after pang passing over the spirit, not only without a murmur, but with cordial acquiescence, and with the experience of His fellow-feeling who was " a man of sorrows "—

> Trial, when it weighs severely,
> Stamps the Saviour's image clearly
>   On the heart of all his friends:
> In the frame His hands have moulded
> Is a future life unfolded
>   Through the suffering which He sends.
>
> Suffering curbs our wayward passions,
> Childlike tempers in us fashions,
>   And our will to His subdues:

Thus His hand, so soft and healing,
Each disordered power and feeling
　　By a blessed change renews.

Suffering keeps the thoughts compacted,
That the soul be not distracted
　　By the world's beguiling art.
'Tis like some angelic warder
Ever keeping sacred order
　　In the chambers of the heart.

Suffering tunes the heart's emotion
To eternity's devotion,
　　And awakes a fond desire
For the land where psalms are ringing,
And with palms the martyrs singing
　　Sweetly to the harpers' quire.

With such a prospect before him the apostle was undaunted—" But none of these things move me, neither count I my life dear unto myself, so that I might finish my course with joy, and the ministry, which I have received of the Lord Jesus, to testify the gospel of the grace of God." Not only liberty, but life itself would be freely surrendered for the highest object—" I hold my life of no account, nor is it so precious to me as to finish my course with joy." This was the spirit of martyrdom, and the prophetic words were verified. The only precious thing to him was the triumphant conclusion of his career —all things else were of no value in comparison. " Yea, and if I be offered," he writes to the church at Philippi, " upon the sacrifice and service of your faith, I joy and rejoice with you all." The joy is the joy of a racer when he touches the goal and receives the garland—the joy that duty and trial are past, and that the longed for prize has been won. If we trace his career from Damascus to the desert of Arabia, and from it to Jerusalem; from Jerusalem to Tarsus, from Tarsus to Antioch, from Antioch to Cyprus, from Cyprus to Antioch in Pisidia, forward to Iconium, Lystra, and Derbe, and retracing his steps through these towns to report to the church in the Syrian Antioch; thence up to Jerusalem and back, and then through Syria and Cilicia, Phrygia and Galatia, down to Troas, and over to Philippi, Thessalonica, Berea, Athens, and Corinth; from Cenchrea direct by sea to Ephesus, and up as before to Jerusalem; down, as was his wont, to Antioch, over "all the country of Galatia and Phrygia in order" till he came to Ephesus; across another time to Macedonia, west as far as Illyricum and on to southern Greece; north again to Philippi, over the blue Ægean once more to Troas, and from it to Miletus, where he was now addressing the assembled elders—then we shall see that his course had been a long and varied one, and that he had not run in vain, if we think not only of the miles he travelled, but of the sermons he preached, the miracles he wrought, the sufferings he endured, the epistles he wrote, and the churches he founded or confirmed.

That long and arduous course, involving so much labour, stoning at Lystra, scourging at Philippi, and hazards of death in every place—for he says, "I die daily"—is identified by the apostle with the ministry he had *received of* the Lord Jesus—from Him when He appeared to him by the way. He did not take "this honour unto himself" —his were no self-assumed functions; but the commission was laid upon him by the glorified Redeemer. He was not set apart, as Matthias, by his fellow-apostles and the church; nor did any one select and ordain him, as he chose and ordained Timothy. Directly from Christ did he receive his ministry—"Paul, an apostle (not of man, neither by man, but by Jesus Christ, and God the Father, who raised Him from the dead)." "But I certify you, brethren, that the gospel which was preached of me is not after man. For I neither received it of man, neither was I taught it, but by the revelation of Jesus Christ." No one intervened between him and the Master—authority, prerogative, and qualification came at once from Him. What to teach, and why and how to teach it, were in every sense supernatural communications.

The primary duty of that ministry was "to testify the gospel of the grace of God." That gospel was his uniform testimony, and the essence of that gospel is the *grace of God*—His rich and sovereign benignity to sinners. That grace, unbought and unexpected, is *gospel*—good news, tidings which we could not anticipate, nor did we merit them. God was under no obligation to provide salvation, and man had no right to expect it. Grace is opposed to necessity on His part, and to merit on ours. And in His gospel He unfolds to men His gracious purpose, which they could have learned in no other way. Neither creation nor providence afford sufficient data. Shall He punish as He has threatened? or shall He, for His own reasons, remit the penalty? How, then, if He remit the penalty, shall He maintain His veracity, and uphold the honour of His law? Who should have dared to solve or even to propose such a problem? O, it is purest mercy which the good tidings convey to us. For it is not a respite or a mitigation, but complete deliverance through grace. It is not some boon fitted for the present, the enjoyment of which may fill up the time previous to the period of infliction. It is not some vindication of God's equity to induce the culprit's unmurmuring submission; but it is a free, perfect, and joyous salvation—not from one section of the penalty, but from its entire sweep and circuit. Pardon, peace, purity, healthful progress to perfection, the resurrection of the body, and the life everlasting—do not these deserve the name of good news? And he that felt this grace in himself, and pitied the souls of men, could not but spend himself in testifying the gospel of the grace of God. No wonder that when his work was done, and he had nearly completed his cycle, he could say with all humility and hopefulness—" I am now ready to be offered up, and the time of my departure is at hand. I have fought a good fight, I have finished my course, I have kept the faith: henceforth there is laid up for me a crown of righteousness, which the Lord, the righteous Judge, shall give me at that day; and not to me only, but unto all them also that love His appearing."

But this address was not only a record of his labours and trials among them; it was not simply an intimation of his departure from them—it was a final farewell— "And now, behold, I know that ye all, among whom I have gone preaching the kingdom of God, shall see my face no more." He approaches this idea with reluctance, and wishes them to note it, that his subsequent charges may have the greater solemnity. If they were hearing his voice for the last time, and if they were never to look on him again, what he now said would fix itself in their memory by the mournful impression which it would make on their hearts. He appeals to the tender tie subsisting between them; for he had gone among them preaching the kingdom of God, and they had listened, believed, and been admitted to that kingdom. The connection now to be severed was close and tender, as between a spiritual father and his spiritual family. When they thought on what precious truths he had brought, what enterprise he had displayed, what intensity of emotion he had manifested, and what courage and disinterestedness marked his unwearied labours, they could not but be attached to him in no ordinary degree, and the termination of their intercourse could not but oppress and grieve them, and this the more surely that they were to see his face no more. Of this painful fact he assures them—"I know." How he knew we cannot tell, or whether he spoke simply from present impression. According to the chronology held by some, the apostle was liberated after a first trial at Rome, and made another and last missionary tour, being probably at Philippi, and certainly at Ephesus. In this case we would say that the apostle spoke here from strong feeling, but from apprehensions which were not verified. Yet he says—"I know;" as if nothing could be more certain. It will scarcely do to say that he might return to Ephesus, and yet see none of his present audience; for we cannot imagine so great changes to have happened in so brief a period, and we cannot suppose him to have been in Asia Minor without being in Ephesus at all. Nor would it suffice to lay emphasis on the mere word "all"—that is, that he would never see all of them again; for that is so true of any assembly, that the apostle could not introduce such a commonplace with all this solemnity. The plain meaning is that he understood and declared the parting to be final; for he expected never to return to them. He writes, indeed, to Philippi, when he was imprisoned at Rome, that he had strong hopes of liberation—" I know that I shall abide and continue with you all." The words—"I know" in the speech, declaring a final farewell, are fairly balanced by the words—" I know" in the epistle, affirming a speedy return to the neighbourhood. Both were not correct, but both might be used under present impression and expectations; for as to his personal future, as he has already said in this address, he was not specially enlightened—only he was generally and continuously warned of coming dangers and trials, " bonds and imprisonment."

Part III.

HIS CHARGE.

Recurring still to the past the apostle adds—"Wherefore I take you to record *this day*—this very day—that I am pure from the blood of all men." Having done his duty—served the Master in the Master's spirit, laboured with many tears, not quailing before Jewish conspiracies; having kept back nothing profitable, but taught them in public and in their own dwellings, in more formal address and in more simple and friendly conversations; having proclaimed to all classes repentance and faith, testified the gospel of the grace of God, and preached the kingdom of God; having done all this labour from the purest of motives and with all humility, might he not appeal to the elders and say—"I am pure from the blood of all men?"

Yea, he adds with conclusive emphasis, gathering up into one brief sentence what had preceded—"For I have not shunned to declare unto you all the counsel of God." He had not shrunk from a full and faithful announcement of the entire will of God. It is implied that portions of that will might tempt a man to shrink from declaring them—those portions which are repugnant to fallen nature, which curb our pride, humble our intellect, and are a stumbling-block to one class of minds, and foolishness to another. But he had not desisted from speaking them, and he had not modified them from fear of giving offence. He had told them how guilty and undeserving they were, and how utterly unable to save themselves; had presented salvation to them in a plain story of one who had been hanged on a tree in Jerusalem; had dwelt on the necessity of an entire change of life, and of the immediate and complete abandonment of such sins as were common in Ephesus, so common as to bring no scandal with them; and had shown them what a marked and visible line of demarcation should exist between them and the world round about them. All the counsel of God—every atom and element of it, what was cardinal and what was subordinate, what was primary and what was relational, what was doctrinal and what was experimental, what belonged to ecclesiastical and what to common life, the proof that guarded and the inference that might be deduced, the sphere of faith and that of hope and of love—all had been expounded by him who had "rightly divided the word of truth." O to be able, amidst all shortcomings, to adopt the apostle's language, or to be able at least to avow that we have aimed, in dependence on divine grace, to declare the whole counsel of God, and that we cannot charge ourselves with wilful treachery to Him whom we serve. What need have we to offer the constant supplication in all fervour and humility that He would fill us with the grace of fidelity, and enable us not only to labour, but to watch for souls; that He would endow us with ingenuity in devising times and means for the successful application of the truth; and give us a living resemblance to Him who went about doing good, in season and out of season, praying by night and labouring by day, His heart being set on His Father's glory and the world's deliverance from sin and death.

From himself the apostle turns to the elders: "Take heed, *therefore*"—since the supervision henceforth devolves solely on you, and since such is the example of vigilance, anxiety, and love I have set before you, "take heed unto yourselves, and to all the flock over the which the Holy Ghost hath made you overseers, to feed the church of God." Themselves were the first object of thought. You are sinners in need of the same salvation, and unless you have accepted that salvation yourselves, you are not fitted to save others—your own souls first, the souls of others afterwards. To the doctrine which they taught they were to take heed, lest error should mingle with their instructions. They were to impart the truth pure and simple, not corrupted by the "rudiments of the world" and "traditions of men," or tinctured with "philosophy and vain deceit." Nor were they to be less careful of their example, of their own growth in the spiritual life. The apostle has himself stated the melancholy issue which he strove by self-command to avoid—"Lest that by any means, having preached the gospel to others, I myself should be a castaway." He warns Timothy, when placed over this Ephesian church, thus—"Take heed unto thyself and unto the doctrine." Their life should be in such harmony with their labour as to be a commentary upon it: for example gives power to precept—one reason, among others, why overseers of the flock belong to the flock, and are "men of like passions" with those whom they teach and govern. As under the former economy the priesthood was of human origin, that those vested with it might "have compassion on the ignorant, and on them that are out of the way," so, under the second dispensation, there is a peculiar propriety in appointing men to the task of interpreting the books of the New Testament. Might not such a trust have been reposed in angels, those high and spotless intelligences who are not involved in the common apostacy of our species, and whose rank would command respect and attention? Had such glorious beings been commissioned to descend on wings of love from their aerial abodes to our forlorn habitation, the world might indeed have been awed by their visits, and these messengers of grace might have commanded impression over a cowering assemblage; yet, while they preached with unimpassioned argument and appeal, and, from the stores of their own celestial eloquence, urged reason after reason on man to embrace the Saviour; or while they narrated how they watched the craddle of the infant Jesus, ministered to Him in the wilderness, opened the portals of His grave, and formed the escort of His ascension; or while they spoke of the evils of sin, and referred to their fellows whose rebellion had cast them out of heaven, and enlarged on that sovereign affection which had selected men as the objects of restoring mercy—while such might have been the themes of angelic address, so interesting in themselves and in the vehicle of their communication, still there would be a repulsion in the visage of these white-robed ambassadors— the radiancy of their countenance would prohibit a free access to them—their words might strike, but not affect, because the eloquence that springs from experience is wanting—the heart of man would feel an utter destitution of that assurance of succour and sympathy which community of nature alone can inspire, and which, arising from a feeling of common misery and common salvation, passes from heart to heart with electrical suddenness and power. Teachers of Christianity propose to others that remedy which they have embraced themselves. "Restore unto me the joy of thy salvation; and uphold me with thy free Spirit: then will I teach transgressors thy ways; and sinners shall be converted unto thee." There is an appropriate efficacy in the thought that he who invites has himself been welcomed—that he who reasons has been induced by the force of his own arguments—that he who warns has known, but escaped the dangers against which he instructs—that he who encourages has felt the joys he proposes, or the perplexities he attempts to unravel. He believes—therefore he speaks; his audience hear, and are inclined to believe. What in other teachers is enthusiasm, is in him but sobriety. "Whether we be beside ourselves, it is to God; or whether we be sober, it is for your cause." "Now we live, if ye stand fast in the Lord."

Then they were to "take heed to all the flock *over the which*"—literally in which—the Holy Ghost had made them overseers. The "flock" is a term which naturally originated in a pastoral country, and is a favourite with the Hebrew prophets. They pictured the flock lying down in "green pastures," or led to the "still waters;" or exposed to wild beasts, but guarded by the sling and staff; or torn and scattered "in the cloudy and dark day," becoming "meat to all the beasts of the field;" or wandering far away into the arid desert, and with difficulty brought back again; or safely reposing in the fold "on the high mountains," under the charge of a shepherd, who must defend them against wolf and bear, while he seeks the lost, and binds up the broken. Or if he be not thus tender and vigilant, he brings upon him the denunciation, "Woe to the shepherds that do feed themselves; should not the shepherds feed the flock?" The flock had indeed once "gone astray," but the divine Shepherd went out after them and found them; opened up a path of return, and carried them back to the fold where they are fed and tended—"the flock that was given Him, the beautiful flock." He is indeed the true and good Shepherd, who calleth "His own sheep by name, and they follow Him," and "go in and out and find pasture;" who does not desert them when they are in danger, and flee like an hireling; who knows His sheep, and is known of them, and has given His life for them. This flock, so dear to Christ who died for them, and who feeds and rules them as the "chief Shepherd," had been committed to the charge of the Ephesian elders as under-shepherds by the Spirit; and such a charge, so divinely given, they were on no account to neglect. These elders were bishops or overseers by the highest consecration—the unction of the Holy Ghost. They were not to assume any despotic authority over the flock, for they were still in it themselves, still a portion of it. And they were to take heed to *all* the flock—to every member of it, whatever his position or calling. They were to "warn them that are unruly, comfort the feeble-minded, support the weak, be patient toward all men," "speaking the things which become sound doctrine;" urging "that

CARE OF THE FLOCK. 331

the aged men be sober, grave, temperate, sound in faith, in charity, in patience. The aged women likewise, that they be in behaviour as becometh holiness, not false accusers, not given to much wine, teachers of good things; that they may teach the young women to be sober, to love their husbands, to love their children, to be discreet, chaste, keepers at home, good, obedient to their own husbands, that the word of God be not blasphemed. Young men likewise exhort to be sober-minded."

The inspection which they were thus to practise must be loving and watchful, as the duty demanded, and after the example of Christ, the " great Shepherd of the sheep." Their office was no sinecure; it needed every gift which nature could confer, and every grace which the Spirit can furnish. To "watch for souls"—how terrible the possibility that remissness may be laid to the pastor's charge, if by his errors, his indifference, or his defective example, the souls of any of the flock be thereby endangered. And when we consider what the perils are which threaten the flock, how frail our nature is, and how hardly beset with temptations; how the duties of the world are apt to encroach upon it, and its pleasures to seduce it; how the idea of eternity is so apt to fade away under the pressure of time and its ordinary business; how one step in a wrong direction may morally necessitate a widening deflection, which may end in a final apostacy—when we consider these jeopardies we may know of what moment it is to "take heed to all the flock." A word spoken in season may prevent incalculable evils—a word to the man of joyous nature, before he learn to love the social bowl; to the man of more sordid inclination, before he come to idolize his gold; to the man of intellectual tendency, before he be seduced away from the simplicity of the gospel; to the maiden who is fond of dress and admiration; or to the wife, that she may not care too much "for the things of the world, how she may please her husband;" to the afflicted or tried, that they make full proof of Christ's sympathy; and to the dying, that they may bear testimony to the power and grace of Him who has abolished death: giving "a portion to seven and also to eight," yea, giving them "their portion of meat in due season." As the Holy Ghost made them overseers, He would qualify them for this supervision, but He would also take account of their stewardship; and woe to them if they were found guilty of breach of trust.

What they were to take heed to do especially, was "*To feed* the church of God"—to do the work of shepherds to it, to rule and protect it, as well as to lead it to "pastures fat and good." Every element of their office they were to discharge—to maintain "the due order," and to impart spiritual instruction, being pastors according to God's heart to "feed with knowledge and understanding." The church has food provided for it by the primary Shepherd—the truth concerning Himself, His character and work; the truth Himself announced when He said—"I am the good Shepherd; the good Shepherd giveth his life for the sheep." For evangelical truth satisfies every desire and longing of the heart; comes home to all its fears and allays them; to all its yearnings and fills them; and to all its expectations, and so supports them that they can never be too ardent, nor yet promise too much: for the pledges which "in Jesus Christ are yea, and in Him amen," shall all be realized in God's good time and method. Christ himself is the nutriment of the flock, as they know Him, trust Him, love Him, and obey Him; Christ everywhere; Christ as source of salvation and peace; Christ as motive to duty and holiness; Christ as theme of praise and object of imitation; Christ as basis of hope and centre of fervid affection; Christ in teaching as prominently as He is in scripture; Christ in all the ordinances as pervadingly as He is in the scheme of redemption. And the elders were also to prevent disorders; to apply discipline; checking the presumptuous and stimulating the sluggish; administering Christ's law with perfect impartiality and in His spirit; and forward ever to "reprove, rebuke, exhort with all long-suffering and doctrine;" "able, by sound doctrine, both to exhort and convince the gainsayer:" "in meekness instructing those that oppose themselves; if God peradventure will give them repentance to the acknowledging of the truth; and that they may recover themselves out of the snare of the devil, who are taken captive by him at his will." Surely such a function so set before them must concentrate all their energies upon it, that by divine strength they might be able to discharge it. It was to be their one study, and they were to be always in it; giving themselves wholly to it; realizing what he afterwards said to one in spiritual office in the same church—" Meditate upon these things; give thyself wholly to them, that thy profiting may appear to all. Continue in them: for in doing this thou shalt both save thyself, and them that hear thee." The end presented was a noble one, and ever to be kept in view:—

> "An ignorance of means may minister
> To greatness, but an ignorance of aims
> Makes it impossible to be great at all.
> I tell you rather, that whoever may
> Discover true ends here, shall grow pure enough
> To love them, brave enough to strive for them,
> And strong to reach them, though the road be rough."

The apostle adds the remarkable clause—"which He has purchased with His own blood." The reading of the previous clause is doubtful, some manuscripts having "the church of God," and others "the church of the Lord," and there are also other variations. On the one hand, the "church of the Lord" is an uncommon phrase, but not less uncommon is the idea of the blood of God. We can easily conceive reasons why "God" should be altered to "Lord," the expression of the last clause being so peculiar; but we cannot also understand why a copyist should have altered Lord to God—the usual idiom, "church of God" being a favourite phrase, and used by Paul no less than ten times in his epistles. The meaning is not materially different, for "the Lord, He is God," and the divinity of Jesus does not depend upon a disputed text. It pervades the New Testament, and underlies the whole scheme of redemption. He has acquired that church for Himself, made it in His own possession. Therefore it is called the "purchased possession," the "peculiar people"—"peculiar" not meaning singular, but, according to its Latin signification, denoting what is one's own by a special right. He has made the church His own, by shedding

His own blood for its ransom. What a price! His own blood; nothing less, and nothing else!—implying grace, condescension, incarnation, obedience, suffering, and death. Jehovah says to the ancient church—"I gave Egypt for thy ransom; Ethiopia and Sheba for thee," but the appeal to the church of the New Testament is—"Ye know that ye were not redeemed with corruptible things, as silver and gold, from your vain conversation received by tradition from your fathers; but with the precious blood of Christ, as of a lamb without blemish and without spot"—

> "The ransom was paid down; the fund of heaven,
> Heaven's inexhaustible, exhausted fund,
> Amazing, and amazed, poured forth the price,
> All price beyond: though curious to compute,
> Archangels fail'd to cast the mighty sum:
> Its value vast, ungrasp'd by minds create,
> For ever hides and glows in the Supreme."

The church is therefore His by the firmest of all bonds, for He has bought it, and with a price beyond all value. He has also redeemed it—put forth His gracious power in actually securing His purchase; nay, He has taken incipient possession of it by His own Spirit, sent down into it in His name, and as His representative.

All this counsel was the more needful, because of coming perils—"For I know this, that after my departing shall grievous wolves enter in among you, not sparing the flock." I know *this*—giving special emphasis to what he is about to state, as something additional to what he has stated. "After my departing" may be either, after my leaving you, or absolutely, after my death; and "grievous wolves" signify ferocious and unsparing ones. The "wolves," for they devour the flock, are in contrast to the tender and faithful "overseers." This havoc may be accomplished either by the teaching of error, or the introduction of immoral practices under guise of higher Christian freedom; "turning the grace of God into lasciviousness." In the first instance, those wolves come from without—they were to enter in among you—itinerant errorists making merchandise of souls. But not only from without them, from within them too should spiritual foes spring up. "Also of your own selves shall men arise, speaking perverse things, to draw away disciples after them." These men, in their very bosom, not precisely among the presbyters before him, were to start up, speaking *perverse things*— things not in accordance with truth, or pernicious distortions of truth. Their design was to draw away disciples after them, and sad to tell, in such an attempt they would succeed. In an age of inquiry and religious excitement, such forms of error are always sure to appear, and they did appear in that century. There is a restlessness in many minds, an eager and morbid desire for novelty—something more than has been taught, or something different from it, or some modification of it which errs either from excess or defect. The Anabaptists were such an off-shoot from the Reformation; the fifth monarchy men sprang out of English puritanism; and revivals in some places become at length spasmodic caricatures. God speed the time when men will take truth as He has given it; simply and lovingly take it, without exercising their own ingenuity upon it, either cutting the gem to set it, or placing it in some capsule which themselves have invented to increase its lustre.

The apostle's prophecy came to pass. Cerinthus, supposed to be of Alexandria, travelled to Ephesus, and promulgated his heresies in the face of the beloved disciple. Others may have followed him, and disseminated the "oppositions of science falsely so called." Timothy, when superintending the church of Ephesus, is warned of certain false teachers inculcating asceticism—" Speaking lies in hypocrisy; having their conscience seared with a hot iron; forbidding to marry, and commanding to abstain from meats, which God hath created to be received with thanksgiving of them which believe and know the truth." The same evangelist is also warned thus—" This charge I commit unto thee, son Timothy, according to the prophecies which went before on thee, that thou by them mightest war a good warfare: holding faith and a good conscience; which, some having put away, concerning faith have made shipwreck: of whom is Hymeneus and Alexander, whom I have delivered unto Satan, that they may learn not to blaspheme," These heretics, " men of corrupt mind, and reprobate concerning the truth," confounded the resurrection with regeneration, holding that as matter was essentially sinful, the rising of the body was impossible, and that the resurrection was simply the resuscitation of the soul from spiritual death to spiritual life. Their philosophy damaged their theology —a thing not uncommon in every age of the church. It is, however, to be borne in mind, that these warnings seem to have accomplished their purpose, for the Ephesian church is thus praised in the apocalyptic letter—"Thou hast tried them which say they are apostles and are not, and hast found them liars."

If, then, such be the case—if these dangers are so imminent; if virulent foes are either plausibly to intrude themselves among you, or some of yourselves are to swerve from the truth, and introduce seductive and pernicious novelties; if the flock be really in such jeopardy—there is all the more reason why unwonted vigilance should characterize the pastors: "Therefore watch, and remember, that, by the space of three years, I ceased not to warn every one night and day with tears." They were to *watch*—to exercise a close and earnest superintendence—at no time to be remiss —and this after the apostle's example. They were to remember how he had acted when he was among them, during those *three years*—a round number employed for a somewhat shorter period. When he was among them, he *warned* them—warned every one of them; spoke in solemn words to each of them, of his condition and destiny; of the truth, and of the tenacity with which he ought to hold it; of the danger of error, and of the fascinating appearance which it so often presents. This warning was continual— "day and night"—on every available opportunity; at every period of contact and fellowship with them. Nay, he *ceased* not to warn them—never thought that they had been sufficiently guarded; never felt as if another warning would be superfluous, or as if he had said all that could or need be said. Another warning and yet another, such were his zeal and anxiety; for he warned them with tears. Those tears were not for his unbelieving countrymen, as already referred to; they were for his converts. Ah! those tears show us the apostle's heart. He was not cold and pure intellect—an icicle radiating the light of a winter's sun. His great mind was not lifted above emotion to a high and gelid empyrean. His soul was as profoundly sensitive as that of a child under its first trials. Nor had his numerous cares and disappointments hardened him into apathy. He felt what a soul is in value, and what heaven and hell are in destiny; how brief man's period is here, and what a hold sin and error have upon him; and he burst into tears as he prayed men "in Christ's stead" to be reconciled unto God. The touching nature of Christ's promises to sinners filled his eye as he repeated them. Tears fell at the memory of Christ's tears, and at the thought of man's hard and impenetrable heart. He wept as he imagined the possibility of any of them descending to the place of weeping and wailing and gnashing of teeth. His moist eyes and agitated bosom are now remembered by him as the signs of his earnestness, and he does not stir them to admiration by a reference to his miracles, but he moves them to sympathy by an appeal to his tears—tears which fell upon his roughened hands as he bent over his daily labour, and furrowed his cheeks as he warned them so incessantly of coming death and an awful eternity.

Part IV.

THE FAREWELL.

The apostle has been drawing to a conclusion more than once, but he cannot. He has still something more to say, and he prolongs the address in the fulness of his heart. He is loath to say farewell—shrinks from uttering his last words to them; he lingers with them, and has yet some additional counsel or appeal to present to them. But he must leave them, and with no hope of another meeting. This was their last interview; they were to see his face no more. But they were not to be left comfortless; a higher power than his would protect and bless them. "And now, brethren, I commend you to God, and to the word of His grace, which is able to build you up, and to give you an inheritance among all them which are sanctified." He committed them to the highest guardianship—to God Himself; handed them over to Him of infinite power and love—to God, and to the word of *His grace*—for by it He works out His purposes. His word is in itself the embodiment of His grace, and also the means by which His grace operates. Here it means that gospel which Paul had proclaimed—for as yet there was no written New Testament. By their believing reception and continued grasp of the doctrine of grace, would they be kept from danger and woe. They who forsake God's truth cast themselves out of God's keeping. He keeps them through their confidence in Him, by deepening it; by opening up to them the meaning of His promises, and enabling them to take fuller draughts of consolation from them; by showing them the path of duty, and guiding and upholding them in it; by inducing them to rely upon His grace, and evermore to cling to that word which reveals and contains it. He does not throw any mystic shield around them, and the stars in their courses fight not for them. But they draw near to God, and they keep near Him; His grace contained in His word cheers and supports them. What they want He has promised, and He will give it, when they ask it. "I will never leave thee," is His pledge. "I will instruct thee," is His promise.

The Ephesian elders were thus left in God's hands, and they could not be left in better hands than His; for He is able to build them up. It is probable that it is to God, and not to the "word of His grace," that this clause refers. Edification is God's work. The figure is common in the apostle's style, and is found in fuller reference in his letter to the Ephesian church. There he speaks of the holy edifice resting on "the chief corner-stone," and "fitly framed together;" preserving its symmetry as it rises in altitude, —a spiritual temple in which believers are inbuilt as living stones; its object being "an habitation of God through the Spirit." But the living stones forming the great temple or church universal, are singly and each also a temple; each a shrine of the Holy Ghost reared up by God's truth and love, compactly built together in its various graces—a scene of divine residence and worship. For God not only saves, but He perpetuates the safety. He not only converts, but He also confirms. Not only does He put believers on the path, but He preserves them in it—" Shall I bring to the birth, and not cause to bring forth? saith the Lord." Not only are they begotten of Him, but the life is fostered and strengthened. Not only does He infuse the hope of the inheritance, but He cherishes it, and deepens it, and brings it to realization. Progress is the law of the spiritual life—God is " able to build you up." Will you doubt His ability to build you up, when you compare autumn with spring, the crop with the seed, the oak with the acorn, the man with the babe, the hill with the rocks of which it is made up, this goodly world with " the highest part of the dust," or original elements of which it is composed, or Israel in the days of Solomon with the miserable horde of fugitives escaping by night from Egypt?

But not only have believers spiritual progress here, they are assured of glory hereafter. They get an *inheritance* —a possession, as Canaan had been to the Jews; among the *sanctified*—those made meet for the inheritance; and among *all* of them—as if not a few should be so changed and endowed. An inheritance is something one can call his own and can enjoy as his own—not something which is his by fiction or unauthorized tenure. And so the happiness of heaven is truly an inheritance. It is ours by God's gift, and its happiness is felt in our perfected natures. It is not around us, but it is within us. It is not a gift we may only lay our hands on, but it is in our hearts and there by a charter which can never be cancelled, and by a sanctifying power which seals the perfection which it has developed. Any other inheritance without us may fail; the ten talents are taken from him who has not improved them. But that which is sanctified is the soul—that which constitutes his consciousness or himself, and therefore it is his inheritance. And God bestows it— it is His prerogative "to give" it, for He has provided it. God bestows it—it is not won from Him as a reward, or earned from Him as a prize. He gives it in His grace, and in the word of that grace He has described its nature, shown how it may be obtained, and what preparation is indispensable for it.

Part V.

CONCLUDING APPEAL TO THE PAST—HIS DISINTERESTEDNESS.

The apostle again comes back to himself. He has spoken of his labours and watchfulness, his trials and tears, what he had suffered and what he had still to endure, and now he refers to the disinterestedness of his toils. No mercenary motive urged him, he was far above the sphere of vulgar greed or ambition—" I have coveted no man's silver, or gold, or apparel." Apparel is mentioned as being an article highly valued in the East; " changes of raiment " being a common present, and no little money being often expended on them. It was not theirs, but them, that the apostle coveted—not what they had, but what they might come to be. He cared nothing for what the world desires; gold would have been but a burden; and a well-filled wardrobe was no object to the pedestrian traveller. Food and raiment were all he needed, and he did not always get them; for he was often " in hunger and fasting, in cold and nakedness." He could not sometimes procure the barest necessaries of life; and if he was at any time unable to work, he must have been sorely pinched. What cared he, therefore, for wealth or finery? He did not demand, far less expect, pecuniary enrichment. Souls were his hire; his highest compensation was in winning men from sin and Satan. His reward was in heaven, under the eye of the Master, and inaugurated by the Master's greeting. What a contrast to many of the "grievous wolves," who make a gain of godliness, and strip the flock of their fleece as they prey upon them; whose object is selfish ease and indulgence at the expense of their victims who are as infatuated as the Jews at Horeb, when they brake off their golden earrings, and made a lavish contribution of them for the beloved calf. The apostle acted in the spirit of the aged Samuel. When the form of government was changed, Samuel, who had been judge for so long a period, took farewell of the people in the memorable appeal—"Behold, here I am: witness against me before the Lord, and before His anointed; whose ox have I taken? or whose ass have I taken? or whom have I defrauded? whom have I oppressed? or of whose hand have I received any bribe to blind mine eyes therewith? and I will restore it you. And they said, Thou hast not defrauded us, nor oppressed us, neither hast thou taken ought of any man's hand. And he said unto them, The Lord is witness against you, and His anointed is witness this day, that ye have not found ought in my hand. And they answered, He is witness."

But he not only asserts his disinterestedness, he produces positive proof, in which all of them must at once have acquiesced. For he appeals to their knowledge—"Yea, ye yourselves know, that these hands have ministered unto my necessities, and to them that were with me." The fact was patent, quite as well known as the fact of his residence among them. Not only did he work to supply his own wants, but the wants of them that were with him. His generosity was, therefore, unchallenged; he laboured to support his colleagues as well as himself; for his was the energy of a master-mind in things of business, as well as in spiritual functions. And he could say—These hands have done it — these hands, stained and peeled by the manipulations of his daily industry. What a noble appeal! corroborated also by what he writes to Corinth at the period referred to. From Ephesus, during the time that "these hands were ministering to his necessities," he wrote his first epistle to the Corinthians, where he says—"Even to this present hour we both hunger and thirst, and are naked and are buffeted, and have no certain dwelling-place, and labour working with our own hands." In these words there is a very touching allusion—"We have no certain dwelling-place." It reveals the longing of one conscious of advancing age and the approach of its infirmities. His apostolate demanded a continuous journeying, and he was not unlike his Lord who had not "where to lay His head." But as years passed on, his unsettled life began to be felt more than previously as a self-denial. Age comes to like repose. Many a one who has spent his youth as waywardly as the butterflies which he chased in the fields, and whose manhood brooked no control, is glad to creep in his old age to the workhouse. The sailor who, braving the battle and the breeze, has roamed for half a century, and been as unsettled as the waves on which he toiled and fought, finds his desired haven in the palatial asylum provided for him by the nation. They who have no certain dwelling-place are usually under stigma, and vagabond is synonymous with lawless; while the steps of a labouring man homewards, avoiding the haunts of temptation and intemperance, are usually steps heavenwards also. Men get tired of wandering—repose is coveted; and the apostle was, as a man, no exception, though his journeys were made in God's name, and for the purpose of dispensing God's blessings. The rest he sighed for soon came to him—two years' detention at Cesarea, and as many at least in Rome.

The conclusion of the address is in the same strain. "I have showed you all things, how that so labouring ye ought to support the weak; and to remember the words of the Lord Jesus, how he said, It is more blessed to give than to receive." I have showed you *all things*—as to all things; or rather in all ways. By the *weak* must be understood not weak in faith, but simply the poor, needing support from the fruits of the industry of their Christian brethren. The apostle *showed* this—taught and enforced it, yea, exemplified it in his own conduct. Their labours were not to be solely for themselves, but in generous sympathy with others: *so labouring*—as I did, and with the end which I had in view. In the same spirit he afterwards wrote to them—"Let him that stole steal no more: but rather let him labour, working with his hands the thing which is good, that he may have to give to him that needeth."

Such generosity is truly Christian. It is the spirit of Him who "came not to be ministered unto, but to minister;" the spirit of that brotherhood which He has formed, and the basis of that eulogy which He pronounces at last. For oneself and for no one else, for oneself in everything, for oneself in thought, labour, and enjoyment—as if this were either happiness or the image of it —that is in utter antagonism not only to Paul's example, but to the divine Master's maxim—"It is more blessed to give than to receive." The saying is not recorded, for, if all that Jesus said had been recorded, "the world would not contain the books that should be written." Many sayings of the divine Teacher must have been in the mouths and memories of the early church; those precious sentences, as terse in expression as pregnant with thought —winged words, wafted through the churches like the seeds of the thistle-down through the air. The apostle had formerly uttered the saying, and now he bids them remember it. The term "blessed" was a favourite one with the Lord. The Old Testament had ended with threatening and a "curse," but the New Testament opens with beatitude and promise. Blessing is Christ's work, "blessed" is His epithet, as in the sermon on the Mount.

The Saviour does not cast any slur upon receiving. No, it is good to receive, but it is better still to give. It is good to receive, for we are needy—in want of all things; and all we have God gives us—life, and breath, and all things: good to receive, for He has offered His best gift in His Son, and seals it by His spirit: good to receive, for we need pardon, holiness, life, joy, and spiritual maturity. Our prayer is for more gifts, and for a fuller receptivity. "Open thy mouth wide" is the command, "and I will fill it" is the promise. But though it is blessed to receive, it is more blessed to give. It shows that you have, and can part with what you have; that you have been blessed, and, in being blessed, are made a blessing to others. Receiving makes us happy, but by giving we impart happiness—a work which is noble and godlike. In giving we are doing what

God is doing, and blessed must be such an imitation of Him—the cistern parting with the waters poured into it from the fountain. Creation depicts the same doctrine: the sun shines not for himself, the clouds pour down their showers upon us, the flowers shed abroad their perfume, and the earth yields her increase. Selfishness is wholly unlike God and the works of his hands; love is the law of nature as well as of grace, and is on all sides divine. An old commentator has remarked, that the rich man in the parable had no need to form the resolution of building a larger storehouse for his increasing goods, for "the poor man's belly should be the rich man's granary." "I felt more pleasure," says a distinguished seaman, who had bravely borne himself during a wreck, "in restoring an infant only three weeks old to its mother, than ever I felt in the proud moment of victory." Even Julius Cæsar could say, that no music was so sweet to his ear as the requests of his friends for assistance; and Mark Antony, when in the depth of adversity, could remark that he had lost all save what he had given to his friends. So true is it universally that what men keep they lose, and what they part with they retain, and that the highest happiness is to create and diffuse it. There was a family reduced to penury by a series of disasters, and no one was told of it. Pieces of furniture were quietly parted with, that the little ones might not break the mother's heart by crying for bread in vain. But there was no appeal made, save to Him who heareth "the young ravens which cry." Suspicions were at length aroused, for the children were seen to gather and devour the crumbs which fell from the hands of their playmates. The curious eye of a neighbour watched the movements of the father, and saw him gather in the dark such husks as swine do eat, and carry them stealthily home. A chink in the window revealed the household revelling in the coarse and unsatisfying fare, over which the provider reverently asked the accustomed blessing. The story was confidentially imparted to a benevolent friend, who at once and anonymously sent by an untraceable channel a handsome relief. The joy of the family that evening, on receiving from Providence what they deemed an answer to their prayers, was beyond telling, though in years of future prosperity they were glad to tell it, but it was not equal to the blessedness of the kind bestower; even though their joy was similar in nature, though not in degree, to what was felt in the home of Bethany that first night which he who had lain three days in the grave spent with his sisters after his resurrection. The joy of a benefactor is an image of the happiness of the divine Wonderworker, whose moments of ecstacy after a miracle compensated Him for daily scorn and privation —the joy He still feels when He sees of the travail of His soul and is satisfied. The happiness of the saint who has received and is before the throne, is far inferior to that of Him who has given it and is upon the throne. No new emotion is this blessedness, it is as old as the patriarch of Uz—" When the ear heard me, then it blessed me and when the eye saw me, it gave witness to me; because I delivered the poor that cried, and the fatherless, and him that had none to help him. The blessing of him that was ready to perish came upon me, and I caused the widow's heart to sing for joy." How unlike those words of the Lord Jesus to the heathen proverb, "Silly the giver, happy the getter."

The tender and solemn discourse was followed by a prayer. In praying with them, he *knelt down*—that unusual posture being a token of his fervour, and how much he was overcome by the scene. The usual posture for prayer was standing, both in the Jewish church and in the early Christian church. In special circumstances, as those of Solomon at the dedication of the temple, Daniel in his chamber, Peter on the housetop, and Stephen in the act of martyrdom, kneeling was naturally resorted to. But in the public assemblies they stood, being commanded "to stand up" to engage in devotional exercise in the days of Ezra; and our Lord alludes to the same custom when he says, "when ye stand praying." Those whom the apostle addressed were profoundly agitated by his last words— "They all wept sore, and fell on Paul's neck, and kissed him; sorrowing most of all for the words which he spake, that they should see his face no more. And they accompanied him unto the ship." They saw him on board, and they could not but stand on the beach and behold with tearful eyes the vessel unfurl her sails; and there would be tokens of recognition and farewell exchanged again and again as the distance widened, till the hull sank out of view, and canvass and spars lessened into a speck, and at length disappeared.

XIV.—PAUL AT JERUSALEM.

I.

SPEECH FROM THE STAIRS OF THE GARRISON.

Acts xxii. 1—30.

THE departure from Miletus had been a scene of great tenderness and sorrow. The sacred historian says, "After we were gotten from them," literally, after we had been torn from them. They could not bear to separate after such a sermon, such a communion, and such a wondrous deed of resuscitation. It had been a revival, and the life stimulated by that preaching and fed from that sacrament, was imaged out in that miracle. They looked upon the preacher and life-restorer, and could not keep their eyes off him; took another wistful look, and yet another, for "they should see his face no more." "They all wept sore, and fell upon Paul's neck and kissed him," unable to restrain their grief as the memory of his past labours and trials pressed upon them, followed by the thought that this was a last farewell. Could he have held out the possibility of return, had he but said that he should make an effort to come back, their misery might have been moderated. But to see his face no more threw over them the pall of death, it was as if they had stood by his sepulchre. Depart on thy old mission, pursue thy path of threatened dangers, thou brave and gentle heart; shadows are closing around thee and thickening before thee. Farewell, and again farewell!

The weather was propitious, and the ship ran that day before the wind forty miles down to the fertile island of Coos; the next day it reached Rhodes, famed for its Colossus, or huge statue of Apollo, at its harbour, and thence entered the port of Patara—a maritime city a short way to the east of the mouth of the river Xanthus. The vessel proceeded no farther, but "finding a ship sailing over unto Phœnicia, we went aboard, and set forth." On the voyage they sighted Cyprus, and "passing it on the *left hand*," that is, to the east, "sailed into Syria, and landed at Tyre, for there the ship was to unlade her burden." While the crew were employed in discharging the cargo, Paul and his companions were also busy "*finding* disciples;" having sought them out, "we tarried there seven days." These disciples, who may have seen the apostle at an earlier period, when he "went through Syria," urged him not to proceed to Jerusalem. They knew from supernatural intimation what dangers awaited him, and they implored him to avoid them. But his martyr-spirit would not listen, and both parties as they separated offered prayer on the beach to God. Taking ship, they came to Ptolemais—called Acco in the Old Testament, and now St. Jean d'Acre—and remained one day. On the morrow they travelled by land to Cæsarea, a distance of about forty-four miles, and took up their abode with Philip the evangelist, one of the seven deacons appointed at an earlier period, and whose four virgin daughters enjoyed the gift of prophecy, as Joel had predicted of the latter times.

During their sojourn at Philip's house, a Judean prophet named Agabus joined them—"And when he was come unto us, he took Paul's girdle, and bound his own hands, and said, Thus saith the Holy Ghost, So shall the Jews at Jerusalem bind the man that owneth this girdle, and shall deliver him into the hands of the Gentiles." This prophecy and its dramatic accompaniment produced a deep effect on the whole company, and they unanimously besought Paul to pause in his journey: "Then Paul answered, What mean ye to weep and to break mine heart? for I am ready not to be bound only, but also to die at Jerusalem for the name of the Lord Jesus." He was not to be deterred by any danger from what he believed to be the path of duty. He wished to carry to Jerusalem the collections made in the Gentile churches, in the hope of healing the division between Hebrew and heathen believers. He had assumed what he regarded as a sacerdotal function, being the "minister of Jesus Christ to the Gentiles, ministering the gospel of God, that the offering up of the Gentiles might be acceptable, being sanctified by the Holy Ghost." The Gentile churches were his oblation prepared for Pentecost, a living "tribute of a free-will offering." He was ready not to be bound only, but also to die. He did not court martyrdom, but he did not shrink from it. The prospect of it did not alarm him, for he had risen far above the fear of death. Faith achieves what philosophy fails to do. The calm and contemplative Hobbes was often terrified at the idea of martyrdom, lest the Leviathan he had so laboriously created should devour him. The great mind of Samuel Johnson lay under solemn terror many a day at the thought of death. Vexation and disappointment, affecting their vanity or their ambition, have also killed not a few. On the other hand, the leonine heart of the German reformer approached that of Paul, but Paul made no boast. Luther avowed that he would go to Leipzig, though it should rain Duke Georges for nine days, and that he would enter Worms though there should be as many devils in it as there were tiles on the roofs of its houses. The humble spirit of the apostle did not indulge in such hyperboles; he had neither the natural buoyancy nor physical robustness of the hearty Saxon. As they proceeded to Jerusalem, it is said, "We took up our carriages," or, as the Geneva version has it, "trussed up our fardels"—packing up the luggage necessary for the journey. Arrived at Jerusalem, they were gladly welcomed by the brethren, and seem to have dwelt with Mnason of Cyprus, an *old disciple*—a disciple from the beginning, or from the commencement of the new dispensation, perhaps a personal follower of the Lord. Paul lost no time in visiting James and declaring "particularly what things God had wrought among the Gentiles by his ministry," and James and the elders, when they heard such a report, "glorified the Lord."

But what course should be now pursued? The apostle of the Gentiles, spite of all his efforts to win them, was an object of extreme dislike to the Jewish zealots—"the many thousands which believe, and are all zealous of the law."

James proposed a compromise to which Paul assented. We enter not on the question whether Paul did right in submitting in such a matter of formal ceremonial to the Mosaic statute; whether he did not venture beyond the legitimate range of his own principle of becoming "to the Jews as a Jew." Suffice it to say that the unforeseen result was—the peril of his life and the visit to Rome, on which his heart had been set, but which was accomplished in a way which he had not anticipated.

Some of the Asiatic Jews, that is, from Ephesus, imagined that he had profaned the temple by bringing an Ephesian into it, whom they had seen with him in some parts of the city. A tumult was easily raised during the feast, and the apostle was dragged out of the temple, for his enemies would not pollute it with his blood. The military governor of the city, during the festivals when popular commotions so often broke out, had his men under arms in the neighbouring fortress of Antonia which jealously overlooked the temple, and on a report of the emeute being carried to him, ran at once "with soldiers and centurions" to the spot and rescued Paul, after he had been roughly handled and beaten. Would not the scene appear to Paul like a repetition of that in which he had taken so prominent a part— the martyrdom of Stephen? It was simply because the mob was without weapons that the apostle survived; and they still pressed so violently upon him, that he was lifted up the garrison stairs by the soldiers, "lest he should be torn in pieces." As he was about to enter the barracks of the fortress, he said to the chief captain, "May I speak unto thee?" who, surprised at hearing himself addressed in this language, replied, "Canst thou speak Greek?" Claudius Lysias had evidently taken him for the ringleader of a recent rebellion. The answer of the apostle satisfied him, and, as requested, he permitted him to address the furious rabble. One wonders at the permission, but the manner and aspect of the prisoner must have showed that he was no rebel, that he was not fitted to be a political or military leader, that he had neither the hardy frame nor the browned aspect of a guerilla chieftain. The apostle had spoken in many a place, but never in a scene of such excitement—the stricken deer turning to the hounds whose tongues were lapping her blood in anticipation. He had preached in the synagogue amidst clamour, and had declaimed on Mars-hill to a sneering and indifferent audience, and he would have gone into the theatre at Ephesus had his friends not dissuaded him. But now in Jerusalem, with the temple in view—the sacred spot of his people and himself—under the shadow of the smoke which arose from the great altar, after an assault in which he had been rudely jostled and savagely struck, his clothes torn and his cheeks streaming with blood, he calmly faces his infuriated foes; and without trepidation, and as if there had not been but a step between him and death a few moments before, "beckoned with the hand unto the people." He had spoken to the chief captain in Greek, but he now addressed them *in the Hebrew tongue*—the Syro-Chaldaic which they were now in the habit of speaking as their mother-tongue. They expected him to address them in Greek, and might be able to understand him, but "they kept the more silence" when he bespoke their attention in a Hebrew preamble. They took it as a national compliment, and their fury at once subsided before the words of the orator who stood above them upon the stairs, the tribune behind him, and beside him two soldiers to whom he was "bound with two chains."

Thus he begins—"Men, brethren, and fathers, hear ye my defence which I now make before you. I am myself a Jew—of Tarsus in Cilicia it is true, yet brought up in this city at the feet of Gamaliel, educated according to the strict doctrine of the law of my fathers, being zealous toward God, like as ye all are this day. I was one who persecuted this way unto the death, binding and throwing into prison men and women, as also the high-priest bears me witness (he being still alive), and all the council from whom, having received letters also to the brethren, I was journeying to Damascus for the purpose of bringing those who were there to Jerusalem in fetters, that they might be punished. And it came to pass, as I was journeying and drawing near Damascus, about noon, suddenly from heaven there shone a great light round about me. And I fell to the ground, and heard a voice calling to me—Saul, Saul, why persecutest thou Me? and I answered—Who art Thou, Lord? and He said to me—I am Jesus the Nazarene whom thou persecutest. And the men who were with me saw indeed the light, and were terror-struck, but they heard not (understood not) the voice of Him that was speaking to me. And I said—What shall I do, Lord? And the Lord said—Arise and proceed to Damascus; there it shall be told thee of all the things which it is appointed thee to do. But as now I did not see on account of the glory of that light, being led by the hand by those who were with me, I came to Damascus. And one Ananias, a devout man according to the law, having a good report among all the Jews who dwelt there, coming to me and standing over me, said to me—Brother Saul, receive thy sight (look up). And the same hour I looked up upon him (received my sight). And he said—The God of our fathers has foreappointed thee to know His will, and to behold the righteous One, and to hear the voice of His mouth; for thou shalt be a witness for Him to all men of what thou hast seen. And now why delayest thou? Arise and have thyself baptized and thy sins washed away, calling on His name. And it came to pass, after I had returned to Jerusalem, and while I was praying in the temple, that I fell into an ecstacy, and saw Him saying to me—Haste and get thee quickly out of Jerusalem; for they will not receive thy testimony concerning me. And I said—Lord, they know themselves that I was ever imprisoning and beating from synagogue to synagogue those that believe on thee; and when the blood of thy martyr, Stephen, was shed, I myself also was standing by and consenting heartily and keeping the raiment of those who slew him. And He said to me—Depart; for unto the heathen afar off am I about to send thee."

Now, first, we may notice what may be called the artfulness of this address. He does not obtrude offensive matter; now that he is out of their hands, he does not speak to chafe them, that he may enjoy their futile rage. No; he speaks honestly, but he speaks with wondrous skill, that he may carry them along with him. He uses their favourite tongue, though himself a Hellenist, and for the purpose of propitiating them. He styles them out of respect brethren and fathers; tells them his relationship to Gamaliel and his education as a zealous Pharisee; refers to the high-priest who had sanctioned his proceeding; calls the Jews in Damascus "the brethren;" names Jesus only when he quotes what He said; describes Ananias as "pious according to the law" and in high repute among his countrymen, while the previous narrative names him a "disciple;" speaks of Jehovah by the Israelitish term, "the God of our fathers;" and informs them how after his change he came back to the temple and did as all devout Jews did—prayed in it. The orator did not wish to give unnecessary provocation, but he makes a calm and impressive statement.

Again, he appeals for confirmation to themselves. Theophilus, the high-priest from whom he received his letter or commission to Damascus, was alive, and might be present; while many of the sanhedrim might also survive. What he wished them to infer was, that he had not changed for light reasons—that he could not but change—that the glory which enveloped him at mid-day was no deception—and that his ears had actually heard the voice of the Nazarene. It was the Nazarenes, as they were contemptuously termed, that he was going to capture and bind in Damascus; and his interceptor styled Himself Jesus the Nazarene—the simplest, but in the circumstances the most alarming and stinging epithet which could be employed. He hoped that they who knew what he was might seek to know what he had become, and why he had abandoned his previous course. This we have already considered in our second chapter—" Paul at Jerusalem."

The account of his conversion here given by himself differs but slightly from the narrative in the ninth chapter. He groups together its more prominent incidents, as they bore upon the object which he had immediately in view. The very fact, that the author of the book of the Acts has left some discrepancies, when he could easily have moulded them into uniformity, shows that he regarded them as in perfect harmony. Speaking from his vivid recollection, the apostle calls the light a "great" light, and he names the precise period of the day—variations from the historical account, but natural to the orator describing earnestly his own experience. The historian relating the circumstances says that the companions of Saul were speechless—the orator simply says they were *afraid*—alarmed. In the ninth chapter it is said—"They heard the voice, but saw no one"—dazzled with excess of light; but here it is said that they "saw the light, but heard not the voice"—the meaning being, that though the splendour enveloped them, they saw not Him from whose glorified humanity it flashed; and though they heard the sound, they could not distinguish the articulate words which it pronounced to the ear of the apostle. The speaker omits what the narrator has told as the dialogue of the Lord with Ananias, but he brings out other features—that Ananias was a Jew, a devout observer of the law, and held in high repute by all the Jews in Damascus. What the apostle reports as being said to him by Ananias is not given in the previous account, but the substance was spoken by the Lord to Ananias, and he naturally repeated it when he visited Saul in the street called Straight. But the appearance of the Redeemer is specially dwelt upon, as this placed Paul on a level with the other apostles as " eye-witnesses of His majesty." From the Saviour's lips he received his commission, and having seen Him, he could testify as truly as Peter and John that He was risen from the dead.

The apostle's main end is to show that he did not disown the religion of his fathers as a creed which he had ceased to believe in—that he had been profoundly attached to it, and still venerated it as divine in its claims and origin—that he had only gone beyond it under a supernatural summons which he durst not resist—that he had espoused the religion of Jesus as the fulfilment of Judaism, and not as a hostile or a rival faith—that he did not cease to be a Jew on becoming a Christian, or renounce the ties of country and kindred—and that his Christianity did not prevent him from revisiting Jerusalem, the chief city of his people, and offering prayer in the temple, their one holy place.

The populace listened till he uttered his commission to the Gentiles: they bore with him till he came to this hated word, and in a moment the sea of faces beneath him lashed itself into fury, and they shouted—"Away with such a fellow from the earth, for it *is not fit* that he should live"—literally, was not fit—he should not have been rescued by the chief captain from our hands. He had been accused of sacrilege—of profaning the holy place—and they imagined that his words were tantamount to a confession of his guilt and a vindication of his conduct. In their phrenzy they cried out, tossed about their clothes in wild excitement, and "threw dust into the air," in token of exasperation. Lysias the tribune, not knowing what the apostle said, and seeing what commotion his foreign words had produced, commanded that he should be taken into the garrison, and put to the torture, that the nature of the charges against him might be discovered. As they bound him with thongs in such a way as to prepare him for the scourge, he felt that it was his right to secure immunity, and put the quiet question to the presiding centurion—"Is it lawful for you to scourge a man that is a Roman and *uncondemned*"—not even put upon his trial? He did not turn in anger and dare or defy them to lay a hand upon him, or tell them what vengeance should fall on them if they did. He states the simple query, and the few words acted like magic. The centurion reported them at once to his tribune, and warned him of the hazard. "Then the chief captain came, and said unto him, Tell me, art thou a Roman? He said, Yea. And the chief captain answered, With a great sum obtained I this freedom. And Paul said, But I was free-born." The prisoner stood on higher ground than his interrogator; they who should have put him to the question left him, and Lysias was afraid, as if he had gone too far in even preparing to scourge a Roman citizen. To bind the prisoner for safe-keeping was no crime, but to bind him into the posture for flagellation was an infringement of the law and the majesty of Rome. But not knowing well what to do in the case, not understanding the nature of the popular enmity and clamour against his prisoner, and "because he would have known the certainty wherefore he was accused of the Jews," he summoned the sanhedrim, "the chief priests, and all their council," "on the morrow," "loosed him from his bands," "and brought Paul down and set him before them."

II.

BEFORE THE SANHEDRIM.

ACTS xxiii. 1—11.

The council are met, not in the old hall, Gazith, where they were wont to assemble—a chamber into which from its position none but a Jew might enter—but in some place beyond the sacred precincts of the temple, and to which the Roman power could have immediate access. The apostle is brought in by his guards, and set before them. It is likely that he had once occupied a seat in that high court himself, but he who had been the judge is now the prisoner. All eyes must have been turned upon him; for his career and character had been notorious, and the agitation of yesterday had scarcely subsided. Some were there who might have known Saul in the school of Gamaliel, and been his competitors in rabbinical studies. They had not only witnessed his piety and admired his erudition, but they must have marked the zeal, energy, and downrightness which had distinguished him, the absence of indifference in his nature, his formation of high and definite purposes and the integrity and tenacity with which he pursued them, the keenness of his intellect and the ardour of his temper, the conscientiousness with which he chose a side, and the chivalrous energy with which he flung himself at once into its defence. Many of them might not have seen him for years, and they could not but be struck with his altered appearance—his furrowed brow and shattered frame. Twenty years of toil, travel, and suffering had told upon him, and he was now such an one as "Paul the aged;" for scourging, stoning, shipwreck, cold, hunger, and rags, continual perils in every place, and perpetual corrosion of heart from the "care of all the churches" had broken down his constitution. Eagerly as the eyes of the sanhedrim scanned him, he quailed not, but calmly and steadily returned their gaze. There stood Paul "earnestly beholding the council," trying whom he could recognize, learning the composition of the assembly on whose votes his fate depended, and balancing the hopes of a fair and impartial investigation.

His lofty moral courage did not desert him, and he begins—"Men and brethren, I have lived in all good conscience before God until this day"—my public life to God has all along been a conscientious one. His life as a member of the theocracy, prior to his change and since his change, had been regulated by conscience. Once, indeed, he persecuted, and now he "built up the faith which he once destroyed." But in both cases he had acted not only sincerely, but in perfect deference to the theocratic principle. Before he understood Christianity he strove to suppress it as an impious innovation, and after he embraced it he felt it to be only the spiritual renovation and development of the old economy. He was a conscientious Jew at both periods—in blaspheming as well as in preaching Christ. He was wrong, indeed, far wrong in the first action, and he honestly and deeply repented it; but he had acted up to his light, and when new light was thrown in upon him he was bound to follow it. He had not become a renegade as they imagined, or renounced his circumcision. He gloried still in Abraham, but more in his faith than in his blood. He had not ceased to love Jerusalem, "the city of solemnities," and he had again and again paid it a visit. He worshipped in the temple, but thought more of the spirit of the service than the mere ceremonial; and he regarded the altar not so much in its present victims as in the real and glorious propitiation which it had prefigured. He had renounced Judaism in the sense that a child leaves the nursery and enters the world, but still remains a member of the same household. He never acted against conscience, allowed no inferior considerations to move him, cast all aside for conviction's sake, yea, had sacrificed all for truth and God. It was this idea that filled his bosom, as he rose to address the council. Nay, he had not forfeited his right to sit there, by obeying the prophets and believing the promised Messiah. Why should one who accepted the national Messiah forfeit any national right? Was any one, by acting as the inspired teachers bade him, to denude himself of any privilege? He will not admit a charge of inconsistency, for he has only taken the step for which Moses and Aaron, David and Isaiah, had prepared him. He had once sat on those benches, and why should not he sit now? He will not allow that he has done anything to disinherit himself, and therefore he says, "Men-brethren," as if he were yet one of themselves—a judge speaking to his colleagues in office. Old scenes revive; he has not cast off his judicial comrades, and though he spoke to the infuriated crowd as "Men, brethren, and fathers," he simply styles the sanhedrim "Men-brethren," not, as Peter had styled them, "Ye rulers of the people, and elders of Israel."

Ananias the high priest could not bear such an introduction. It was not an appeal to clemency, nor even an admission that matters of high moment were in debate. It was more than a plea of not guilty—it was a protestation of positive rectitude, containing in it an implied charge against the judges. Ananias ordered the mouth that uttered these sentiments to be struck, as a penalty for its sin. He had spoken so wrongly that he must be symbolically punished—his "cheek-bone" hit with a sandal, and perhaps his "teeth broken" by the blow. This sudden outbreak of temper was a virtual judicial sentence from the head of the council, and many of them must have acquiesced in it as a just punishment for contempt of court.

The apostle would not bear such an indignity from a court with which he felt himself quite on a level. He wished his case to be tried, and his reply to be fully heard; and it was heartless on the part of Ananias so to treat a man who but the day before had been in danger of his life, and was now defenceless and in the hands of the Roman power. Paul sought only fair play; he wanted no partiality shown him, and he would have scorned to say a word for the mere purpose of ingratiating himself with his judges. But that mouth must be struck, if this ebullition of temper on the part of the president be obeyed—the mouth which had so often dropped those precious pearls, which had given utterance to so many blessed truths in Asia and in Europe, and all because mention was made of conscience, a monitor which Ananias possessed not, or it had so often warned him in vain, that it had ceased to whisper any suggestion or reproof.

The apostle at once answered, and that in no common tone—" God shall smite thee, thou whited wall: for sittest thou to judge me after the law, and commandest me to be smitten contrary to the law?" These words can scarcely be regarded in any other light than a prophecy; no idle malediction or passionate recrimination, but an oracle of doom pronounced on one who had so shamefully outraged the office which he filled. He was a hypocrite, notoriously venal and ambitious; and the sacerdotal robes, made "for glory and for beauty," covered a depraved and cruel heart. His office was to judge according to law, and by evidence calmly weighed; but he violated alike its letter and its spirit by his peremptory order. Ananias, the son of Nebedæus, obtained the office of high priest under the procurator, Tiberius Alexander, and he held it also under the procurator Cumanus. Involved in a quarrel between Jews and Samaritans, he was sent a prisoner to Rome by Quadratus, prefect of Syria, but the emperor Claudius decided in his favour. On his return he retained his office till superseded by Ismael, a short time before the departure of Felix from Judea. After his deposition from the pontificate, " he increased in glory every day," as Josephus says. Bribery and violence had characterized his possession of power, and he occupied a princely palace in the Upper city. But his crooked and nefarious policy provoked a tragical retaliation, and at length, at the commencement of the Jewish insurrection, the sicarii, or lawless assassins, surrounded his house and set fire to it. Ananias fled in haste and took refuge in an aqueduct, out of which he was dragged and slain.

The apostle's words may be regarded as in this way fulfilled. The sentence, however, contains a general principle often illustrated in divine providence. "The Lord is known by the judgment which he executeth: the wicked is snared in the work of his own hands." Thus the maimed Adonibezek confessed, "As I have done, so God hath requited me;" "As thy sword hath made women childless, so shall thy mother be childless among women," said Samuel to Agag; Nathan foretold a retributive fate to David; Daniel's accusers met the punishment which they had plotted for him; and Haman was hanged on the gallows which he had erected for his adversary.

The apostle had no sooner spoken than he was checked. "And they that stood by said, Revilest thou God's high priest?" The rank of Ananias is at once insisted on, as if that could shield him from the awful fulmination. The apostle at once replied—"I wist not, brethren, that he was the high priest: for it is written, Thou shalt not speak evil of the ruler of thy people." The meaning of this verse has been much questioned. It has been said that the apostle means to reply that Ananias was not high priest, but had only usurped the office, and that Paul did not recognize him—a hypothesis that has no sure historical foundation, nor does the apostle speak as this theory supposes. Nor can it mean that Paul did not identify the high priest, inasmuch as he had been long absent from Jerusalem, and might not be acquainted with his person. But the apostle does not say that he had made a mistake of persons, or that he was ignorant of the rank of Ananias, who must have been president of the council. Others imagine that the apostle pleads defective eye-sight, and that his vision had been seriously impaired ever since "the glory of that light" had blinded him. It may be replied that the scales fell from his vision, and that all miracles of restoration are perfect in final result. Or even if his sight remained under partial weakness, it was yet so good as to enable him to work at his occupation as a tentmaker, and to travel by himself in a strange country. Nay more, he had surveyed the council before he began, and must have seen the position of its supreme judge. The word rendered in the first verse "earnestly beholding," does not denote, as some would seem to think, the gaze of one who sees imperfectly; it is rather a steady eager look, and is rendered variously in our version. Thus in Luke iv. 20, where it is said that the "eyes" of all the synagogue with wonder and curiosity "were fastened" on Jesus; Luke xxii. 56, A maid beheld Peter, and "earnestly looked upon him," scanning his features so as to recognize him; or Acts i. 10, The eleven disciples "looked stedfastly toward heaven," to catch a glimpse of the ascending Lord; Acts iii. 4, Peter "fastening his eyes" upon the lame man at the beautiful gate of the temple, said, &c.; or Acts vi. 15, As the face of Stephen became like the face of an angel, all that sat in the council were "looking stedfastly on him," &c.

None of the previous explanations hold for another

reason. The passage of scripture quoted by the apostle refers not exclusively to the high priest, but to any ruler, and was violated if evil was spoken of any ruler or any one of the assembled council. It was no real apology, therefore, that he did not see that it was the high priest who offered him this insolence. It happened, indeed, to be the high priest who spoke, and the apostle answered, "I wist not, brethren, that he was high priest"—words that cannot mean, I did not know that such a man could be a high priest, or, I know the law to which you allude, but, in speaking as I have done, I have not broken it; for, if he was not high priest, and though the apostle might deny his title, he was at least a ruler, and under the shield of the old statute. Had he wished to refuse Ananias all claim to the pontificate, might he not have used the language of those "that stood by"—"I know him not for God's high priest," whatever title he may derive from man's authority? The conclusion, then, seems to be that the apostle had not the knowledge present to his mind that it was the high priest whom he was addressing. He does not formally apologize, but perhaps he intimates that the words might have been differently couched—that he might have uttered the malediction more solemnly, and with less of personal feeling mingled up with it. Nor does he retract it, though he may regret that it did fall upon a successor of Aaron. What a terrible thought that one whose function it was to represent the people, pass beyond the vail, and stand before the ark, should be so foredoomed to be smitten by God!

This incident must have made some commotion, which

allowed the apostle to perceive more clearly the temper of his judges. It must have kindled resentment against himself on the part of those who thought themselves affronted by the insult offered to their president. Justice was not to be expected from an impassioned and prejudiced bench, of the members of which Ananias might be a fair specimen.

The apostle now discerned the composition of the council, and measured his advantage. It was in vain for him to plead any farther—one party were bound by their previous creed to deny the very possibility of his most striking proofs. So that he suddenly threw in a statement which acted like the explosion of a bomb among his judges. "But when Paul perceived that the one part were Sadducees, and the other Pharisees, he cried out in the council, Men and brethren, I am a Pharisee, the son of a Pharisee: of the hope and resurrection of the dead I am called in question. And when he had so said, there arose a dissension between the Pharisees and the Sadducees: and the multitude was divided." The apostle only stated the truth. Not only was he a Pharisee, but the son of a *Pharisee*—or rather Pharisees, his ancestry being Pharisees for many generations back. The phrase—"hope and resurrection of the dead," does not mean merely the hope of a resurrection, but probably contains two distinct ideas—"hope" as a specific thing—that hope in all likelihood being the Messiah—the grand hope of the nation; and the "resurrection of the dead" proved indeed and exemplified in His. Had the prisoner been allowed to proceed, he would soon have unfolded his views, and shown that every consistent Pharisee must follow him to that Saviour who had glorified the law to which they were so deeply attached, and provided that righteousness of which they were so eagerly in quest.

What he was charged with was no novelty. It was as old as the first promise. It was found in the "adoption" as its blessing, in the "covenants" as their peculiar heritage, in "the giving of the law" as its grand object, for it was a schoolmaster till Christ, and in "the promises" as their very centre and fulness. Prayer had been offered, and victims had bled for it. It was what the nation had been originally organized for, and what it lived and longed for. For this hope he was called in question, for a hope alike dear to saint and patriot; and his plea is, that in accepting that hope when presented in the fulness of the time, he had acted with perfect consistency as a Jew, and with honest faith as a believer in God. He had only done as an individual what the nation should have done as a body, and had done simply what God had intended they should do—ay, and had long trained them for doing. His conversion had only anticipated what might have been and ought to have been the national decision as to the nation's hope.

The resurrection of the dead had been an article of the national creed, but it was confirmed and illustrated by the resurrection of Him who brought life and immortality to light. The resurrection implies a future state. That future state did not occupy any place among the ratifications of the Mosaic code, which was guarded by a special providence, nor does it come into prominence among the Hebrew prophets. But it is there—though in comparative obscurity. Isaiah sings—"Thy dead men shall live," and the figure in Ezekiel as to the valley and the dry bones, is based upon the popular belief and conception of the reality. The Pharisees held by this faith, but the Sadducees denied it. These rationalists were also materialists—saying that there is "no resurrection, neither angel nor spirit;" either denying a spirit-world altogether, or affirming that mind is but the result of cerebral organization—that there is no soul in man, or that it dies with his body. How they received the Old Testament, and explained away the passages in which angels and supernatural beings are so often spoken of, we do not know. Only we know that a similar process is not uncommon, and that men in our days profess to accept scripture, and yet explain away its natural meaning—declaring the story of creation to be a myth, and that of the deluge a fable; regarding angels but as names of such messengers as a "flaming fire," and devils but as the dreams of a dark superstition; holding that prophecy is but sagacious conjecture, and miracles but dexterous feats; and even affirming that the language of Jesus in reference to demoniac possession and the resurrection from the dead, was merely a conformity to current forms of thought and language. Men may profess to take the Bible, and thus eliminate all that characterizes it—as if there might be salvation without a saviour, and without human souls to be saved.

The council was at once divided. "And there arose a great cry: and the scribes that were of the Pharisees' part arose, and strove, saying, We find no evil in this man; but if a spirit or angel hath spoken to him, let us not fight against God." The commotion became violent—the disputants waxed very angry. Fierce polemical passions were at once let loose. The Pharisees suddenly discovered that their old adherent might be used as a champion against their Sadducean foes, and at once they took his side—ceased to be judges, and sank into partisans. It was a strange reaction when they shouted—"We find no evil in this man"—a sentiment which they could not in their hearts believe, but what he had spoken was an opportune war-cry. And they added in their new-born zeal and patronage—"But if a spirit or an angel hath spoken to him" . . . and the rest of the sentence was drowned in the uproar. The one word rendered—"Let us not fight against God"—does not appear to form a portion of the text, and the abrupt sentence has a special emphasis, the very reference to spirit and angel exasperating their opponents into a yell which interrupted the speakers. Thus orthodoxy clamoured, and heresy retorted with similar din—nay, the debate was intensified into action, hands were laid on the apostle, and he was clutched hither and thither by his unexpected allies and their antagonists. Then the chief captain feared "lest Paul should have been pulled in pieces of them"—some assaulting, and others defending him; and there being no hope of the restoration of quiet, and not knowing how far the unseemly excitement might be carried, Lysias "commanded the soldiers to go down and to take him by force from among them, and bring him into the castle."

During the following night, when strange thoughts must have occupied his mind—the scenes of the day starting up before him, and the events of his previous life, from the martyrdom of Stephen and his departure under the high priest's commission to Damascus, rising vividly in his recollection, while his mind was profoundly impressed by the truth of the repeated warning that imprisonment awaited him in Jerusalem, and he might be wondering as to the issue, and whether his fate should be that of the protomartyr, or whether he should be able to accomplish his earnest wish of visiting Italy—the Lord stood by him and said, "Be of good cheer, Paul, for as thou hast testified of me in Jerusalem, so must thou bear witness also at Rome." His heart was at once relieved and comforted. The cloud was lifted. The Lord was his shield, and had been a witness of all the procedure. Faithful service is never overlooked; His eye is never dimmed. "Be of good cheer" is His frequent salute, and His words do their own errands, creating what they command. They come in the crisis, and men wonder at the martyr's courage. How is it that fetters and stripes, and every form of refined cruelty, do not quench the soul; that the sight of the rack or the gibbet, the cage of wild beasts, or the fagots piled up before the stake, do not terrify a prisoner into weakness or recantation? Is it not that Jesus has spoken, and the words are yet ringing in his ears—"Be of good cheer?" May not every one who works and witnesses for Jesus enjoy the same blessed consolation? Shall He withhold His words from the faithful spirit that bows to no will but His, relies on no strength but His, and covets no assistance but His? Nay, such loyalty reposing on such confidence brings Jesus ever near, as He still repeats the same syllables—"Be of good cheer."

The sanhedrim could not destroy the apostle; an invisible hand interposed and stayed their fury. No matter what delays might happen, or what obstacle the tardy and hostile operations of law might create—Rome is the goal. There were compearances before Felix and Festus, and two years of captivity at Cesarea; the storm raged fiercely in the Mediterranean, sending the ship of Alexandria far out of her course, and casting her upon an island a total wreck; but another vessel received the prisoner, and he whose name and fame had preceded him, landed safely at Puteoli, where some of the brethren welcomed him—" and so we went towards Rome."

XVI.—PAUL AT CESAREA.

II.

BEFORE FELIX.—ACTS XXIV. 1-23.

THE apostle's work was done in Jerusalem, and so the words of Jesus had intimated. But how he was to reach Rome he could not tell, and events were happening around him which threatened to defeat the Master's promise. Disappointed of their prey, more than forty Jews "banded together, and bound themselves under a curse, saying, that they would neither eat nor drink till they had killed Paul." This conspiracy indicates the rancorous fanaticism which characterized the people. Probably those men were sicarii, or zealots—that desperate class who, pleading the example of Phinehas, took the execution of the law into their own hands, and at length sank into hired assassins—paid agents of private revenge. To show the state of feeling and morals, we are told that they made their purpose known to the sanhedrim, who, from the report of Paul's nephew, seem to have acquiesced in the murderous project. Such a conspiracy was quite in accordance with the temper of the people. Josephus tells us of ten men who combined in a similar way against the life of Herod, because he was deemed an apostate; and Philo, another contemporary of the apostle—a calm, meditative, and philosophical Jew—given to speculation rather than political or ecclesiastical policy, thus writes—"It is highly proper that all who have a zeal for virtue should have a right to punish with their own hands, without delay, those who are guilty of this crime; not carrying them before a court of judicature, or the council, or, in short, before any magistrate; but they should indulge the abhorrence of evil, the love of God, which they entertain, by inflicting immediate punishment on such impious apostates, regarding themselves for the time as all things—senators, judges, prætors, sergeants, accusers, witnesses, the laws, the people—so that, hindered by nothing, they may without fear, and with all promptitude, espouse the cause of piety." But Providence has many modes of working out its ends. It is not the tribune or his centurions who are to save Paul; nor is there to be any bold or sagacious unravelling of the plot. A young man suddenly steps upon the scene, and frustrates it. Gaining a knowledge of it by some means, he first informs his uncle, and by him is sent to the chief captain to give him similar insight. Lysias was well aware of the unscrupulous nature of the men with whom he had to deal, and at once took measures for his prisoner's safety and sent him the same night under a strong military escort to Cesarea.

And thus Paul finally left Jerusalem—a prisoner guarded by a troop of soldiers. He had come to it in early youth with bright hopes and eager purposes. His rabbinical studies had delighted him, and he outstripped many competitors. The juvenile emotions of the student, as he first gazed upon the metropolis—the city of God, and the scene of so many glories and disasters—must have been in strange contrast to his feelings, when as a prisoner, and to escape assassination, he issued from one of its northern gates, in the midst of four hundred soldiers, and took the road to Cesarea. He had left it on one memorable occasion for Damascus, and come back three years after totally changed in soul and pursuit. Again and again had he visited it, but now he takes leave of it for ever—a foreign power protecting him from its lawless and vengeful populace; the clatter of those hoofs, and the glitter of those spears in the starlight, ever and anon impressing him with the strangeness of his situation, and showing him that Christ can make the enemies of his nation his shield and defence. A few years later and the Roman engines compass the "holy city." Assault after assault is made upon it; point after point is gained through successive breaches; murder, faction, plague, and famine reign within it; the temple is set on fire; the streets run with blood; wild shrieks rise high above the uproar—Jerusalem has fallen. It had been Melchizedek's citadel and David's capital—the place of sacrifice and worship—the scene of the national gatherings at the Passover and Pentecost—and the dwelling-place of the ark and the cherubim. But its reverses had been as marked as its glories. Shishak and his bands from the Nile had sacked it; Arabians and Assyrians had captured and plundered it; Necho and his Egyptian legions had levied contributions from it; Sennacherib had invested it, but was utterly smitten by its guardian angel; Nebuchadnezzar had left it a heap of stones and dust, but it had been rebuilt; Alexander of Macedon had approached it with hostile intentions, but spared and honoured it; Ptolemy of Egypt ruthlessly spoiled it; Antiochus Epiphanes ravaged it with characteristic ferocity; the Maccabean chieftains restored and purified it; Herod adorned and beautified it—but its days were numbered, and in a brief period it became a mass of ruins, and yet is "trodden down of the Gentiles." But as the apostle went out of it for the last time, he could not but feel the power of early associations; not only the memories of old historic times—of Solomon's glory, Hezekiah's revival, and Ezra's patriotic enterprise—but also of more recent events which had hallowed Siloam and Gethsemane, and shed an undying lustre on Calvary and the Mount of Olives.

Along with the prisoner Lysias sends a despatch to Felix the governor. The despatch states the case with truth in its general features, but in such a way as to produce the impression that the tribune had done his duty from another motive than the real one. He writes—"This man was taken of the Jews, and should have been killed of them: then came I with an army, and rescued him, having understood that he was a Roman." But it was not true that he had rescued him from the knowledge that he was a Roman citizen; for he was not aware of this fact till after the capture, and when he was about to do him the worst of all indignities—to scourge him. But the credit which he so adroitly takes to himself verifies the document as the report of a Roman officer who wishes to stand well with his superior. Felix, on receiving the letter, asked of what province he was; and when he understood that he was of Cilicia—"I will hear thee, said he, when thine accusers are also come. And he commanded him to be kept in Herod's judgment-hall."

After five days Ananias the high priest and the elders

came to Cesarea, and along with them a *certain orator*—a professional pleader, who was to lay the charges against Paul before the governor. The trial began, and Tertullus set forth the various points of accusation—unsparing in his invective, throwing out insinuations against Lysias the chief captain, and screening the Jews from blame. But the orator told a falsehood when he said—" Whom we took and would have judged according to our law;" for the mob would have put the apostle to death without any trial, had the chief captain not prevented them. But Tertullus represents him as impeding " by great violence" an ordinary process of Jewish law. The charges against Paul were artfully laid by a forensic debater, " and the Jews also assented, saying that these things were so."

The prisoner at the bar had no counsel—had the benefit of no professional skill—but rose to reply for himself when the governor beckoned to him. His answer is a plain statement of facts. He had heard the charges, and he calmly refutes them, count by count—showing the impossibility of some of them, and the absurdity of others. He began by the usual complimentary appeal—not false and fulsome, as that of Tertullus, but one that only spoke the truth—referring to the long period of six years during which Felix had been governor, and the consequent knowledge which he must have acquired of Jewish character and customs. He then refers to the knowledge which Felix could easily obtain as to his actings since he had come into Palestine. His whole conduct during that brief period could bear the closest inspection—" Because that thou mayest understand, that there are yet but twelve days since I went up to Jerusalem for to worship. And they neither found me in the temple disputing with any man, neither raising up the people, neither in the synagogues, nor in the city: neither can they prove the things whereof they now accuse me." Those twelve days have been variously counted, but may be thus given—first day, his arrival; the second, his interview with James; the third, his assumption of the vow; the fourth, fifth, and sixth, its continuance; the seventh, his apprehension; the eighth, his appearance before the council; the ninth, his nocturnal departure for Cesarea; the tenth, eleventh, and twelfth, at Cesarea; the thirteenth, being the day of the trial, for five days after his departure from Jerusalem, Ananias came down to Cesarea.

During this interval, the apostle did none of the things with which he was charged. He entered into no disputes, and addressed no popular assembly, in any supposable place, for he was under a vow. Not only had he not committed those misdemeanours, but he had not even had the requisite opportunity. Therefore he defied them to the proof. Their allegations against him were baseless. He was no pest, and no mover of sedition. Nay, he goes on to affirm that he was a better or more consistent Jew than his accusers. "But this I confess unto thee, that after the way which they call heresy, so worship I the God of my fathers, believing all things which are written in the law and in the prophets." He does not deny his Christianity; and he admits that they called it *heresy* or schism, as Tertullus had already said. This portion of the accusation was true, but far from true in their sense. He adored no new God, he still worshipped the paternal God—using a classic epithet of special significance before a Roman judge. The Roman law allowed this toleration to the Jew, and the apostle claimed its protection. None other God than the national God—the God of Abraham, Isaac, and Jacob—the God who had done such wonders for them, and for whose service that temple had been erected—the God owned by the nation, and still standing in a covenant relationship to it—none other God did the apostle acknowledge, worship, or preach. He was therefore no apostate or innovator—no setter forth of strange divinities. Nay more, he worshipped the God whom his nation had always worshipped, in the way which Himself had prescribed, for he was "believing all things which are written in the law and in the prophets." He honoured God by crediting His oracles. He would not discredit Jehovah by denying His revelations. It was his pure and comprehensive faith in the Old Testament that made him what he was. He held by the national creed as well as by the national God. He had virtually uttered the same sentiment before—maintaining, that when he became a Christian, he had not ceased to be a Jew; nay, that the only consistent Jew is he who becomes a disciple of Jesus of Nazareth—of Him of whom the law, the prophets, and the psalms, are so full—and follows out the teaching and predictions of Moses and his inspired successors. Had not he believed the Old Testament foreshowing Christ, he had never been a Christian believing in Christ. Warned by God of a Christ to come, he simply accepted Him when He had come at the time and in the place predicted: so that he held by the national faith more intelligently, honestly, and piously than did his accusers. He had done nothing that they were not bound to do, if they would only obey the God of their fathers "with a perfect heart, and with a willing mind." He believed that God had been true to His promises, but they did not. He believed that God had sent the great Deliverer at the period predicted, but they did not.

He subjoins farther—" And have hope toward God, which they themselves also allow, that there shall be a resurrection of the dead, both of the just and unjust." He and they had the very same hope. They were at one in acknowledging the same God, and the same scriptures, and they had also the same hope for futurity. That hope is the hope of a resurrection, or what he had already expressed in his address before the sanhedrim, but always connected in his mind with the resurrection of Jesus as its pledge and pattern. The Pharisees, and indeed the nation generally, held this view—the Sadducees being always a minority. Having this great similarity of faith with his nation, he differed only in this—that he believed God had verified his oft-given pledge to them, and held that this belief, " the way which they called heresy," was yet the highest homage to the God of truth. Then he repeats the sentiment, for the utterance of which before the Jewish council Ananias had commanded him to be smitten on the mouth. " And herein do I exercise myself to have always a conscience void of offence toward God and toward men." That is— in consequence of this belief—my worship of my fathers' God, my faith in the law and the prophets, and my hope of a resurrection—I discipline myself so as to have and to hold an offenceless conscience in every way toward God and toward men. I have nothing to charge against myself. I have uniformly followed conviction. In becoming a Christian, I have obeyed God; and since I became a Christian, I have acted toward men honestly—not stirring up strife unnecessarily, but labouring to bring them to the same belief. He had not been a pest, though he strove to disseminate his views; nor yet a mover of sedition, though his enemies had broken the peace and tried to inculpate him. No, he was a consistent member of the theocracy, and the gospel which he had espoused and preached was only its fruit and fulfilment. He had simply followed whither God had pointed, and his conscience was void of offence toward Him; and as he had striven to make his countrymen think with himself, had taught them no error nor asked them to forsake Jehovah, their fathers' God, so his conscience was void of offence also toward men. And this was a perpetual work with him, no periodical task, or detached effort of casuistry—" I exercise myself," I put it before me as an aim, and ever nerve myself to realize it. His ends were not his own—he obeyed God, and served man.

The apostle now comes to the special charge which had led to his apprehension—" Now, after many years, I came to bring alms to my nation, and offerings." Several years had elapsed—four, or it may be five—since his last visit to the capital. But he had not come as a sower of sedition. He has said already that he came to worship, and he adds more precisely as to the purpose of his journey, that he came to bring alms to his nation, and offerings. He does not mean that he brought the offerings in the same sense as he brought the alms. The offerings were those made in the temple in connection with the vow which he had taken upon himself, and with the purification of the Nazarites, whose expenses, at the suggestion of James, he had engaged to defray, perhaps out of the same fund which had been collected among the foreign churches. The offerings are introduced also as a kind of afterthought. No mention is made in the history of the alms and offerings, but there are many references in the epistles—Rom. xv. 25, 26; 1 Cor. xvi. 1—4; 2 Cor. viii. 1—4; and this is one of those undesigned coincidences which attest the credibility of the New Testament. His object was to bring alms to the poor, but he also presented offerings in the temple. How could he then be accused of disloyalty or irreligion when he had so sedulously gathered alms for his poorer brethren, and when he frequented the temple and engaged in its most solemn acts of devotion? He thus boldly, and by a bare statement of facts, disposes of the allegations made against him. How the disturbance which had involved him came to be made he next states—"Whereupon certain Jews from Asia found me purified in the temple, neither with multitude, nor with tumult." "Whereupon" is literally—"in which," or "amid which" occupations showing my love to my nation, and my fidelity to the law. The verse is variously read. Literally it is, "In the midst of which they found me purified in the temple, neither with multitude nor uproar, but certain Jews from Asia"—gathered the crowd and made the tumult.

THE BASELESSNESS OF THE PROSECUTION. 389

The apostle was in the temple, a devout conscientious Jew, and, so far from being disorderly, he was found "neither with multitude, nor with tumult." He had caused no disturbance and gathered no crowd, but, as quietly and devoutly as the throng of worshippers around him, he had entered into the ceremonial service. The Jews from Asia were from Ephesus, and had known him there. They surmised that he had brought Trophimus into the temple and profaned it, and raised an immediate alarm and outcry—no difficult thing amidst the crowds assembled at Pentecost. He had not been seized by any officers of the law on any definite charge which might be substantiated by legal evidence, but he had been set upon by a disorderly mob. Besides, the very persons who made the accusation, and "shouted—Men of Israel, help!" should have been produced in evidence against him, or, as he says, "Who ought to have been here before thee, and object, if they had ought against me." This statement is a legitimate objection to the entire proceeding. Where were the witnesses? What could they depone? Ananias and the deputation from the sanhedrim could bear no witness, for their witness was but hearsay. The Ephesian Jews were the proper parties to hear, if they had ought against him. But they were not brought forward. The conclusion the apostle comes to is, that without these there could be no case against him. Why should a man be prosecuted in absence of all the principal witnesses?

The prisoner makes another appeal to his very enemies—"Or else let these same here say if they have found any evil-doing in me, while I stood before the council, except it be for this one voice, that I cried standing among them, Touching the resurrection of the dead I am called in question by you this day." If the Ephesian Jews cannot be brought into court, let the men who had come to Cesarea and now accused him—let them tell what they knew against him. They could, indeed, depone nothing as to the original charge, but let them say what crime they found in him when under their own cognizance. Nothing could they allege except this one voice, the bold statement he had made at their tribunal. The inference is, that this saying can surely be no sufficient foundation for a charge, for it was only the utterance of a faith held by the people as a body. The repetition of the sentiment shows that the apostle was not ashamed of it, that he sought not to conceal it, but gloried in it, as showing his own consistency as a Hebrew disciple, and as disproving the accusations of religious disaffection and anti-national feelings and deeds which were so rifely brought against him.

Such is the brief report of the apostle's reply. It deals in no generalities. It is no laboured response, artful in its statements, bringing into bold relief what was for him, and throwing into shadow what might tell against him; pressing into his service a variety of subsidiary arguments; making strong protestations of innocence, with magnificent disclaimers of all animosity, and of all intention to create tumult. But it is a bare statement of facts, so clearly and succinctly put, that none but a man of conscious innocence could have spoken it. He invites examination, and appeals to the means of conducting it. He holds that his original accusers should have been cited, and he appeals to the members of the sanhedrim as to his conduct when before them. The majesty of the Roman law, allowing him to finish his reply without interruption, presents a striking contrast to the rude and unmannerly exhibition of temper in the Jewish council. Anarchy is worse than tyranny, and Cæsar's sword was less to be dreaded than the daggers of the zealots.

The apostle's address produced some effect on Felix—" And when Felix heard these things, having more perfect knowledge of that way, he deferred them, and said, When Lysias the chief captain shall come down, I will know the uttermost of your matter." This rendering is correct. The phrase, "having more perfect knowledge" of that way, does not mean that the knowledge of Felix was made more perfect from Paul's address, but that from his position and long experience he had a knowledge of Christianity not usually found in his rank and station. From his better information of *that way*—of Christianity—he saw the hollowness of the accusation, and ought at once to have acquitted the apostle. But a man of his character was afraid to offend the Jews, and therefore he adjourned the diet, on the pretext of waiting till Lysias, so much implicated in the matter, should come down to Cesarea. The real motive, however, appears to have been what is afterwards stated—the expectation of being bribed by the prisoner to grant his release.

But the main point is gained. The high priest and elders were evidently very wishful to have Paul under their own jurisdiction, and Tertullus blames Lysias for his interference, while he also hints at the inconvenience of being forced to come to Cesarea and conduct the trial. But Paul is detained at Cesarea, safe from Jewish malice—from mobs and conspirators. During his detention he is kept in "free custody," not confined to a prison, but under charge of a centurion, who "should forbid none of his acquaintance to minister or come unto him." Of these there might be not a few in Cesarea, Agabus and his four daughters, as well as Aristarchus and Luke.

II.

BEFORE FELIX AND DRUSILLA.

ACTS XXIV. 24—27.

The baffled accusers of the apostle returned to Jerusalem. Their prey had escaped; nay, as was very strange, Cæsar had delivered him from a successor of Aaron. The affair must have excited some commotion, and Felix must have talked of it to Drusilla. The curiosity of the young and beautiful Jewess was excited, and "after certain days" Paul was sent for by the governor to gratify himself and his wife. The character of both was notorious. As a prefect Felix was rapacious and dishonourable, though not without energy in repressing disorders. Brought to Rome as a slave, he became a freedman of Claudius, and crept up, through meanness and unscrupulous subservience, to the position he filled. His brother Pallas and himself had been flagitious plunderers of the public exchequer. Booty and bribery he took in every form during his government of Judea. Several worthy priests, friends of Josephus, he imprisoned for a frivolous reason, and sent them to Rome; nay, by means of hired assassins he secured the death of Jonathan the pontiff, who had been so honest and patriotic as to expostulate with him on his misgovernment. During his procuratorship, the Jewish historian says, "he saw Drusilla; and being captivated with her beauty, persuaded her to desert her husband, transgress the laws of her country, and marry himself." Drusilla was the youngest daughter of Herod Agrippa I.—the Herod who killed James, and soon after died at Cesarea, "eaten up of worms." She was betrothed at her father's death, and when she was only six years old, to Epiphanes, prince of Commagene; but on his refusal to submit to circumcision and become a Jew, as an indispensable condition of the nuptials, she was married to Azizus, king of Emesa, from whom Felix, aided by a sorcerer named Simon, from Cyprus, induced her to elope. Herself and her son by this union perished during an eruption of Vesuvius in the reign of the Emperor Titus.

Felix and Drusilla being seated in pomp, the prisoner was introduced and asked to discourse "concerning *the faith in Christ*"—in that Messiah which the Jewish books foretold, and of whom Drusilla, as a Jewess, must have often heard, both as the hope of the nation, and as being identified by many with the child whose birth had so alarmed her great-grandfather, that he slew the babes in Bethlehem; whose herald's fidelity had so enraged her grand-uncle that he beheaded him for Herodias' sake; and the progress of whose religion had provoked her father to "kill James, the brother of John, with the sword." The topics on which the apostle discoursed were connected with the "faith in Christ." You cannot suppose him to entertain his august auditors with mere ethical discussions, when they wished him to speak of his theology; for he well knew that no virtue can be truly practised without a sufficient motive, and that this ruling power in the soul must be its love to Christ; nay, that the soul must escape danger through faith in the

Saviour ere it can possess righteousness or exercise temperance or self-command. Righteousness and temperance were, therefore, discussed and enforced not with the speculation of a philosopher, but with the directness and power of an apostle. What faith in Jesus is, he must have told them—what it implied, and on what foundation it rested; what blessings spring out of it, and what a profound and happy change it works on the heart and character. Before Drusilla he must have adduced the proofs of the Messiahship, as she still held by the national faith; and before Felix and her he could not but expatiate on some elements of that holiness which the gospel inculcates and the Lord Jesus had exemplified. Those elements referred to are selected by the historian, probably because they bore so directly on the conscience of the guilty pair to whom the prisoner delivered the requested sermon.

He discoursed on *righteousness*—not as the means of justification, but as the result of sanctifying influence; not merely the equity, which a judge like Felix should display, but that rectitude which underlies the entire code of morality—that sense of duty which leads a man to be what he ought to be, and to do what he ought to do to all around him and on all occasions. Such integrity springs from that love which is the fulfilment of the law. It will not only not injure, but it will also benefit; for this is a duty. It will not merely abstain from wrong, but it will rejoice to impart good; for this is right. It is benevolence expressed under the form of right, and conditioned by human relationship. Let us picture such a man acting under law to Christ. Should a wild beast be found in his property, he will not merely drive it out of his own domain, heedless of the ravages it may commit on his neighbour; a farther duty is demanded. In any scene of general danger and loss, he will not simply look after himself and secure himself against harm; something more is laid upon him. If he can in any way benefit another, he cannot refrain from doing it, either by a kind suggestion, a word of warning, or a deed of beneficence; and all the while he feels that he is but doing what is incumbent on him. This generosity is not something which he can dispense with, or indulge in as he pleases; it ever shapes itself into the form of a righteous obligation. He must do it; it is an element of duty, of righteousness—of equity robed in love. The apostle dwelt on this in its connection with faith in Christ; for He has enjoined it, and has shown in Himself what it is. And it must have struck the mind of him of whom the great Roman painter of character says —" that he thought himself licensed to do all crimes with impunity." The idea of obligation had neither power nor existence within him; duty was a term foreign to his depraved nature, which sought immediate gratification at all hazards, and cared for nothing else. The great master just referred to depicts him in another of his inimitable strokes, as one "who through every extent of ferocity and lust, exercised the power of a king with the soul of a slave." No wonder that such a man as he, when he saw himself read so thoroughly and all his turpitude exposed, winced, and was startled under the calm gaze and searching sermon of his prisoner.

The apostle discoursed on *temperance*—self-restraint generally, but with special reference to continence; the command of appetite, and particularly of such appetites as are indulged among men without restraint and without loss of social position. For a higher motive should act than the fear of man or respect of caste—every motive which reason urges and revelation hallows—honour, his own dignity, regard to the end for which God has made him, homage to the law under which he is placed in prospect of the judgment he is soon to undergo, and in imitation of that pure and perfect example which the Divine Model has set before him. How a man degrades himself and deletes the image of God within him when he dethrones his mind and conscience, is chafed into a demon or degraded to a brute, takes the bridle off his tongue or power of locomotion from his limbs, by excessive indulgence in stimulants. How far and how ignominiously he falls from the chief end, when he lives "in chambering and wantonness," glories in his shame, has no object but enjoyment, and, living in pleasure, is dead while he liveth. For when impurity—

> "by lewd and lowest arts of sin,
> Lets in defilement to the inward parts,
> The soul grows clotted by contagion,
> Imbodies and imbrutes, till she quite lose
> The divine property of her first being."

Is not the social evil of great cities a reproach to civilization and Christianity? character, modesty, health, and happiness being all forfeited by criminal indulgences: for, when night

> "Darkens the streets, then wander forth the sons
> Of Belial, flown with insolence and wine;"

and the "lips of the strange woman," who prowls about,

"drop as an honeycomb, and her mouth is smoother than oil, but her end is bitter as wormwood." Felix, as we have said, had seen Drusilla during his procuratorship in Judea, and had seduced her from her husband. The victim of his libertinism was by his side when the apostle thus reasoned. In fact, Felix, though imported into Italy as a slave, was "husband of three queens," as a Latin biographer calls him, soaring high, and being successful, too, in his amours. The words of the apostle may have only affronted the adulteress, but they shook her paramour.

And *judgment to come* was another topic more awful still which rung through that hall. Felix had no creed—was not even fortified by stoical pride. He took "the good the gods provide," with no thought for the morrow, save for further indulgence. The earnestness of the apostle must have impressed him—the conviction that he believed all that he spoke with such startling energy. As he reasoned of a future judgment he must have showed the grounds of it, and proved its certainty; he must have told what it was—a perfect inspection of man's whole character by Him who knows us altogether—not our life only, but ourselves—not action, but heart with all its passions and purposes; by Him who, as He knows us with infallible accuracy, will pronounce upon us with unimpeachable equity. No subterfuge can avail; the soul is laid open to its core, and all that it ever thought, felt, or purposed is read under the eye of Omniscience. It feels its doom, if it be impenitent, ere the Judge pronounce it; and He who is love, who died in pity and reigns in grace, shall speak in thunder and in sorrow, and his words are all the more thrilling that they come from the lips of Him who is Saviour, and was willing to save even those whom He condemns. "Depart from Me," and He is the source of all nobleness and felicity. He had often bidden them come; had opened His bosom—the bosom pierced with a spear; and stretched out His arms—the arms nailed to the cross, and implored them with tears to come; had wrestled with them by His Providence, His Word, and His Spirit; had argued and threatened; had invited and allured; and all that they might come. But they would not come; and the righteous sentence is—" Depart from Me." "Cursed" they are; for they have forfeited mercy, and brought down upon themselves an indescribable penalty. The "fire" into which they are exiled for ever was not originally kindled for them, but "for the devil and his angels," with whom they have allied themselves in guilt, and under whose temptations they have irretrievably fallen. Oh, can it be that any one with the knowledge of such a hazard—any one able to realize it—will yet incur it by wayward and incorrigible unbelief. God of his infinite mercy forbid! But the crisis of destiny will come, and it is right that it should come. Reason acquiesces in the thought—" Know thou that for all these things God will bring thee into judgment;" yea, "God shall bring every work into judgment, with every secret thing, whether it be good or whether it be evil." And the prisoner must have told his judge of the glory of that higher tribunal before which even he must stand and give account; that the man Jesus is Judge; that His majesty shall eclipse the sun, for before it the earth and the heaven shall flee away; that the resurrection precedes the judgment, and that they who "sleep in the dust of the earth shall awake, some to everlasting life, and some to shame and everlasting contempt."

The voluptuary was deeply moved by the picture so vividly presented to him. His past history could not bear inspection. He was conscious that he was guilty, that his life had been stained by knavery and blood, by cruelty and profligacy, by practices, at some of which humanity blushes, and others of which it scorns and reprobates. He felt that he would be loathed and execrated if men knew all of him, and what then should he answer before God? The prospect of being judged—inspected by an Omniscient eye from which no vail could screen, and judged by an impartial Arbiter whom no pretext could deceive—filled him with alarm. The scene impressed him, he partially realized it, felt himself in the presence and under the glance of the Searcher of hearts, and he *trembled*—becoming afraid or seized with a panic; and he replied—"Go thy way for this time." If he was anxious to hear him begin, he was as anxious that he should close. He could not bear this dissection of his character and motives—this allusion to a coming judgment. He was wholly unprepared for such an appeal, for he was but an illiterate and sceptical libertine, and his shallow nature vibrated with the impulse of the moment. Like many men of sensual depravity, he was far from being pleased with himself. Amidst all his success and splendour, twinges of uneasiness may have often shaken his conscience—the fate of many dashing profligates—

> " As a beam o'er the face of the waters may glow,
>   While the tide runs in darkness and coldness below,
>   So the cheek may be tinged with a warm sunny smile,
>   Though the cold heart to ruin runs darkly the while."

But the impression made upon Felix was soon charmed away. Depart, said he to the prisoner, but in courtesy he added—"When I have a convenient season, I will call for thee"—literally, when I have got time or opportunity. That opportunity came often, and he and Paul had many a colloquy. But there was a sordid motive mixed up with his conduct. At the very time he was so solemnized as to make this reply, he formed the resolution of securing a bribe if possible—" He hoped also that money should have been given him of Paul, that he might loose him: wherefore he sent for him the oftener, and communed with him." Avarice put on the guise of an anxious inquirer, took an interest in the prisoner to make money out of him, and hoped to be well paid for all the communing which it held with him. Felix would risk another discourse on righteousness, temperance, and judgment to come, and even submit to the alarm produced by it, if he might win compensation in a few shekels and talents. To what base subterfuges hypocrisy will stoop. Balaam could only speak as God allowed him, but he would only speak for hire; his heart clung to " the wages of unrighteousness" as fondly as it longed for " the death of the righteous." While Saul was planning to increase the king's flocks out of the spoils of Amalek, he was religiously professing that he had been only collecting victims for God's altar. Herod, while he is sharpening his poniard, devoutly says— " Bring me word again, that I may come and worship Him also." Felix pretends concern for his soul, that he might charm some money from the preacher. He knew that the apostle had come to Jerusalem in possession of money, as he had stated in his answer before the tribunal, and he thought that, like the most of men, he would do anything or give anything for freedom—that he would not scruple to offer a bribe of what did not belong to him. He judged Paul by himself, and was disappointed; for Paul preferred to liberty a good name and a clear conscience. He would not aid a Roman magistrate in violating the law, or buy his freedom with the wages of iniquity. What Felix was is indicated by those words, and under his prefecture no one would be punished who could purchase a pardon, and the locks of the prison might be opened by a golden key.

Two years passed, and yet the prisoner remained under military surveillance. No farther crime was alleged against him, nor was he again brought to trial. If Lysias came down, nothing resulted. Felix yet hoped for a bribe, or perhaps he had begun to despair of triumphing over Paul's rectitude. But at length he was superseded. Clamour had been raised against him—his rapine and tyranny had provoked the nation, who complained of him to the emperor. The people had borne long, but their patience was exhausted. Felix, aroused to his peril, and ever alive to his interests, thought ere he left to propitiate the Jews, and gain some popularity with them. Knowing what would gratify them, and perhaps induce them to abandon a formal charge against him, he "left Paul bound." He had been in free keeping, friends having access to him, but now his liberty was abridged, and he was put into strict military custody, chained to a soldier, and he wore that chain, when shortly afterwards he appeared before Agrippa. Felix did this against his own convictions, for he knew that no charge could be substantiated against the prisoner; in fact, that in strict justice he should have been liberated long ago. It was therefore an act of wanton tyranny to place him in closer durance, and from such a motive. His oratory had terrified Felix, but the impression was so evanescent that he could subject the orator to an ignoble fetter—sacrifice the man who had made him tremble—to propitiate the Jews. He had no scruple about the means, provided the end were obtained. On arriving at Rome, the procurator was tried before the emperor, and was with difficulty acquitted through his brother's interest.

Those two years at Cesarea were a breathing time to the apostle. Then and there probably the third Gospel was written by Luke, and the mind of Paul was nerved by meditation and prayer for the close of his career. It was like the leisure of a sick-bed to a dying saint—a repose among the flowers that grow upon the brink of the river, ere he is summoned to cross it.

III.

BEFORE FESTUS.

Acts xxv. 1—12.

Felix was recalled, and Porcius Festus sent out to Judea by Nero, at the beginning of his reign. As a magistrate, his character and conduct were greatly superior to those of his predecessor. Three days after his arrival at Cesarea the Roman capital, he went up to Jerusalem the national capital, prompted no less by curiosity than by a desire to meet with the men who swayed to a large extent the destinies of the people, and upon whose feelings and measures no little of the peace and prosperity of his administration would depend. The enemies of the apostle, unable to gain anything from Felix, at once beset his successor. "The high priest" (Ismael) " and the chief of the Jews" informed him against Paul, made it a special request, and put the granting of it on the footing of a personal favour—that he would send for Paul to Jerusalem, that is, transfer his trial to Jerusalem, their object being to assassinate him by the way. The governor, whether aware or not of their motives, would not listen, but replied that Paul should be kept at Cesarea, and "that he himself should depart shortly thither"—"Let them, therefore, said he, which among you are able, go down with me, and accuse this man, if there be any wickedness in him." By the epithet "able"—"which among you are able"—is to be understood, not those who had ability to attend the court at Cesarea, but persons of power or of rank—the magnates. There is in the proper text no word corresponding to "wickedness," and the clause is more emphatic without it—"if there be anything in this man." Having sojourned in Jerusalem not more than eight or ten days, Festus returned to the seat of government, and the very next day, "sitting on the judgment-seat" the symbol of his authority, "commanded Paul to be brought." The Jews who had come down to Cesarea "stood round about" him, and laid numerous and heavy complaints against him, but on examination they could not prove them. Their charges of apostacy, sacrilege, and treason, being unsupported, fell at once to the ground.

The apostle's various replies, made by him from time to time as opportunity offered, are thus summed up— "Neither against the law of the Jews, neither against the temple, nor yet against Cæsar, have I offended anything at all." The accusations were much the same as those brought before Felix, and his formal answer would also be similar—a distinct denial of all those charges, and a challenge to any one to prove them against him.

The procurator was bound in equity at this point to have acquitted the captive at his bar, but he was most anxious to ingratiate himself with the men in power, and, like Pilate and Felix before him, "to do the Jews a pleasure;" and perhaps he might imagine that means of proof might be found in Jerusalem which were not forthcoming at Cesarea. He does not yield their entire request to the Jews; but, as if he suspected their fairness, he proposes that himself should be present in their council, and wishes also to obtain the prisoner's consent to change the venue. His question was, "Wilt thou go up to Jerusalem, and there be judged of these things before me?" The question was a treacherous one. It was put from a bad motive—to please the Jews; and it was subjecting the prisoner to a new trial, and for the same unproved offence. The apostle felt at once what the question involved, and what injustice it meditated; that it was an unwarranted change of jurisdiction which would make his sworn enemies his judges, and he nobly answered—"At Cæsar's judgment-seat I am standing, where I ought to be judged; the Jews in nothing have I wronged, as thou knowest better (than thou choosest to confess). For if I am guilty, or have done anything worthy of death, I do not refuse to die, but if there be not one of the things of which they accuse me, no one can deliver me unto them. I APPEAL TO CÆSAR."

The apostle's life was at stake, and he would not be the victim of injustice. He was at that moment at Cæsar's judgment-seat, to be tried by his delegate and under his authority, and there, and there alone, could his trial as a Roman citizen be conducted. Let him be pronounced guilty or not guilty at the proper tribunal. He had done no injury to the Jews, and he hints that Festus must have been convinced of this during the trial, or by the record of the previous one. Let him be found guilty on proper evidence, and he *refuses not to die*—does not beg off from death. But let him be found innocent, then surely no one had legal power to remand him to Jerusalem, this want of power being even implied in the procurator's question—"Wilt thou go up to Jerusalem and be judged?" But the apostle knew the hazard, saw the procurator's weak desire to please the Jews, felt that his case had been too long delayed, and therefore took it out of the hands of Festus and out of the hands of the sanhedrim, and appealed to Cæsar. It was a wise and also a necessary step, and as a Roman citizen he was entitled to take it—to carry his case from the inferior court at Cesarea to the imperial tribunal at Rome. It needed no written document or formal reasons—the simple sentence was enough, such was the power and sweep of the Roman law through all the provinces of the empire. Festus may have been surprised by the sudden termination; but after consulting for a moment with his assessors, for the privilege of appeal was guarded by some exceptions, he said, "Thou hast appealed unto Cæsar, unto Cæsar thou shalt go." These last words must have cheered him after two years' detention, and revived his hope of seeing Rome. Hope so long deferred may have made his "heart sick," but the way was at length providentially opened, and Christ's promise, harmonizing with his own fervent desire, was at length to be fulfilled.

IV.

BEFORE FESTUS AND AGRIPPA.

Acts xxv. 13—27; xxvi. 1—32.

Agrippa was a son of the Herod who was struck with mortal and loathsome agony " by the angel of the Lord," during the celebration of games in honour of the emperor at Cesarea. Acts, xii. 23. At the period of his father's death he was at the court of Claudius Cæsar at Rome, and only seventeen years of age. Motives of policy kept the emperor from allowing so young a man to succeed his father as king over a people so turbulent as the Jews, and Cuspius Fadus was sent in his room as procurator. But the small kingdom of Chalcis was conferred upon the prince, with the supervision of the temple in Jerusalem; and a short time afterwards he was raised to royal sovereignty over those tetrarchies which had belonged to Philip and Lysanias. He is not called " the king of the Jews," but only king; for Judea was still under a procurator and attached to the province of Syria. Bernice, his eldest sister, was of great beauty, and of as great depravity. She was married first to her uncle Herod of Chalcis, and after his death she lived with Agrippa under the stain of an incestuous attachment. To divert the scandal, she married Polemon, king of Cilicia, but soon left him and came back to her brother. In subsequent years she became mistress of Vespasian, and of his son Titus, who was obliged by popular clamour to part with her—as reluctant, indeed, to dismiss her as she was to be dismissed. Josephus records her career, and she has not escaped the pencil of Juvenal.

No sooner had Festus taken possession of his government than Agrippa and his sister came to *salute* him—to offer their formal congratulations to him, and through him to the emperor. During their residence with him, Festus mentioned Paul to them, as "a certain man left in bonds by Felix;" and after detailing the circumstances, and the bearing of the Roman law upon them, contemptuously narrowed the case to a point, that the whole controversy was—"of one Jesus which was dead, whom Paul affirmed to be alive." It was true; the entire dispute did hang on this—Was He who died on Calvary raised again from the dead? The gospel rests solely and wholly upon the affirmative answer, and that affirmative was the soul and substance of the apostle's preaching. On this statement of the matter, "Agrippa said unto Festus, I would also hear the man myself. To-morrow, said he, thou shalt hear him. And on the morrow, when Agrippa was come, and Bernice, with great pomp, and was entered into the place of hearing, with the chief captains and principal men of the city, at Festus' command Paul was brought forth."

Before this lordly assemblage Festus again gives a brief account of the trial of the apostle, with the special declaration—"I found that he had committed nothing worthy of death." But the entire question was beyond the range of his experience, and he did not know how to word his despatch to Rome—"Of whom I have no certain thing to write unto my lord. Wherefore I have brought him before you, and specially before thee, O King Agrippa, that, after examination had, I might have somewhat to write." Agrippa being thus appealed to as the principal personage, at once addressed the prisoner in these words—"Thou art permitted to speak for thyself. Then Paul stretched forth his hand and answered for himself—

"On all the counts with which I am charged by the Jews, King Agrippa, I think myself happy in being about to defend myself this day before thee, especially as thou art so experienced about all customs and also questions belonging to the Jews: wherefore I beseech thee to hear me patiently. My manner of life from my youth, which from the beginning was among my own nation in Jerusalem, know all the Jews, who previously knowing me from the beginning, can give witness, if they are willing, that in accordance with the strictest sect of our religion I lived a Pharisee. And now for the hope of the promise made to our fathers by God, I stand on my trial—which promise our twelve tribes, intensely engaging in divine service night and day, hope to reach: for which hope I am charged by the Jews, O king. What! is it reckoned by you a thing beyond belief, if God raises the dead? Well, then, I thought with myself that I was under necessity to do many things contrary to the name of Jesus the Nazarene; which also I did in Jerusalem. And many of the saints did I shut up into prisons, having received the (requisite) authority from the chief priests; and when they were being put to death, I gave my vote against them. And punishing them often through all the synagogues, I forced them to blaspheme; being exceedingly mad against them, I persecuted them as far as even to foreign cities.

In which business being engaged as I was on my journey to Damascus, with authority and commission from the chief priests, at mid-day I saw, O king, in the way a light from heaven, beyond the brightness of the sun, shining round about me and those who were journeying with me. And we all having fallen to the ground, I heard a voice speaking to me and saying in the Hebrew tongue—Saul, Saul, why persecutest thou me? Hard for thee it is to kick against the pricks. And I said—Who art thou, Lord? And He said—I am Jesus, whom thou persecutest. But rise, and stand upon thy feet: because for this end I have appeared unto thee, to ordain thee a minister and a witness both of those things which thou hast seen, and of the things in which I will appear to thee; delivering thee from the people and from the Gentiles, to whom (both of whom) I now send thee, in order to open their eyes, so that they may turn from darkness to light, and from the power of Satan unto God, that they may receive forgiveness of sins and inheritance among the sanctified—by faith that is in Me. Whereupon, O King Agrippa, I did not become disobedient to the heavenly vision: but to those in Damascus first, and also in Jerusalem, and throughout all the region of Judea, and to the Gentiles I preached, that they should repent and turn unto God, doing works worthy of repentance. On these accounts the Jews, having seized me in the temple, attempted to kill me. Having, therefore, obtained help from God, unto this day I have stood, testifying both to small and great, saying nothing except what Moses and the prophets did say should come —whether the Messiah was to be a suffering one, whether as the first from the resurrection of the dead, He is to proclaim light to the people and to the Gentiles."

The apostle pursues to some extent the same argument which he had delivered to the Jewish crowd from the stairs of the temple garrison. He professes his happiness that King Agrippa is to hear him; for as a Jew he had some acquaintance with the themes of Jewish controversy, and had not the passionate antipathies of the sanhedrim. He tells what he was, how he was educated as a zealous Pharisee in the first seat of learning. He held by the nation's hope — that hope which they all cherished, and which they were so eager to reach. "Our twelve tribes" is the name which he gives his nation. Ten of them had gone into hopeless captivity, but a scanty remnant may have come back with Judah and Benjamin. But the full theocratic number is given, and all of them possessed the same hope, whatever their diversities of character and position. Reuben, "unstable as water," might fall short of excellence; Simeon might wield the instruments of cruelty, and be scattered through the commonwealth; Levi might exult in his Urim and Thummim as he offered sacrifice and burned incense; Judah might recline in his vineyard, and wash his clothes in the blood of grapes; Issachar might stoop to servitude; Zebulun might dwell in his haven, and suck the treasures hid in the sand; Dan might occupy the seat of the judge, and Napthali that of the bard; Gad might clothe himself in armour, and Asher realize the blessedness in his name; Joseph might be crowned with benediction, and revel in fatness and wealth; and Benjamin might crouch as a wolf

RESURRECTION NOT BEYOND GOD'S POWER. 413

among his fastnessess—but whatever their peculiarity and history, whatever their temperament and locality, the twelve tribes agreed in claiming the one hope, and anticipating it, as they engaged in divine service. The inference of Paul is, that he had preceded them—that he had found what they were in quest of, and that they were bound to follow him, as he pointed out the way to the blessed discovery.

Then he throws in the question—"Why should it be thought a thing impossible with you, that God should raise the dead?" Agrippa had been taught this doctrine—that God could raise the dead; that He who made the body could reorganize it; that He who had caused what was not to be, could surely bring back to being what had been; and if He did raise a dead man on any special occasion, no one with the Old Testament in his hand could say that the statement was in itself, and of necessity, incredible. That He had raised up Jesus could be easily and satisfactorily demonstrated; and His resurrection points Him out, and glorifies Him as the hope of the twelve tribes.

But he passes away from this theme, and then tells what he had become, dwelling on the strange phenomenon which had so suddenly produced the change. He is minute in his specification. He was not one of those creatures of such facile temper and constitutional indifference, as to have so few settled convictions that a change of opinion may happen either one way or another, and yet scarcely disturb their mental equilibrium. Nor was he one of that class who are liable to continual oscillation, whose sentiments of to-day cannot be safely predicted to be those of to-morrow, and in whom, therefore, any alteration of view excites no surprise. He had held very fixed opinions and acted tenaciously up to them; did many things from conviction contrary to the name of Jesus of Nazareth; persecuted many of the saints under a commission from the chief priests; recorded his vote for their death when they were tried before the sanhedrim; punished them often in every synagogue; laboured by torture to induce them to blaspheme; nay, his rage was not bounded by his country—" being exceeding mad against them, I persecuted them even unto strange cities."

Why and how, then, had he changed — changed so suddenly and so decidedly as not only to cease to be a persecutor, but to become a preacher of the new faith with unexampled activity, to suffer the loss of all in connection with it, and to be a willing martyr for it? How came that change? It was not by argument, or as the result of a mental conflict. It was not by close intercourse with Christians and a more thorough acquaintance with their creed and character. The ingratitude of his employers did not drive him from them, nor did he petulantly go over to Christianity, because some other agent had superseded him in their favour. Nor did he grow colder and colder in his attachment to Judaism, and at length openly recant when the sanhedrim withdrew their confidence from him. Ambition could not prompt him, nor the prospect of wealth allure him. No; it was in the midst of his bold and enthusiastic career, as he went to Damascus with authority and commission from the chief priests to imprison, torture, and slay the Christian disciples, that he was changed. Therefore, the ordinary inducement to change opinion and party were not applicable to him.

Why and how, then, had he changed? His simple answer is—that Jesus, the founder of Christianity, met him and spoke to him; that He was enveloped in a glory "above the brightness" of the noonday sun; that this scene was no hallucination, for it happened "at mid-day;" and that the light also dazzled them which journeyed with him, and they could attest the truth of his statement. Jesus then accosted him, told him who He was, and why He had appeared. The challenge was, "Why persecutest thou Me?"—He and His being one. "It is hard for thee to kick against the pricks." Such wildness only multiplies and deepens the wounds. Had Saul some misgivings already? Did the scene of Stephen's martyrdom haunt him; and were the tones of that prayer still lingering in his ear? Had he begun to feel the pricks, and to recalcitrate ere the Master spoke? At all events his mind was opened at once to conviction, and would persecute Jesus no more. He durst not; those words touched his soul, and filled it with a new power. Jesus then gave him that evangelical commission to declare what he had seen and heard, and to carry the gospel of salvation to the gentile world.

The inference which he silently pressed upon Agrippa was, Could any one remain unconvinced after such a manifestation—any one whose eyes had been dazzled by such glory, and his ears appalled by such an address? It was no inner impression, which a fanatical imagination might create; but an outer and a palpable display before his very senses, so vast and so public, as to be accounted for in no way by any ocular deception. He had seen the Nazarene in a glory which the sky could not furnish, and He had spoken to him; what else could he do but obey? He durst not refuse—there could be no rebellion against such a command; and, therefore, he honestly obeyed the commission which he received. He did as he was told, and he could not do otherwise. It was impossible for him to be " disobedient to the heavenly vision "—he " showed first unto them of Damascus, and at Jerusalem, and throughout all the coasts of Judea, and then to the Gentiles, that they should repent and turn to God, and do works meet for repentance." This conviction was deep and indelible. It nerved him to suffering and perseverance. It made his nation his enemy, but he would die rather than cease to believe and do the work of an apostle.

And thus he describes his labours—" Having therefore obtained help of God, I continue unto this day, witnessing both to small and great, saying none other things than those which the prophets and Moses did say should come; that Christ should suffer, and that He should be the first that should rise from the dead, and should show light unto the people and to the Gentiles." This is a *résumé* of his preaching, as he spoke in Damascus and in Jerusalem, throughout the coasts of Judea and among the Gentiles. He discussed the question as to the character of Messiah; proved that He was capable of suffering, and was to be distinguished by suffering, as at Thessalonica. He held that He was risen again, as he had done at Antioch in Pisidia. He maintained that He was to enlighten the Jew first and then the Gentile, and this he had done in the same Antioch. Everywhere he had proclaimed these truths—a Messiah who had come, who had been characterized by suffering, who had risen again from the dead, and who had by His apostles instructed Jew and Gentile on the momentous topics of sin and salvation, God and eternity. Everywhere he had shown that these events and these blessings were in perfect accordance with the Hebrew scriptures, with Moses and the prophets, and that, therefore, Christianity is the genuine and orthodox Judaism. The address is still meant for Agrippa. The apostle again maintains his consistency as a Jew, and that he propounded no novelty in preaching a Messiah that should suffer, rise again, and illumine both Jew and Gentile, but had spoken in perfect harmony with the utterances of Moses and the prophets. The fulfilment of prophecy in the sufferings of Christ has been considered by us under previous heads—" Paul at Antioch in Pisidia," " Paul at Thessalonica."

The Jewish colouring of this address, its reference to Jewish prophecy and its fulfilment, its use of special terms—such as "forgiveness," "Satan," "inheritance," "sanctified"—and its allusions to a resurrection, made it unintelligible to Festus, and he broke in with loud and impetuous tones—" Paul, thou ravest, much learning has thrown thee into madness." " Much learning" is, literally, many letters—many books of the same class as the Jewish scriptures referred to; and the continuous study of them, according to Festus, had subverted his reason. He was regarded by the governor as an unfortunate monomaniac, heated into fanaticism by intense application to occult and superstitious learning. Ah! truly the apostle must have often appeared as beside himself, for he acted in opposition to maxims of worldly prudence, and cared not for what most men labour and struggle. A sceptical age like his, when selfishness reigned supreme, and men lived but for the pleasure of the hour, and had no thought of a God who governs or a judge who will scrutinize; when serious thought and settled conviction had ceased to be felt, and every one was fluttering among opinions and creeds like an insect among flowers, pleased with all of them by turns, but attached to none of them—such an age must have branded as a madman the homeless old man, cold, hungry, ragged, scourged, and shipwrecked—yet unwearied in his zeal and labours as he travelled, preached, wrote, and suffered—his life in danger, and a chain upon his wrist. They could not gauge his soul — they had no plumb-line of sufficient length. And yet they were the fools. He had studied the chart and foreseen the danger, and his feet were now upon a rock—while they were making merry in a vessel which was gliding round the outer edge of the whirlpool, soon to narrow the circle with increasing velocity, till amidst shrieks and despair she plunged into the terrible abyss. Yes, as thou spakest in synagogues, didst declaim on Mars-hill, bare thy back to the lash, fabricate those tents, shiver on the wreck, or answer before governors and kings, resolved to die rather than recant; while thou didst hold thy life in thy hand, and priests and zealots sought to snatch it from thee,—all this while thou wast carrying the truest wisdom with thee—wise in doing the Master's work—wise in winning souls—soon to shine wisest among the wise, "like the brightness of the firmament," and having "turned many to righteousness," to be an orb of surpassing radiance among "the stars for ever and ever."

The rude and bold interruption of Festus did not disconcert the apostle, but he calmly replies—"I am not mad"—and he withholds not his title—"most noble Festus, but words of truth and sanity am I uttering"—not the mere hallucinations of a disordered intellect. Then he turns with graceful tact away from Festus, to whom he was not speaking, and who had heard and judged him before, and appeals to the king—that he was no stranger to these things—that they were not done in a corner, for his conversion had been effected on the highway, and his public life had been matter of notoriety. What might appear insanity to a Roman like Festus, might yet be an intelligible and self-consistent narrative to a well-informed Jew like Agrippa. The appeal burst suddenly—"King Agrippa, believest thou the prophets?" and the reply follows as a master-stroke—"I know that thou believest." The king was educated in that belief, and had not apostatized from it; held that "the prophets" were inspired of God, and that their oracles were true in fact and divine in origin. The tacit inference was, that Agrippa's faith in the prophets should lead him to faith in the Christ, to whom they all gave witness. Agrippa saw at once the design, and replied in compliment to his eloquence—"Almost thou persuadest me to be a Christian." It is universally admitted that the phrase rendered "almost," cannot bear that translation. If it have a temporal sense, it may mean

—in brief space thou art persuading me to become a Christian. Or it may have a quantitative sense—with little trouble, or with little argument, you would make me a Christian. What the motive was that prompted the declaration we do not know. It was probably a complex one. He was so far moved by the apostle's earnestness and sympathy, and he had also some information on the subject; but such an impression was not conviction. The sense may be—really, without much ado, thou art trying to make me a Christian; you would make a Christian of me as easily and in as off-hand a way as you were made yourself: the name Christian, of heathen coinage, in his mouth, does not imply any sincere or decided emotion, for he was a haughty and light-minded voluptuary.

God had done much for the Herods, but their worldliness and ambition ruined them. The first of them had been visited by the Magi, and might have hallowed the great event of his reign—the birth of Jesus. Another of them had the ministry of apostles, if he had chosen to enjoy it; but he beheaded one of them, and imprisoned a second. And this last of them so specially appealed to on this occasion, listened without conviction, and allowed the precious opportunity to pass. He still fawned upon the Roman power, as he did on this visit to Festus; but his courtly demeanour could not stay its final fury, and he lived to see the destruction of Jerusalem.

Agrippa having thus replied, the apostle rose at once to the occasion, and uttered his last public words for Christ in Judæa—" I would to God, that not only thou, but also all that hear me this day, were both almost, and altogether such as I am, except these bonds." This peroration reaches sublimity—so brief is it and so compact—sweeping round the bench and the audience, and ending with a touching allusion to his own captivity. The apostle's reply may be rendered—" I could pray to God, that not only thou, but also all that hear me this day, might become, both in little and in much, such as I am, except these bonds;" or, with another reading, " I could pray to God that whether (persuaded) with ease or with difficulty, not only thou, but all that hear me this day, might become such as I am, except these bonds." The answer corresponds to the statement, and is to be understood accordingly. The apostle could pray, or found it in his heart to pray—could at once pour out an ardent supplication, were it convenient at that moment; and the prayer is, that all that heard him might become as he was —a genuine, decided, active, and patient Christian—wholly Christ's, and wholly in His work as he was, or precisely in his condition. But he checks himself at once, and admits one exception—" these bonds "—as he points to the fetter upon his arm, or lifts it to view; " except these bonds "— and by an instinctive movement of his arm, the words found an echo in the clang of his chain. What better prayer could the apostle present—what nobler wish could he entertain? His prayer could not be that Festus should be transferred to a richer province, that Agrippa should succeed to a larger kingdom, or that the aristocracy of Cesarea should enjoy the coveted patronage of the emperor. But it was that their hearts should be as his, their ambition as his, and their life as his—vitalized by the truth and Spirit of Christ, for then they should possess peace, joy, and hope—working for Him who had blessed them, and preparing to pass into His presence and be crowned with His rewards. Yet filled as his soul was with ecstacy, he forgot not his loss of liberty, and referred to it with a delicacy which pleaded for him more powerfully than an open and bitter complaint.

On the assembly breaking up, a favourable opinion was expressed of his character—he had not spoken in vain. Agrippa uttered the formal decision—"This man might" or "could have been set at liberty, if he had not appealed unto Cæsar." That is, he ought to have been released prior to his appeal; and Felix and Festus are virtually condemned for their partiality or carelessness. But his discharge was impossible, now that an appeal had been taken; for an appeal could not be withdrawn, even with the consent of both parties. His appeal, however, secured the visit to Rome on which his heart was set, and by which he should have the honour of proclaiming the gospel for a long period in the eternal city.

XVII.—PAUL ON THE VOYAGE TO ROME.

Acts xxvii.

THE great goal of the apostle's life is now to be reached. The name of Rome must have been familiar to him from his youth. Images of its military and architectural grandeur must have often floated before him; the City of the Seven Hills must have stood out to him as the centre of the world's pomp and power. Wherever he had been, at home in Tarsus, in Judea, in the Levant, in Asia Minor, and in Europe, Roman authority and law prevailed. Roman roads had been often trodden by him, and he had seen the eagles of Rome under every sky. He longed to visit the great metropolis, and he had already written a large and argumentative letter to the church there. He did not reach it so soon as he had anticipated, or by such a journey as he might originally contemplate. But God had promised it, and the divine promise was in God's own way fulfilled. In self-defence he had appealed to Cæsar, and he must sail for Italy to prosecute his appeal.

The time of departure at length came, and Paul and certain *other* prisoners—of a different class, were placed under the care of Julius, "a centurion of Augustus' band;" perhaps a captain in the imperial life-guards returning to Italy. The ship in which they embarked at Cesarea belonged to Adramyttium, and was apparently on its homeward voyage, "meaning to sail by the coasts of Asia," the usual route for vessels engaged in this traffic. Several of the apostle's friends were with him—Luke the narrator, and Aristarchus the Macedonian, whom he afterwards names his "fellow-labourer" and "fellow-prisoner." On touching at Sidon the next day, the centurion, who, from the report of Festus, must have been aware of the frivolous charges preferred against him, "courteously entreated Paul," and allowed him to go on shore to see his friends and *refresh himself*—the reference in the last word being to corporeal frailty, perhaps increased by sea-sickness. Leaving Sidon, they sailed *under* Cyprus, that is, under the lee of Cyprus, or to the east of it, the direct course being to the south of it; for so the contrary winds compelled them, and they might take advantage of a strong current which, running with great strength to the westward, would enable them to make way against the gale. They thus "sailed over the sea of Cilicia and Pamphylia," and "came to Myra, a city of Lycia." At Myra vessels were changed, and the prisoners were put into a "ship of Alexandria sailing into Italy"—probably a corn-ship, and, like others of the class, a regular trader, of large size and with a well-appointed crew. On loosing from Myra, the wind was adverse. Small progress was made, and after "many days" they had with difficulty come opposite to Cnidus, a distance of not more than one hundred and thirty miles. The prevailing wind in those regions, and at that season of the year—the close of summer—is still the north-west wind, against which the ship could scarcely work up. In consequence of this they ran under the lee of Crete, or to the east of it, so as to be sheltered by it. Having with difficulty rounded the point of Salmone—"hardly passing it," they coasted the south side of the island, and, unable to pass Cape Matala, where the shore suddenly trends to the north, they put in to the Fair Havens, not far from Lasea—a town, the ruins of which were for the first time identified in 1856 by Mr. Tennent, a merchant of Glasgow, and the friends who were cruising with him in his yacht.

The season was, however, far advanced—"the fast was now already past"—it was the end of September or beginning of October, and therefore perilous to undertake a long voyage. Navigation was not actually interrupted till about six weeks later, but sailing "was now dangerous." Warning comes from an unexpected quarter. It is not the centurion in anxiety for his charge, the captain afraid of his ship, nor the owner apprehensive about his cargo. It is not the crew who refuse to put to sea, nor the passengers who protest on account of the roughness of the weather. It is one of the prisoners who takes it upon him to warn them, and to foretell disaster—damage to the cargo and ship, and the jeopardy of their own lives. The apostle was no coward himself, and he knew that he should reach Rome. But he had regard to those who were with him. He knew the dangers of the season, and may have had a supernatural intimation. He felt that no one should tempt Providence, and he was willing to remain, though assured of a divine safeguard. Nor was he without previous experience—"Thrice I suffered shipwreck, a night and a day have I been in the deep." This is the first time he speaks, and his words are unheeded; but in a brief time he commanded attention, and the safety of the passengers was owing to his courage and presence of mind. On deck, though in bonds, he grows in importance among soldiers and seamen who knew nothing of his history, and cared as little for it; nay, rises ultimately into supreme command, captain and centurion being for a season superseded by the insignificant Jewish prisoner. Thus mind and character will assert themselves in every situation, and shine through every disguise. These forces of soul defy repression and burst into ascendancy—guiding with facility, and governing with universal compliance. The centurion, however, would not listen to Paul, but rather "believed the master and owner of the ship," both of whom were anxious to get to the end of the journey. They had lain long wind-bound at Fair Havens, but it was not a good winter station, and the greater part joined in opinion with the captain and supercargo, hoping to get to Phœnice, about forty miles west, and a more commodious roadstead to winter in, as from its position it was secured from the prevailing storms. They seem now to have given up all hope of reaching Rome before next spring; but on a favourable change of breeze, when the "south wind blew softly," they made for Phœnice which lay to the north-west, and, hugging the shore, "sailed close by Crete." But they were soon overtaken by a hurricane, blowing down from the highlands of the coast, and called Euroclydon—perhaps more correctly Euroaquilo—or a north-east wind. The adjective rendered tempestuous is in the original "typhonic," or like a typhoon, the tempest which is accompanied by whirlwinds driving the clouds in circling conflict, and raising the sea in columns of spray. The ship was caught in the squall, and "could not bear up into it," literally, look it in the eye, and was therefore forced to scud before it. "Running under" the islet of Clauda, they "had much work to come by the boat," that is, taking advantage of the smooth water under the lee of the island, with difficulty they hoisted on board the boat which was usually towed behind the ship, showing that they were preparing to resist the storm. Then they used "helps," "undergirding the ship," a common precaution in those times, passing a stout cable several times round the hull, so as to tighten the planks which might be strained by the heavy seas. Being driven still to the south-west, and being naturally afraid of falling "into the quicksands," or the shoals of the Syrtis on the northern shore of Africa, they *strake sail*—rather, lowered the mainyard and its sail—and "so were driven," keeping the ship's head off shore, and her right side to the wind. The tempest did not abate, and the next day they "lightened" her—threw out a portion of the cargo. But the danger still increasing, "we cast out with our own hands the tackling of the ship"—all portions of the heavy gear or rigging—others, according to this reading, beside the crew being employed in the work, or the apostle himself and Luke putting a hand to the labour. In a short time such a vessel must have foundered and gone down, a common fate with ancient ships. The sky had closed dark and angry around them, and "neither sun nor stars in many days appeared," while the gale increased in fury, and they abandoned hope; for the ship was leaking, and they could not tell where they were, on what coast they might be driven, or how long the opening timbers would resist the violence of the waves. The darkness of night was above them, with a raging sea around them, and the labouring bark, though frapped and eased of its heavier freight and furniture, was drifting helplessly before the wind.

In this crisis of dismay and danger, the voice which had warned them at Fair Havens was heard again. And the apostle now spoke from divine authority. We know not what were the feelings of the passengers, or how they expressed them, though we can well imagine the confusion and fear among two hundred and seventy-six persons during a tempest of such force and duration. Perhaps, as in Jonah's voyage, they cried every man to his god, and bethought themselves of Paul's early counsel. As "the sea wrought and was tempestuous," the master might exhaust his skill, and the centurion betake himself to Neptune, but Paul resorted to secret prayer to Him who "commandeth and raiseth the stormy wind which lifteth up the waves." They would not listen to his advice, and the hurricane had enveloped them; but still he prayed for them, and he received all their lives as a gift in answer to his intercession. So richly fraught with comfort, he stood forth to cheer and animate them, for they were exhausted with toil, terror, and fasting. He reminds them first of his previous warning, which they had slighted—not to upbraid them indeed, nor even to elicit the conclusion that he was a true prophet, but to show them that he had spoken not from opinion, but from certain knowledge, and that, therefore, what he was now to say demanded credence—" And now, I exhort you to be of good cheer: for there shall be no loss of any man's life among you, but of the ship. For there stood by me this night the angel of God, whose I am, and whom I serve, saying, Fear not, Paul; thou must be brought before Cæsar: and, lo, God hath given thee all them that sail with thee. Wherefore, sirs, be of good cheer; for I believe God, that it shall be even as it was told me. Howbeit, we must be cast upon a certain island."

The brief speech is remarkable; the Master, by an angel, had appeared in the crisis to reassure His servant. The apostle does not disguise his position—" Whose I am, and whom I serve "—and the language shows why such a vision had been vouchsafed to him. Had there been five righteous persons in Sodom it would have been saved, and for Paul's sake the lives of all his fellow-passengers are preserved. He had appealed to Cæsar, and the appeal must be heard. He was the principal person on board, and invested with peculiar dignity. The ship is his by God's charter. Her cargo may be cast into the sea, and the ship herself be lost, but the apostle must get to Rome. " God hath given thee *all them* that sail with thee "—their life; that of nigh three hundred persons was bound up in his life. The effect of such a speech at such a time may be easily conceived. It was no flattering prophecy which he uttered. He made no attempt to buoy up their spirits by predicting that the storm was approaching its end, that the clouds were breaking, or that the wind was veering. There is a distinct assurance of safety, but as distinct an assurance of wreck. They should not founder, or be engulphed among the quicksands they dreaded, but they must be driven ashore, and that "upon a certain island." The prophecy was minute and circumstantial, and could not but impress them who listened to it. If they rejoiced in safety, they must have rejoiced with trembling when they thought that they were to be cast away in the storm. It was life in the midst of destruction which was pledged to them —they were to be snatched from a watery grave. Deliverance was not to come from God's stilling the "noise of the seas," but the turbulent surges were to throw the ship on land, and break her to pieces in their fury.

It was now the fourteenth night since they had left Fair Havens in Crete, and they were still tossed about in the Adriatic—"They mount up to the heaven, they go down again to the depths; their soul is melted because of trouble. They reel to and fro, and stagger like a drunken man, and are at their wit's end." Unable to ascertain their position, "about midnight the shipmen deemed that they drew near to some country"—literally, that some country drew near to them—common but graphic nautical language, in which land rises or sinks, comes near or disappears. The *shipmen*—seamen—came to this conclusion, as they could from many signs unperceived by soldiers, prisoners, and passengers, such as the noise of breakers rising above the sound of the storm. Fearful of the close proximity of the shore, "they sounded, and found its depth twenty fathoms;" and in a short time, heaving the lead again, "they found it fifteen fathoms." This rapid shallowing alarmed them, and they feared to be dashed on the rocks over which the waves were breaking. To stay the progress of the ship, and keep her if possible in her present position, they cast four anchors out of the stern—not an unusual fashion in ancient navigation. On that coast the land is too low to be seen, though the breakers might be both audible and visible; and soundings of similar depth are yet found by mariners in the same locality. The alarmed inmates of the ship, groaning " in the sides " or crowded upon deck, now anxiously waited for the day. They might go down at their anchors, unable to ride out the gale if it increased; and they could not tell the nature of the coast till morning broke. Their purpose now was to strand the ship, and she was anchored so that her head was to the land, but they could not tell whether there might be a beach which should afford them the opportunity. In this moment of awful suspense, when wreck was certain, and the object was to be prepared for it, the sailors lost heart, and would have deserted the vessel. They pretended that it was necessary to lower the boat, which some days before they had taken in with difficulty, for the ostensible purpose of carrying out anchors from the prow to steady the pitching vessel. This manœuvre shows how critical they reckoned their situation—when, in such a night of gloom and tempest, they would take to the boat which could scarcely be expected to live in such a sea. Their purpose, as they had the working of the ship, could not be easily detected by the landsmen, whom they would have so selfishly abandoned.

But there was one on board who had the gift of discerning spirits. He divined the treachery, and for the third time spoke. His stern words were—" Unless these abide in the ship, ye cannot be saved." He had already assured them of safety; but that safety so absolutely promised depended upon means. They were to run the ship ashore as soon as it was day; and the operation could not be done except by the practised seamen, who alone could handle the vessel so as that she might be carried to the most promising part of the beach, and as high on the beach as possible. Neither the soldiers nor the landsmen on board could be depended on for this difficult task. The soldiers at once, on hearing Paul speak in such a tone, cut the ropes by which the sailors were lowering the boat, and it fell into the sea, and was either capsized or drifted away. From this period till day began to appear, the apostle was exhorting them all to take food. The crisis was at hand, and it would need all their strength and presence of mind to take advantage of it. The last desperate effort to save their lives by swimming or floating on broken spars was to be made, and it must not be made by them in a dull and exhausted state. The apostle had special care of them, for their lives were given him; and he who could discourse as he had done before Felix, Festus, and Agrippa, can descend to speak of common duty, and inculcate obedience to physical law. His topic had been usually the salvation of the soul, but now it is the preservation of life; it had been generally the deliverance of their spirits from hell, but now it is the rescue of their persons from a watery grave. The great and the little, the mighty and the minute, the spiritual and the temporal, dietetic necessity and evangelical enterprise, were equally within his grasp. Raising his voice above the storm, he said to his fellow-voyagers, and it was his fourth utterance—" The fourteenth day ye this day complete without food, expecting (the storm to abate), and having taken nothing. Wherefore I exhort you to partake of food, for this is for your safety, for of none of you shall there fall a hair from the head. And when he had thus spoken, he took bread, and gave thanks to God in presence of them all; and when he had broken it, he began to eat. Then were they all of good cheer, and they also took some meat. And we were in all in the ship two hundred threescore and sixteen souls." The apostle now stands out the commander of the ship, the guiding spirit in the emergency—her officers and crew are passive and helpless. For a fortnight they had had no regular meals—the usual result of a hurricane; and day after day they had been looking for it to moderate. But as the moment of danger and deliverance was at hand, they were to strengthen themselves by food, and rest assured of ultimate safety. Displaying his lofty presence of mind, he set the example, gave thanks—for this brief service was not to be forgotten —and began to eat. His words cheered them all, and there were many of them—for the store ships were large and roomy, and the trade between Egypt and Rome was great and constant.

That they might run the ship as high upon the beach as possible, they lightened her again, and cast out the wheat into the sea—the remainder of her cargo. As day broke, they could not tell where they were, but they discovered a bay, not rocky and bold, but having a *shore*

—sandy beach—and on it they resolved to run the ship. For this purpose, and to lose no time, they cut away the anchors and left them in the sea; at the same time, as ancient ships were steered by two large paddles or oars, one on each quarter, which in this case had been lashed away while the ship lay at anchor by the stern, they loosed these "rudder-bands," when she got under way; and that she might be steered to the likeliest spot, they also hoisted the foresail, and "made toward shore." "Falling into a place where two seas met," or a narrow channel between two portions of the sea—between the island of Salmonetta and the larger island of Malta—they succeeded in stranding the ship; and the sharp prow being forced into the tenacious clay and mud of the beach, "stuck fast and remained immoveable;" but the stern was broken by the billows which so violently struck it and washed over it. The anxiety and consternation at the first shock must have been great, as each looked to the readiest means of safety. The sternness of Roman discipline next showed itself amidst the confusion, and the soldiers proposed "to kill the prisoners, lest any should swim out and escape." Had not Paul been among them, a military execution might have ensued; but the centurion was willing to save him, and the other prisoners were saved along with him—for as he had said already, God had given him the lives of all on board. In fact, Paul was invulnerable, and the military counsel was folly. The sailors, in selfish panic, would leave the ship, but they cannot; the soldiers would slay the prisoners ere they secured their own safety, but they dare not shed a drop of blood. The centurion then gave orders that all should make for the shore; that those "which could swim should cast themselves first into the sea;" and that the rest should float themselves through the surf *on boards*—deck planks, or any suitable portion of the wreck. His commands were obeyed, and the divine pledge was fulfilled—" and so it came to pass, that they escaped all safe to land."

XVIII.—PAUL IN ROME.

Acts xxviii.; Ephes. iii. 1; vi. 20; Phil. i. 12—14; iv. 22; Coloss. iv. 18; Philemon 9—13.

The island on which the ship had been cast was Malta, and the entire account of the voyage and of the storm confirms the statement. The rain was pouring down in torrents; the weather was intensely cold; and the wet and shivering voyagers were kindly received by the natives, called "barbarians," as not being of Greek descent, but a Punic colony. "They kindled a fire and received us every one." The apostle, having saved his fellow-travellers from death, exerted himself for their comfort, and helped to keep up the fire by gathering fuel; but in arranging a bundle of sticks on the burning heap, a viper, roused from its torpor, glided "out of the heat and fastened on his hand." The native onlookers expected instant death for him. They knew the viper's bite to be mortal; observing Paul to be a prisoner, they concluded that some heavy crime lay upon him; and seeing in the event a retributive providence, "they said among themselves— No doubt this man is a murderer, whom, though he hath escaped the sea, yet vengeance *suffereth* not to live"— rather, suffered; for in their estimation he was already dead. But the apostle shook the beast off his hand into the fire, and "felt no harm." The rude spectators, seeing it "hang on his hand" and in the attitude of biting him, and knowing what venom was in its bite, at once "changed their minds;" and since he had not "swollen or fallen down dead suddenly," as they most surely looked for and continued to anticipate, they thought him more than man, and concluded "that he was a god"—so contrary was the result to all their experience. And yet it was in conformity with the Lord's promise before He ascended—"They shall take up serpents" without hurt. Strange were the reverses in the apostle's history. The people of Lystra first took him for a god, and then with sudden freak stoned him as an enemy of the gods. The Maltese first suspect him to be a murderer, and then capriciously exalt him into a divinity.

The apostle was "lodged three days courteously" by Publius the "chief man," who may have been the governor of the island, as lieutenant under the prætor of Sicily; and he repaid this hospitality by effecting a miraculous cure on his father—"he entered in and prayed, and laid his hands on him, and healed him." The prayer of Paul superseded the prescriptions of Luke the physician. The report of the miracle spread through Malta, and other invalids were healed. The consequence was that the grateful islanders showed the apostle and his friends uncommon attention, and "when they departed, laded them with such things as were necessary" for health and comfort during the rest of the voyage. After a sojourn of three months they embarked in a ship which, like that which had been wrecked, was of Alexandria, and bore on its prow a figure-head of Castor and Pollux—the tutelary twin-gods of sailors. The ship soon came to Syracuse—the capital of Sicily—a distance of eighty miles, and waited there three days. On leaving Syracuse, the wind being unfavourable, they *fetched a compass*—were obliged to tack—as they came to Rhegium, on the south-west point of Italy. A day seems to have been spent there in waiting for a favourable breeze; then a "south wind" sprang up, and they ran in a day a hundred and eighty-two miles to Puteoli, in a sheltered part of the bay of Naples, and the great harbour of southern Italy and of the Alexandrian grain-ships. "Brethren" were found in this busy emporium, and after a week's stay with them the landward journey to Rome was commenced. Many Christians in Rome, on hearing of the apostle's progress, set out to meet him along the Via Appia; some proceeding as far as the Appii Forum—about forty miles from the capital—and others only as far as the Tres Tabernæ, about ten miles nearer it. The heart of the apostle was cheered when he saw the men who had come so far to welcome him—Christians from the world's centre and metropolis—and he "thanked God and took courage." His sensitive spirit was cheered by this sympathy. On entering Rome, Paul was, as a prisoner, handed over to the *captain of the guard*—the prefect of the life-guards or prætorian camp—probably Burrus; but he was not put in strict confinement, being suffered to dwell by himself with a soldier that kept him, and to whom he was chained. The despatch of Festus and the report of Julius may have led to this lenity.

But, in Rome as elsewhere, the apostle could not be idle. He had come to Rome after being before the sanhedrim, and he did not know what reports of the procedure might have reached the capital. He wished to stand well with his countrymen, and was anxious that no prejudice against himself should impede the reception of the gospel which he preached. He had appealed to them in every city of Asia which he had visited, and they had thwarted his message and sought his life. "When shall he die, and his name perish?" was their daily question, and they often sought to shorten the term of suspense. And now, after a tedious and dangerous voyage to Rome, he allows only three days to elapse before he assembles the representatives of his people. He was not at liberty so as to enter their synagogue, but he invites them to his residence, and thus addressed them — "Men-brethren, though I have done nothing hostile to the people, nor to the customs of the fathers, yet as a prisoner from Jerusalem was I delivered into the hands of the Romans, who, when they had examined me, would have released me, because there was no cause of death in me. But the Jews opposing it, I was forced to appeal to Cæsar, not as having anything to charge my nation with. On this account, therefore, I have called you to me, to see you and to speak with you; for because of the hope of Israel I am surrounded with this chain."

Thus the apostle states his general purpose of the interview. He protests his innocence, and asserts that none of the charges brought against him were true. He had done nothing against his people, either from want of patriotism or in spiteful revenge of their treatment of him. No part of his conduct was dictated by hostility toward them. He had neither flattered nor betrayed them. His entire career showed how profoundly he loved them, and how devoted he had been to their spiritual welfare. But they misinterpreted his message, and had from error become provoked at him. For nothing he had proposed would abridge their national or spiritual privileges, but would rather expand them. What he had done and suffered was for his people, for their highest interest—that they might realize their destiny, and apprehend their theocratic relation, as it had been confirmed and developed by the Messiah through whom the old oracle would be verified—"Ye shall be named the Priests of the Lord: men shall call you the Ministers of our God: ye shall eat the riches of the Gentiles, and in their glory shall ye boast yourselves."

Nor had he done anything "against the customs of the fathers." The old institutions were yet revered by him, though he did not regard the observance of them as essential to salvation. He did not labour to induce men to forsake the temple, but to worship Him who as its Lord had become incarnate. His object was not to get men to desert the "holy convocations," but to show that those assemblies had a definite typical purpose which they should recognize; for the Paschal Lamb had been slain, and the Spirit had been poured out, and the first-fruits had been presented. He did not preach that men should turn their back upon the altar, but that they should betake them to the blood of the great victim slain in these last times for them. The "customs" in themselves he did not despise, but his object was to teach men to honour them by receiving the truths which they imaged, and the blessings which they foreshowed. He had acted in unison with the Mosaic institute in accepting and preaching the Christ; for he had only done as David had taught, and the entire dispensation had prescribed. Christianity was to him not the rival, but the successor of Judaism—not its substitute, but its consummation. This is what he has said already in various forms in his previous defences in Judea.

But the Jews had delivered him into the hands of the Romans—that at least was the spirit of the transactions. They seized him to kill him, and the Roman power rescued him. He had stood before their tribunal, but the council broke into tumult. His Roman judges would have acquitted him as not guilty; but the Jews withstood such an issue, proposing a new trial for the purpose of getting his person into their hands. As a stop to such injustice he had appealed to Cæsar, not to complain against the nation before the emperor. His act in appealing was simply defensive, and he was shut up to the necessity of doing it. It involved no charge against the Jews, and it did not bring their conduct under review. The apostle seems to think that they might suspect this, or might have received such information. This being the state of matters, his appeal being forced upon him in self-vindication, he had sent for them; for he was one of them, attached to his people in every land. And there was an additional reason —the chain upon his arm was the result of his attachment to the hope of Israel. The Messiah was the hope of Israel, and had been so for centuries. Israel ever looked to the future, and lived in it, and longed and prayed for the predicted time to come. Every Jew had this hope set before him, and every consistent Jew should embrace it when presented. He is no renegade who embraces Messiah; rather he is the apostate who refuses Him, and casts dishonour upon seer and altar—the seer who announced and the altar which prefigured Him. The apostle means to say that it was his consistent and enlightened Judaism which had led to his apprehension and trial.

The reply of the Jews is brief—"They said unto him, We neither received letters out of Judea concerning thee, neither any of the brethren that came showed or spake any harm of thee. But we desire to hear of thee what thou thinkest: for as concerning this sect, we know that everywhere it is spoken against."

Some suppose that the chief of the Jews told a deliberate falsehood to the apostle, as they did not wish to be entangled in the dispute. But perhaps the meaning is—that they really had received no oral or written information about the nature and grounds of the apostle's appeal. He had departed for Rome immediately after the appeal had been taken; and the storm which had overtaken him would in all likelihood have detained any other ship in the same seas. Then he had left Malta at the very earliest opportunity, and had arrived at Puteoli before any ship leaving Judea in spring could have reached it. The Jews did not dream of the cause ending in an appeal, and so may have sent no despatch to their countrymen in Rome about it. As may perhaps be inferred from a remark of Suetonius, it was the turbulence of the Jews in their assault upon the Christians that had led to their banishment under the previous emperor, and they were, therefore, very timorous now, lest they should be involved in a second peril. The persons summoned by the apostle could not but see the favour with which he was treated, and therefore they abstained from bringing any charge against him on their own authority; though their obedience to his summons shows that they were by no means ignorant of his history and functions. They, therefore, quietly ask him to speak on the great controversy. Waiving all conversation about his legal position, they inquire as to his theology; such inquiry being professedly prompted by their knowledge that Christianity was everywhere spoken against. They admit that their prepossessions are against the faith which the apostle preached; for it was universally cried down and opposed. If these words signify that this was all they knew about Christianity, then they must have spoken in extreme caution, high contempt, or gross dissimulation; for there was a large and flourishing church at Rome, comprising in its membership many Jews. Or, perhaps, they mean to insinuate that their brethren in Judea may be presumed to be right, from the universal obloquy in which Christianity was held; but since they had one before them so notoriously connected with its spread, they should deem it their duty to listen to his account. They appointed a day to meet with him; *many*—more than on the previous occasion came, and the discussion lasted a whole day in the apostle's lodging.

There he resumed his old work—did what he had done at Thessalonica and Berea, at Ephesus and Corinth. "He expounded and testified the kingdom of God;" that is, in explaining it, he proved it—evidence and information being interlaced. In opening up its nature, he argued its truth. In telling its character, he demonstrated the reality of its existence. As he unfolded what the prophets had predicted of Messiah's reign, he at the same attested that it had come to pass. The point on which all his illustrations converged was this—"persuading them concerning Jesus," that He was the Head of this kingdom, the promised Deliverer. For Jesus was the predicted Messiah—all the olden oracles met in Him. Israel had ever looked into the future, and the hope of Messiah was the star that shone through the night of ages. Their whole history pointed to His coming, and was adapted to it. For this had they been organized, and the destinies of humanity committed to them; since the "Desire of all nations" was to be one of them, born and proclaimed in the midst of them. The apostle wished them to realize their honour as the source of the world's life. His proofs were no extraneous arguments; he did not adduce probabilities or dwell upon ingenious deductions, but fetched evidence directly from their own scriptures, "both out of the law of Moses and out of the prophets." His object was to show that the honest interpretation of the Pentateuch, as it is followed up and illustrated by the prophetical books, should lead them to believe that the Messiah must have come, and that Jesus, in time and place of birth, in qualification, character, work, suffering, and glory, must be that Messiah. The power and eloquence with which Paul could press and demonstrate this, after such experience in the work, may be easily conceived. But the cross was a stumbling-block here as elsewhere, in Italy not less than in Judea; and while "some believed, others believed not."

These solemn colloquies of the apostle produced discord. It had been so in many places before. Jewish nature

JEWISH UNBELIEF. 445

was not softened by an Italian climate—the majority of them remained unconvinced. Ere they departed, and just as they were going, the apostle seized the solemn opportunity to say "one word"—one final word, a farewell pregnant with doom. It is the sad epilogue—the conclusion of his last address to his unbelieving kinsmen according to the flesh—the last of his speeches recorded to us by the Spirit of God. It must have been in deep heaviness and sorrow of heart that he uttered it. It was wrung from him, and it sealed the fate of ancient Israel, for it identified their characters with that of their fathers— "Well"—that is, truly—"spake the Holy Ghost by Esaias the prophet unto our fathers"—rather, your fathers, for he severs himself from them. Ye are their true descendants —inheritors of their character and destiny. What Isaiah said to them may be repeated still to you, for it is equally applicable to you. The message is a terrible one— "Go unto this people, and say, Hearing ye shall hear, and shall not understand; and seeing ye shall see, and not perceive: for the heart of this people is waxed gross, and their ears are dull of hearing, and their eyes have they closed; lest they should see with their eyes, and hear with their ears, and understand with their heart, and should be converted, and I should heal them."

The quotation is from the sixth chapter of Isaiah. The prophet sees Jehovah on His "throne, high and lifted up," guarded and worshipped by the seraphim, while His vast and voluminous mantle filled the temple. The song is chanted, "HOLY, HOLY, HOLY," and the house shakes at the thunder of the anthem. The prophet cannot engage in it, as his lips were unclean; but a seraph flies with a live coal and lays it on them, and they are refined and tuned to the melody. The challenge then issues from Jehovah upon the throne, "Whom shall I send, and who will go for us?" and the prophet no sooner responds, "Here am I, send me," than he receives the commission which the apostle declares to be yet so applicable to the people. It runs thus—

> "Go, and say to this people, hear ye on but understand not,
> And see ye on but perceive not;
> Make fat the heart of this people,
> And their ears make heavy, and their eyes smear up:
> Lest they see with their eyes, and hear with their ears,
> And understand with their heart, and turn and be healed."

The oracle is quoted three times in the New Testament with peculiar variations—twice by our Lord, Matt. xiii. 14, and in John xii. 39, 40. In Matthew, and in this place of Acts, the version is much the same, and it is that of the Septuagint, the passive being used—"their heart is waxed gross, and their ears are dull of hearing." The result is described, the cause being, the neglect of ordinances— vision without perception, hearing without instruction. As quoted in John, the agency of God is recognized— "He hath blinded their eyes, and hardened their heart;" while in the original of Isaiah it is the work of the prophet which produces the infatuation, and his commission is, "Make the heart of this people fat." There is no material difference among these forms. The prophet is bidden preach, and the effect of his preaching is to harden them; as if it were, "Go preach them dull and callous."

Such was the effect, but not the intention of his labours; but God foreknowing the result, simply and bitterly says, "Go and infatuate them." And if the message has such an effect—a message from God Himself—then the result as well as the process may be ascribed to Him—"He hath made the heart of this people gross." There is therefore no difficulty. The responsibility rests with the people who profit not by the oracle. They believe it not, cease to regard it—familiarity with it breeding contempt for it—and they wilfully harden their heart. The oracle is the innocent means of it, and he who utters it may be said in this sense to produce it, as the gospel is to some "the savour of death unto death." Nay, He who gives the oracle and commissions His servant to proclaim it virtually creates the effect, without in any way impeding the freedom or destroying the responsibility of those who profess to see, but apprehend not, and to listen, but regard not.

Isaiah loved his people, though his labour did not benefit them, but rather did them injury through their unbelief. The apostle repeats the oracle, and says that it was verified in his connection with his countrymen. They heard, but did not accept what they heard; saw, but perceived not the truth and beauty of what their vision rested on. Their heart was impervious; they were too dull to detect the tones of divinity in the lesson before them, and too blind to decipher signs and tokens of the fulfilment of prophecy. They would not turn to God, and healing was denied them. Darkness and disease should press upon them to their ruin and death. There was no want of evidence, and there was no lack of instruction. They could not say, let God speak louder, or let God speak fuller, or let God speak oftener. Every available form of lesson was given them, but their fatuity only grew upon them; as it had been in Jerusalem, so it was in Rome. The nation was approaching its end, and daring God to judgment.

And the Gentile races were to occupy their position. "Be it known therefore unto you, that the salvation of God is sent unto the Gentiles, and that they will hear it." The apostle repeated what he had done in every town which he had visited, and especially at Antioch and Corinth—presses salvation upon the Jews, ere he turn to the Gentiles. It had been so predicted. "They will hear it," or accept it; and so it has proved, for they were not prejudiced like the Jews against it. These words have gladdened many a soul, for the gospel is confined by no boundary, and repelled by no barrier. It does not confine itself to any class, condition, or age, but speaks to "this man and that man" of every occupation and character, even though for a season they might refuse to hear it: Bunyan the tinker, John Newton the sailor, Colonel Gardiner and Hedley Vicars the soldiers, Thomas Scott the minister, Wilberforce the senator, Augustine the rhetorician, Lord Rochester the courtier, Africaner the savage, Cowper in his genius, and poor Joseph in his imbecility. The fruits of the gospel are reaped chiefly among the Gentiles, there being still but few converts from ancient Israel. There are churches in Europe among Celts, Saxons, and Sclaves, among the Negroes and Caffres in Africa, among Red Indians and Esquimaux in North America, among Malays and Mongols, among Hindoos and Burmese in Asia—but the synagogue yields only a rare unit to Christ. "They will hear it." We bless him for the prophecy as we discern its fulfilment; as he pronounces it, we hail him as the apostle of the Gentiles, magnifying his office, and encouraging himself in the discharge of it. "They will hear it"—words that have rung through nineteen centuries, and have not spent their force—words that have sped from Rome to London, flown across the Atlantic, and echoed amid the islands of the Pacific—words that shall only cease to have a significance of contrast when God shall bring in his ancient people with the fulness of the gentile nations. "They will hear it"—such are the last recorded words of him who never forgot the Jew, while he preached to the Gentile; who could wish himself "accursed from Christ for his brethren, his kinsmen according to the flesh," even while he rejoiced in preaching a free and unconditioned gospel to men without distinction of race or country. "They will hear it"—our apostle vouches for us: O that all of us verified the prophecy, and in city and hamlet, in crowded lanes and rural highways, heard it with faith and spiritual profit!

The oracle being delivered as a farewell, the Jews departed and disputed keenly with one another. The Roman power meanwhile conceded comparative liberty to the apostle, for he "dwelt in his own hired house, and received all that came in unto him." He could not go to them, but they came to him. His life was secure from Jewish conspiracy, and he availed himself of his privilege. Our last glimpse of him coincides with our first view of him—the aged man is one with the neophyte. On being converted, "straightway he preached Christ." Such is our first intimation of his labours, and our last is told in similar phrase—"Preaching the kingdom of God, and teaching those things which concern the Lord Jesus Christ, with all confidence, no man forbidding him." As he began, so he concluded. During this period of imprisonment, he wrote, saying—"For me to live is Christ." It was so in Damascus, and it is so in Rome, after a lapse of thirty years—the preaching of Christ is still the element of his prison life as it had been that of his public life. He could shake the viper off his arm, but he could not shake the chain off it, for it was the will of God that for two years he should labour under the protection of Cæsar. He tells the result in one of his letters—"But I would ye should understand, brethren, that the things which happened unto me have fallen out rather unto the furtherance of the gospel; so that my bonds in Christ are manifest in all the palace, and in all other places; and many of the brethren in the Lord, waxing confident by my bonds, are much more bold to speak the word without fear." Nay, more wonderful still, he writes in the same epistle—"All the saints salute you, chiefly they that are of Cæsar's household."

What may not be achieved by one man's labour, by the energy of a mighty mind and a great heart? In fact all gigantic movements have but one vital centre, one impelling and controlling will and power. Such a one is usually and justly termed the soul of the enterprise. Other minds unconsciously yield to him, and he transfuses so much of his spirit into them, that they feel and act like portions of himself, or become in turn the centres of a kindred and widening influence. The genius of the apostle possessed this character; it moulded and inspired those who came in contact with it. In the imperial barracks the Tarsean Jew in bonds was noted as no ordinary man, and his words spoken in season touched hearts whose occupation and training were by no means favourable to their susceptibility. There were others in the palace—that scene of indescribable iniquity—on whom a saving change had been wrought by him. Wherever the apostle is he is felt in his power—during the storm in the ship, and under his appeal a prisoner in Rome—" a prisoner of Christ Jesus."

And thus in fine the apostle found himself in Rome, among two millions of human beings, citizens and foreigners; the latter being gathered from all parts of the world, and representing all races and religions. Its streets and forum, its baths and temples, its palaces and theatres studding its seven hills, presented an architectural splendour which was darkly fringed with scenes of squalor, poverty, and vice. It was the world in miniature. Africa and Britain, India and Spain met in it, with sailors from every country, and captives from every province. All lands were tributary to it, and the names of its consuls, prætors, and Cæsars had reproduced themselves in barbarous tongues. The earth bowed at the throne of Nero, and his will was felt over myriads of many colours and climes. Mighty tides of influence streamed out from the city on all sides, and struck on the most distant shores. Therefore, vital evangelical power established in it would soon radiate to the ends of the empire. Pilgrims would carry it in their treasures, it would march with the legions, and returning prisoners would bring back the gladsome news. The apostle aimed at such an end; and though a cause was usually heard within a week of the appellant's arrival, for "two whole years" was the apostle permitted to labour "with all confidence, no man forbidding him." Then was laid the foundation of many churches in the Italian peninsula and over Europe, a vast network of missionary operations, connecting itself with the Jewish bondman at Rome—a prisoner, and yet the apostle of the Gentiles. They who saw him and conversed with him caught his spirit and carried away his words, carried them beyond the Campagna and up the slopes of the Alban and Sabine hills, over the Alps into Gaul, and across the channel to our native isle.

The book of the "Acts" closes with this account of Paul's imprisonment. The gospel is at length preached in Rome by an apostle—an earnest of its universal diffusion, and of the fulfilment of the Lord's own promise. Critics and historians vary as to the period of the apostle's death —some holding that he was released, and that, after more missionary labours and travels, he was again apprehended, brought to Rome, tried, and executed; and others maintaining that soon after the period specified in the conclusion of the "Acts," he was put to death by Nero; tradition placing its time on the 29th of June, and its scene at Aquæ Salviæ, on the Ostian road, about two miles from the city. Thus he who had been "apprehended of Christ Jesus," and "separated unto the gospel;" who had "lived by the faith of the Son of God," and by His grace had "laboured more abundantly" than his colleagues; who had "filled up that which was behind of the afflictions of Christ in his flesh for His body's sake," and entered into "the fellowship of His sufferings," received at length his heart's desire in "being made conformable unto His death."

THE END.

Printed by William Mackenzie, Glasgow

Other Solid Ground Titles

In addition to the book in your hand, Solid Ground is honored to offer other uncovered treasure, many for the first time in more than a century:

ANNALS OF THE AMERICAN BAPTIST PULPIT by *William B. Sprague*
JESUS OF NAZARETH by *John A. Broadus*
THE CHILD AT HOME by John S.C. Abbott
THE KING'S HIGHWAY: *The 10 Commandments for the Young* by Richard Newton
THE LIFE OF JESUS CHRIST FOR THE YOUNG by Richard Newton
LET THE CANNON BLAZE AWAY by Joseph P. Thompson
THE STILL HOUR: *Communion with God in Prayer* by Austin Phelps
COLLECTED WORKS of James Henley Thornwell (4 vols.)
CALVINISM IN HISTORY by *Nathaniel S. McFetridge*
OPENING SCRIPTURE: *Hermeneutical Manual* by *Patrick Fairbairn*
THE ASSURANCE OF FAITH by *Louis Berkhof*
THE PASTOR IN THE SICK ROOM by *John D. Wells*
THE BUNYAN OF BROOKLYN: *Life & Sermons of I.S. Spencer*
THE NATIONAL PREACHER: *Sermons from 2nd Great Awakening*
FIRST THINGS: *First Lessons God Taught Mankind* Gardiner Spring
BIBLICAL & THEOLOGICAL STUDIES by *1912 Faculty of Princeton*
THE POWER OF GOD UNTO SALVATION by *B.B. Warfield*
THE LORD OF GLORY by *B.B. Warfield*
A GENTLEMAN & A SCHOLAR: *Memoir of J.P. Boyce* by *J. Broadus*
SERMONS TO THE NATURAL MAN by *W.G.T. Shedd*
SERMONS TO THE SPIRITUAL MAN by *W.G.T. Shedd*
HOMILETICS AND PASTORAL THEOLOGY by *W.G.T. Shedd*
A PASTOR'S SKETCHES 1 & 2 by *Ichabod S. Spencer*
THE PREACHER AND HIS MODELS by *James Stalker*
IMAGO CHRISTI by *James Stalker*
A HISTORY OF PREACHING by *Edwin C. Dargan*
LECTURES ON THE HISTORY OF PREACHING by *J. A. Broadus*
THE SCOTTISH PULPIT by *William Taylor*
THE SHORTER CATECHISM ILLUSTRATED by *John Whitecross*
THE CHURCH MEMBER'S GUIDE by *John Angell James*
THE SUNDAY SCHOOL TEACHER'S GUIDE by *John A. James*
CHRIST IN SONG: *Hymns of Immanuel from All Ages* by *Philip Schaff*
COME YE APART: *Daily Words from the Four Gospels* by *J.R. Miller*
DEVOTIONAL LIFE OF THE S.S. TEACHER by *J.R. Miller*

Call us Toll Free at 1-877-666-9469
Send us an e-mail at sgcb@charter.net
Visit us on line at solid-ground-books.com

www.ingramcontent.com/pod-product-compliance
Lightning Source LLC
Chambersburg PA
CBHW021826220426
43663CB00005B/141